A guide to
The World Bank

A guide to
The World Bank

SECOND EDITION

THE WORLD BANK
Washington, D.C.

ISBN-10: 0-8213-6694-7 (soft cover)
ISBN-10: 0-8213-6918-8 (hard cover)
ISBN-13: 978-0-8213-6694-3 (soft cover)
ISBN-13: 978-0-8213-6718-6 (hard cover)
eISBN-10: 0-8213-6695-5
eISBN-13: 978-0-8213-6695-0
DOI: 10.1596/978-0-8213-6694-3

Cover design: Rock Creek Creative
Cover photos (clockwise from lower left): World Bank/Jim Pickerell; World Bank/Ami Vitale; World Bank/Gennadiy Ratushenko.

Interior design and typesetting: Circle Graphics
Interior photos: IFC/Rob Wright (page xiv); World Bank/Curt Carnemark (page xvi); World Bank/Simone McCourtie (page 6); World Bank/Thanit Thangpijaigul (page 44); IFC/courtesy of Embraer (page 138); World Bank/Bill Lyons (page 188).

Library of Congress Cataloging-in-Publication Data
Guide to the World Bank. — 2nd ed.
    p. cm.
Includes bibliographical references and index.
    ISBN 978-0-8213-6694-3 — ISBN 978-0-8213-6695-0 (electronic)
    1. World Bank Group. 2. Developing countries—Economic conditions 3. Economic assistance. I. World Bank.
HG3881.5.W57G853 2007
332.1'532—dc22

                                                                    2007019884

CONTENTS

Boxes

Figures

Tables

PREFACE

The World Bank Group is a vital source of financial and technical assistance to developing countries around the world. Our focus is on helping the poorest people in the poorest countries by using our financial resources, staff, and extensive experience to aid countries in reducing poverty, increasing economic growth, and improving quality of life.

Our efforts in this regard are as diverse as the people and landscapes in which we work. In partnership with more than 100 developing countries, we are striving to improve health and education, fight corruption, boost agricultural support, build roads and ports, and protect the environment. Other projects are aimed at rebuilding war-torn countries or regions, providing basic services such as access to clean water, and encouraging investments that create jobs.

In addition to this critical groundwork around the world, various parts of the World Bank Group are involved in activities ranging from conducting economic research and analysis to providing financial and advisory services to governments and private enterprises. These activities reflect the emphasis we place on sharing development knowledge, which is gleaned not only from our decades of experience but also from that of our 185 members—including both developing and developed countries.

This completely revised and updated second edition of *A Guide to the World Bank* provides an accessible and straightforward overview of the World Bank Group's history, organization, mission, and purpose. Additionally, for those wishing to delve further into subjects of particular interest, the book guides readers to sources containing more detailed information, including annual reports, Web sites, publications, and e-mail addresses for various departments.

It is my hope that this second edition continues to help build a better understanding of the World Bank Group's work and awareness of the world's most critical challenge: putting an end to global poverty.

Marwan Muasher
Senior Vice President
External Affairs
The World Bank

ACKNOWLEDGMENTS

The first edition of *A Guide to the World Bank*—published in 2003—was conceived and edited by Paul McClure. This second edition was produced by a team led by Stephen McGroarty.

The book benefited greatly from the advice and feedback of the following people: Anita Ahmed, Timothy T. Carrington, John Didier, Francis Dobbs, Pernille Falck, Alexander Ferguson, Melissa Fossberg, Nicole Frost, Nadine Shamounki Ghannam, Leroy Grassley, Declan Heery, Jung Lim Kim, Natalia Kirpikova, Johanna Martinson, Katherine Marshall, Paul McClure, Roger Morier, Merrell Tuck-Primdahl, Catherine M. Russell, Estela T. Sanidad, Elena Serrano, Abigail Tamakloe, Terence Winsor, and Filippo Zanzi. Additionally, Caroline Banton was indispensable in researching, fact checking, and writing; and Alice Faintich applied her superb editing skills to the manuscript.

Many people in the Bank's Office of the Publisher contributed to or provided assistance to this project. Cindy Fisher expertly managed the design and editorial production of the book, and Nora Ridolfi adeptly coordinated the printing process. Thanks also go to Jose de Buerba, Valentina Kalk, Patricia Katayama, Kathryn Matthews, Paola Scalabrin, Thaisa Tiglao, Jonathan Tin, Mario Trubiano, and Shana Wagger for their input; and to Dirk Koehler, Santiago Pombo, Nancy Lammers, Randi Park, Richard Crabbe, and Carlos Rossel for their continuous support and guidance.

ABBREVIATIONS

CAS	Country Assistance Strategy
CSO	civil society organization
HIPC	heavily indebted poor countries
HIV/AIDS	human immunodeficiency virus/acquired immune deficiency syndrome
IBRD	International Bank for Reconstruction and Development
ICSID	International Centre for Settlement of Investment Disputes
IDA	International Development Association
IFC	International Finance Corporation
IMF	International Monetary Fund
MDG	Millennium Development Goal
MIGA	Multilateral Investment Guarantee Agency
NGO	nongovernmental organization
PIC	public information center
PREM	Poverty Reduction and Economic Management
PRSP	Poverty Reduction Strategy Paper
TB	tuberculosis
UN	United Nations
VPU	vice presidential unit
WBI	World Bank Institute

All dollar amounts are U.S. dollars unless otherwise indicated.

A man works in a timber factory in Bosnia and Herzegovina. The ability to work is the only financial asset of many of the world's poor people. Efficient labor markets create opportunities for work, thereby helping to reduce poverty.

The World Bank Group Mission

To fight poverty with passion and professionalism for lasting results. To help people help themselves and their environment by providing resources, sharing knowledge, building capacity, and forging partnerships in the public and private sectors.

International Bank for Reconstruction and Development
International Development Association

To promote sustainable private sector investment in developing countries, helping to reduce poverty and improve people's lives.

International Finance Corporation

To promote foreign direct investment into developing countries to help support economic growth, reduce poverty, and improve people's lives.

Multilateral Investment Guarantee Agency

A mother and child in Botswana. Nearly half of the world's population today is under 25 years old. Nine out of ten of these young people live in developing countries. Within the developing world the majority of the poor are children and youths.

Introduction

Conceived in 1944 to reconstruct war-torn Europe, the World Bank Group has evolved into one of the world's largest sources of development assistance, with a mission of fighting poverty with passion by helping people help themselves.

We live in a world that is both very rich and very poor. The average person in some countries earns more than $40,000 a year—$110 a day. But in this same world, around 2.6 billion people—almost half the developing world's population—live on less than $2 a day. Of these, almost 1 billion earn less than $1 day. For these people, the many effects of poverty are life-altering. For example, in developing countries, an estimated 33,000 children die every day from avoidable causes, and every minute at least one woman dies in child-birth. Poverty additionally keeps more than 100 million children—most of them girls—out of school.

To further complicate matters, many obstacles exist that make it difficult for people to escape poverty's grasp. Inadequate infrastructure hinders access to health care, education, jobs, and trade; poor health and lack of education, in turn, deprive people of productive employment; and corruption, conflict, and poor governance waste public resources and private investment. In the face of such obstacles, the challenge of reducing poverty is both enormous and complex. But with the world's population growing by an estimated 3 billion people over the next 50 years, and with the vast majority of those people residing in developing countries, it is a challenge that must be met.

The World Bank Group, also referred to as the Bank Group, is one of the world's largest sources of funding and knowledge for developing countries. Its main focus is on helping the poorest people and the poorest countries. Through its five institutions (box 1), the Bank Group uses financial resources and extensive experience to help developing countries reduce poverty,

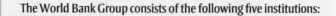

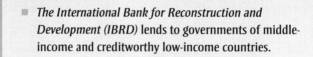

Box 1 The Five World Bank Group Institutions

The World Bank Group consists of the following five institutions:

- The *International Bank for Reconstruction and Development (IBRD)* lends to governments of middle-income and creditworthy low-income countries.

- The *International Development Association (IDA)* provides interest-free loans—called credits—and grants to governments of the poorest countries.

- The *International Finance Corporation (IFC)* provides loans, equity, and technical assistance to stimulate private sector investment in developing countries.

- The *Multilateral Investment Guarantee Agency (MIGA)* provides guarantees against losses caused by non-commercial risks to investors in developing countries.

- The *International Centre for Settlement of Investment Disputes (ICSID)* provides international facilities for conciliation and arbitration of investment disputes.

Even though the World Bank Group consists of five institutions, only the International Bank for Reconstruction and Development and the International Development Association constitute the World Bank.

increase economic growth, and improve the quality of life. The twin pillars of its strategy for reducing poverty are

- supporting the creation of a favorable investment climate, and
- empowering poor people.

Box 2 Millennium Development Goals

- Eradicate extreme poverty and hunger
- Achieve universal primary education
- Promote gender equality and empower women
- Reduce child mortality
- Improve maternal health
- Combat HIV/AIDS, malaria, and other diseases
- Ensure environmental sustainability
- Develop a global partnership for development

The range of interventions includes support for sound governance, sustainable development, inclusive delivery of social services, improved infrastructure, private sector development, and job creation. The Bank Group's work focuses on achievement of the Millennium Development Goals (MDGs), which call for eliminating poverty and achieving sustained development (box 2). The goals are used to set the Bank Group's priorities and they provide targets and yardsticks for measuring results. They are the Bank Group's road map for development.

The Bank Group is managed by its member countries (borrowers, lenders, and donors), whose representatives maintain offices at the Bank Group's headquarters in Washington, DC. Many developing countries use Bank Group assistance ranging from loans and grants to technical assistance and policy advice. All Bank Group efforts are coordinated with a wide range of partners, including government agencies, civil society organizations (CSOs), other aid agencies, and the private sector.

Over the past 20 years, the Bank Group's focus has changed, and so has its approach. Issues related to gender, community-driven development, and indigenous peoples are now integral to the Bank Group's work. Today, the World Bank Group is

- the world's largest funder of education,
- the world's largest external funder of the fight against HIV/AIDS,
- a leader in the fight against corruption worldwide,
- a strong supporter of debt relief,
- the largest international financier of biodiversity projects, and
- the largest international financier of water supply and sanitation projects.

This book guides the reader into the conceptual work of the World Bank Group. Its goal is to serve as a starting point for more in-depth inquiries into subjects of particular interest. It provides a glimpse into the wide array of activities in which the Bank Group institutions are involved, and it directs the reader toward other publications and to Web sites that have more detailed information.

The following chapters explain how the World Bank Group is organized; how it operates; and how its work focuses on countries, regions, and specific topics in development. Appendixes provide further information on Bank Group contacts, on the organization's history, and on country membership and voting shares in the institutions.

We welcome comments on this publication as well as on the many projects and activities of the Bank Group institutions. To provide comments, visit http://www.worldbank.org and click on "Contact Us" or send an email to feedback@worldbank.org.

A woman washes her hands in Vietnam. Better hygiene and access to drinking water and sanitation help to reduce the instances of illness and death caused by preventable diseases each year.

1 How the World Bank Group Is Organized

This chapter explains how the World Bank Group is governed and how it is organized to do its work. It provides detailed information on the five World Bank Group institutions and other major organizational units. The final section explains the World Bank Group's relationship with the International Monetary Fund and the United Nations.

Governance of the World Bank Group

Founding Documents

Each of the five institutions of the World Bank Group has its own Articles of Agreement or an equivalent founding document. These documents legally define the institution's purpose, organization, and operations, including the mechanisms by which it is owned and governed. By signing these documents and meeting the requirements set forth in them, a country can become a member of the Bank Group institutions.

Ownership by Member Countries

Each Bank Group institution is owned by its member countries (its shareholders). The number of member countries varies by institution, from 185 in IBRD to 143 in ICSID, as of April 2007. The requirements for membership and the country classifications the Bank Group uses are explained in chapter 3.

In practice, member countries govern the Bank Group through the Boards of Governors and the Boards of Directors. These bodies make all major policy decisions for the organization (figure 1.1).

Boards of Governors

The World Bank Group operates under the authority of its Boards of Governors. Each of the member countries of the Bank Group institutions

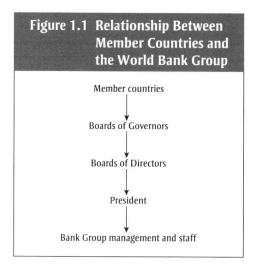

Figure 1.1 Relationship Between Member Countries and the World Bank Group

Member countries

↓

Boards of Governors

↓

Boards of Directors

↓

President

↓

Bank Group management and staff

appoints a governor, who is usually a government official at the ministerial level. If a member of IBRD is also a member of IDA or IFC, the appointed governor serves ex officio on the IDA and IFC Boards of Governors. MIGA governors are appointed separately to its Council of Governors. ICSID has an Administrative Council rather than a Board of Governors. Unless a government makes a contrary designation, its appointed governor for IBRD sits ex officio on ICSID's Administrative Council.

The governors admit or suspend members, review financial statements and budgets, make formal arrangements to cooperate with other international organizations, and exercise other powers that they have not delegated. Once a year, the Boards of Governors of the Bank Group (including ICSID's Administrative Council) and the International Monetary Fund (IMF) meet in a joint session known as the Annual Meetings (more information on these meetings appears in the final section of this chapter). Because the governors meet only annually, they delegate many specific duties to the executive directors.

Boards of Directors

General operations of IBRD are delegated to a smaller group of representatives, the Board of Executive Directors. These same individuals serve ex officio on IDA's Board of Executive Directors and on IFC's Board of Directors under the Articles of Agreement for those two institutions. Members of MIGA's Board of Directors are elected separately, but it is customary for the directors of MIGA to be the same individuals as the executive directors of IBRD. Unlike the other four institutions, ICSID does not have a board. The president of the Bank Group serves as the chair of all four boards (and as the chair of ICSID's Administrative Council), but he or she has no voting power.

IBRD has 24 executive directors. The five largest shareholders—the United States, Japan, Germany, France, and the United Kingdom—each appoint one executive director. The other countries are grouped into constituencies, each of which elects an executive director as its representative.

The members themselves decide how they will be grouped. Some countries— China, the Russian Federation, and Saudi Arabia—form single-country constituencies. Multicountry constituencies more or less represent geographic regions, with some political and cultural factors determining exactly how they are constituted.

The executive directors are based at Bank Group headquarters in Washington, DC. They are responsible for making policy decisions affecting the Bank Group's operations and for approving all loans. The executive directors function in continuous session and meet as often as Bank Group business requires, although their regular meetings occur twice a week. Each executive director also serves on one or more standing committees: the Audit Committee, Budget Committee, Committee on Development Effectiveness, Personnel Committee, and Committee on Governance and Executive Directors' Administrative Matters.

The boards normally make decisions by consensus; however, the relative voting power of individual executive directors is based on the shares that are held by the countries they represent (figure 1.2). For more on the constituencies, voting power, and elections of the executive directors, see appendix E.

World Bank Group President and Managing Directors

The World Bank Group president is selected by the executive directors. The Articles of Agreement do not specify the nationality of the president, but by long-standing, informal agreement, he or she is a U.S. national (by custom,

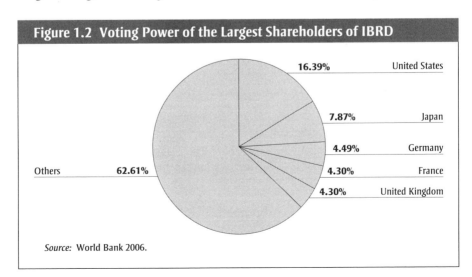

Figure 1.2 Voting Power of the Largest Shareholders of IBRD

16.39%	United States
7.87%	Japan
4.49%	Germany
4.30%	France
4.30%	United Kingdom
Others 62.61%	

Source: World Bank 2006.

nominated by the U.S. executive director), while the managing director of the IMF is a European. The president serves a term of five years, which may be renewed. There is no mandatory retirement age.

The executive vice presidents of IFC and MIGA report directly to the World Bank Group president, and as mentioned previously, the president serves as chair of ICSID's Administrative Council. (ICSID operates as a secretariat whose secretary-general is selected by the Administrative Council every six years.) Within IBRD and IDA, most organizational units report to the president and, through the president, to the executive directors. The two exceptions are the Independent Evaluation Group and the Inspection Panel, which report directly to the executive directors. Additionally, the president delegates some of his or her oversight responsibility to two managing directors, each of which oversees several organizational units.

For more information about the World Bank Group president see box 1.1 and visit http://www.worldbank.org/president. For information about previous presidents of the Bank Group, see appendix C.

Box 1.1 World Bank Group President Robert B. Zoellick

Robert B. Zoellick, a U.S. national, is the World Bank Group's 11th president. Before joining the Bank Group, Mr. Zoellick served as International Vice Chairman of the Goldman Sachs Group and as Managing Director and Chairman of Goldman Sachs' Board of International Advisors. He previously served as Deputy Secretary of the U.S. State Department and as the 13th U.S. Trade Representative in the U.S. cabinet.

Mr. Zoellick has additionally held the positions of Deputy Assistant Secretary for Financial Institutions Policy and Counselor to the Secretary at the Treasury Department, and of Undersecretary of State for Economic and Agricultural Affairs and Counselor of the Department at the State Department. In the private sector, Mr. Zoellick was Executive Vice President of Fannie Mae, the large housing finance corporation.

Mr. Zoellick graduated Phi Beta Kappa from Swarthmore College in 1975. He earned a J.D. magna cum laude from the Harvard Law School and an MPP from the Kennedy School of Government in 1981.

The Five World Bank Group Institutions

The institutions that make up the World Bank Group specialize in different aspects of development, but they work collaboratively toward the overarching goal of poverty reduction. The terms "World Bank" and "Bank" refer only to IBRD and IDA, whereas the terms "World Bank Group" and "Bank Group" include all five institutions (box 1.2).

The World Bank: IBRD and IDA

Through its loans, policy advice, and technical assistance, the World Bank supports a broad range of programs aimed at reducing poverty and improving living standards in the developing world. It divides its work between IBRD, which assists middle-income and creditworthy poorer countries, and IDA, which focuses exclusively on the world's poorest countries. Working through both IBRD and IDA, the Bank uses its financial resources, skilled staff, and extensive knowledge base to help each developing country achieve stable, sustainable, and equitable growth.

IBRD and IDA share the same staff and the same headquarters, report to the same senior management, and use the same standards when evaluating projects. Some countries borrow from both institutions. For all its clients, the Bank emphasizes the need for

- investing in people, particularly through basic health and education;
- focusing on social development, inclusion, governance, and institution building as key elements of poverty reduction;
- strengthening governments' ability to deliver quality services efficiently and transparently;
- protecting the environment;

Box 1.2 Origin of the Term "World Bank"

The term "world bank" was first used in reference to IBRD in an article in the *Economist* on July 22, 1944, in a report on the Bretton Woods Conference. The first meeting of the Boards of Governors of IBRD and the IMF, which was held in Savannah, Georgia, in March 1946, was officially called the "World Fund and Bank Inaugural Meeting," and several news accounts of this conference, including one in the *Washington Post*, used the term "world bank." What began as a nickname became official shorthand for IBRD and IDA in 1975.

- supporting and encouraging private business development; and
- promoting reforms to create a stable macroeconomic environment that is conducive to investment and long-term planning.

Bank programs give high priority to sustainable social and human development and to strengthened economic management, and they place an emphasis on inclusion, governance, and institution building. Additionally, within the international community, the Bank has helped build consensus around the idea that developing countries must take the lead in creating their own strategies for poverty reduction. It also plays a key role in helping countries implement the MDGs, which the United Nations (UN) and the broader international community seek to achieve by 2015.

In conjunction with IFC, the Bank is also helping countries strengthen and sustain the fundamental conditions they need to attract and retain private investment. With Bank support—both lending and advice—governments are reforming their overall economies and strengthening financial systems. Investments in human resources, infrastructure, and environmental protection also help enhance the attractiveness and productivity of private investment.

The International Bank for Reconstruction and Development

IBRD, established in 1944, is the original institution of the World Bank Group and the source of the loans for which the Bank Group is best known. IBRD remains what many people mean when they refer to the World Bank. It has the largest country membership, the broadest mission, and the greatest number of staff in the Bank Group, both at headquarters and in offices around the world (box 1.3).

When IBRD was established, its first task was to help Europe recover from World War II. Today IBRD plays an important role in poverty reduction by providing the countries it now serves—middle-income and creditworthy poorer countries—with loans, guarantees, and analytical and advisory services. It provides these client countries with access to capital on favorable terms in larger volumes, with longer maturities, and in a more sustainable manner than the market provides. Specifically, IBRD

- supports long-term human and social development needs that private creditors do not finance;
- preserves borrowers' financial strength by providing support during crisis periods, which is when poor people are most adversely affected;
- uses the leverage of financing to promote key policy and institutional reforms (such as safety net or anticorruption reforms);

Box 1.3 IBRD Basic Facts

Year established:	1944
Number of member countries:	185
Cumulative lending:	$420.2 billion[a]
Fiscal 2006 lending:	$14.1 billion for 112 new operations in 33 countries
Web:	http://www.worldbank.org

a. As of June 30, 2006. Includes guarantees from fiscal 2005.

■ creates a favorable investment climate to catalyze the provision of private capital; and

■ provides financial support (in the form of grants made available from IBRD's net income) in areas that are critical to the well-being of poor people in all countries.

IBRD raises most of its funds on the world's financial markets. It is an AAA-rated financial institution, but one with some unusual characteristics: its shareholders are sovereign governments and its member borrowers have a voice in setting its policies. IBRD provides loans, guarantees, risk management products, and analytic and advisory services. These services may be packaged together or offered as stand-alone services. Also, unlike commercial banks, IBRD is driven by development impact rather than by profit maximization. IBRD borrowers are typically middle-income countries that have some access to private capital markets. Some countries that are eligible for IDA lending because of low per capita incomes are also eligible for some IBRD borrowing because of their creditworthiness. These countries are known as "blend" borrowers (table 1.1). Hundreds of millions of the developing world's poor, defined as those who live on less than $2 a day, live not in the world's very poorest countries, but in middle-income countries, which are defined as those with an annual gross national income per capita between $876 and $10,725 (For more on country classifications, see *World Development Indicators* or the *World Bank Annual Report,* http://publications.worldbank.org/ecommerce/.)

Countries are considered to have graduated from IBRD borrowing when their per capita income exceeds the level that the Bank classifies as middle income. For more information, including a list of IBRD graduates, see chapter 3 and box 3.2.

Table 1.1 Country Eligibility for Borrowing from the World Bank as of July 1, 2006

Income group and country	2005 GNI per capita[a]	Income group and country	2005 GNI per capita[a]
COUNTRIES ELIGIBLE FOR IBRD FUNDS ONLY			
Per capita income over $6,055			
Korea, Republic of	15,810	Slovak Republic	8,130
Antigua and Barbuda	10,920	Croatia	8,070
Trinidad and Tobago	10,440	Palau	7,410
Hungary	10,050	Lithuania	7,210
Estonia	9,100	Mexico	7,150
Seychelles[b]	8,290	Poland	7,110
St. Kitts and Nevis	8,200	Latvia	6,760
Per capita income $3,466–$6,055			
Chile	5,870	Venezuela, República Bolivariana de	4,810
Libya	5,530	Turkey	4,740
Lebanon	5,510	Panama	4,630
Mauritius	5,260	Argentina	4,470
Botswana	5,190	Russian Federation	4,460
Gabon	5,010	Uruguay	4,360
Malaysia	4,960	Romania	3,830
South Africa	4,960	Belize	3,500
Costa Rica	4,820	Equatorial Guinea	NA
Per capita income $1,676–$3,465			
Brazil	3,460	Peru	2,710
Bulgaria	3,450	Ecuador	2,590
Jamaica	3,370	Suriname	2,540
Fiji	3,140	Dominican Republic	2,470
Namibia	2,990	Jordan	2,470
Marshall Islands	2,980	El Salvador	2,450
Kazakhstan	2,930	Guatemala	2,330
Tunisia	2,890	Colombia	2,290
Macedonia, former Yugoslav Republic of	2,790	Swaziland	2,280
		Micronesia, Federated States of	1,910
Iran, Islamic Republic of	2,770	China	1,740
Belarus	2,750	Morocco	1,730
Thailand	2,750		
Algeria	2,730		
Per capita income $876–$1,675			
Ukraine	1,520	Philippines	1,250
Syrian Arab Republic	1,380	Iraq	NA
Paraguay	1,280	Turkmenistan	NA
Egypt, Arab Republic of	1,250		

Income group and country	2005 GNI per capita[a]	Income group and country	2005 GNI per capita[a]
COUNTRIES ELIGIBLE FOR A BLEND OF IBRD AND IDA FUNDS[c]			
Per capita income $3,466–$6,055			
St. Lucia[d]	4,800	Dominica[d]	3,790
Grenada[d]	3,920	St. Vincent and the Grenadines[d]	3,590
Per capita income $1,676–$3,465			
Serbia and Montenegro[e]	3,280	Bosnia and Herzegovina	2,550
Albania	2,570		
Per capita income $876–$1,675			
Indonesia	1,270	Bolivia	1,010
Azerbaijan	1,240		
Per capita income $875 or less			
India	730	Uzbekistan	520
Pakistan	690	Zimbabwe[b]	340
Papua New Guinea	660		
COUNTRIES ELIGIBLE FOR IDA FUNDS ONLY[c]			
Per capita income $1,676–$3,465			
Maldives[d]	2,390	Samoa[d]	2,090
Tonga[d]	2,130	Cape Verde[d]	1,870
Per capita income $876–$1,675			
Armenia	1,470	Djibouti	1,020
Vanuatu[d]	1,450	Cameroon	1,010
Angola	1,350	Guyana	1,000
Kiribati[d]	1,350	Congo, Republic of	950
Georgia	1,310	Lesotho	950
Honduras	1,170	Nicaragua	890
Sri Lanka	1,160	Moldova	880
Per capita income $875 or less			
Bhutan	870	Mali	380
Côte d'Ivoire[b]	840	Guinea	370
Timor-Leste	750	Central African Republic[b]	350
Senegal	710	Togo[b]	350
Mongolia	670	Tanzania	340
Comoros	640	Tajikistan	330
Sudan[b]	640	Mozambique	310
Vietnam	620	Gambia, The	290
Yemen, Republic of	600	Madagascar	290

(continued)

Table 1.1 *continued*

Income group and country	2005 GNI per capita[a]	Income group and country	2005 GNI per capita[a]
COUNTRIES ELIGIBLE FOR IDA FUNDS ONLY[c] *continued*			
Per capita income $875 or less			
Mauritania	560	Nepal	280
Nigeria	560	Uganda	280
Solomon Islands	560	Niger	240
Kenya	530	Rwanda	230
Benin	510	Eritrea	220
Zambia	490	Sierra Leone	220
Bangladesh	470	Guinea-Bissau	180
Ghana	450	Ethiopia	160
Haiti	450	Malawi	160
Kyrgyz Republic	440	Liberia[b]	130
Lao People's Democratic Republic	440	Congo, Democratic Republic of	120
Burkina Faso	400	Burundi	100
Chad	400	Afghanistan	NA
São Tomé and Principe	390	Myanmar[b]	NA
Cambodia	380	Somalia[b]	NA

Source: World Bank 2006.
Note: NA = estimates are available in range only, GNI = gross national income.
a. World Bank Atlas methodology. Per capita GNI (formerly gross national product) figures are in 2005 U.S. dollars.
b. Loans/credits in nonaccrual status as of June 30, 2006. General information on countries with loans/credits in nonaccrual status is available from the Credit Risk Department in Finance.
c. Countries are eligible for IDA on the basis of (a) relative poverty and (b) lack of creditworthiness. The operational cutoff for IDA eligibility for fiscal 2007 is a 2005 GNI per capita of $1,025 using World Bank Atlas methodology. To receive IDA resources, countries must also meet tests of performance. In exceptional circumstances, IDA extends eligibility temporarily to countries that are above the operational cutoff and are undertaking major adjustment efforts but are not creditworthy for IBRD lending. An exception has been made for small island economies.
d. An exception to the GNI per capita operational cutoff for IDA eligibility ($1,025 for fiscal 2007) has been made for some small island economies, which otherwise would have little or no access to Bank Group assistance because they lack creditworthiness. For such countries, IDA funding is considered on a case-by-case basis for financing projects and adjustment programs designed to strengthen creditworthiness.
e. Following a referendum in May 2006, Montenegro declared its independence from the union of Serbia and Montenegro, resulting in both states becoming independent countries. Data are for both states prior to independence.

Even though IBRD does not maximize profits, it has earned a positive net income each year since 1948. This income funds development activities and ensures financial strength, enabling low-cost borrowing in capital markets and good terms for borrowing clients. Additional information on IBRD loans appears in the next chapter.

The International Development Association

After the rebuilding of Europe following World War II, the Bank turned its attention to the newly independent developing countries. It became clear that the poorest developing countries could not afford to borrow capital for development on the terms offered by the Bank; hence, a group of Bank member countries decided to found IDA as an institution that could lend to very poor developing nations on easier terms. To imbue IDA with the discipline of a bank, these countries agreed that IDA should be part of the World Bank. IDA began operating in 1960 (box 1.4).

IDA helps the world's poorest countries reduce poverty by providing credits and grants. Credits are loans at zero interest with a 10-year grace period before repayment of principal begins and maturities of 20, 35, or 40 years. These credits are often referred to as concessional lending. IDA credits help build the human capital, policies, institutions, and physical infrastructure that these countries urgently need to achieve faster, environmentally sustainable growth. IDA's goal is to reduce disparities across and within countries— especially in terms of access to primary education, basic health, and water supply and sanitation—and to bring more people into the economic mainstream by raising their productivity.

IDA is funded largely by contributions from the governments of its high-income member countries (table 1.2). Representatives of donor countries meet every three years to replenish IDA funds. Since 1960, IDA has lent $170 billion to 108 countries. Annual lending figures have increased steadily and averaged about $9.1 billion over the last three years. Additional funds come from repayments of earlier IDA credits and from IBRD's net income.

Box 1.4 IDA Basic Facts

Year established:	1960
Number of member countries:	166
Cumulative commitments:	$170 billion[a]
Fiscal 2006 commitments:	$9.5 billion for 167 new operations in 59 countries
Web:	http://www.worldbank.org/ida

a. As of June 30, 2006. Includes guarantees from fiscal 2005.

Table 1.2 Cumulative IDA Subscriptions and Contributions

Member	$ millions	Percentage of total
Argentina	69.84	0.05
Australia	2,417.33	1.72
Austria	1,368.44	0.97
Barbados	1.04	0.00
Belgium	2,081.59	1.48
Bosnia and Herzegovina	2.43	0.00
Botswana	1.62	0.00
Brazil	557.19	0.40
Canada	6,219.97	4.42
Colombia	24.66	0.02
Croatia	5.67	0.00
Czech Republic	54.59	0.04
Denmark	2,020.66	1.44
Finland	942.12	0.67
France	10,166.45	7.22
Germany	15,936.56	11.32
Greece	88.31	0.06
Hungary	54.63	0.04
Iceland	39.95	0.03
Ireland	207.18	0.15
Israel	41.03	0.03
Italy	5,183.77	3.68
Japan	28,803.37	20.46
Korea, Republic of	690.80	0.49
Kuwait	755.74	0.54
Luxembourg	122.00	0.09
Macedonia, former Yugoslav Republic of	1.07	0.00
Mexico	138.32	0.10
Netherlands	5,162.09	3.67
New Zealand	180.28	0.13
Norway	2,086.89	1.48
Oman	1.37	0.00
Poland	69.08	0.05
Portugal	140.89	0.10
Russian Federation	262.78	0.19
Saudi Arabia	2,258.21	1.60
Serbia and Montenegro[a]	6.86	0.00
Singapore	36.41	0.03
Slovak Republic	17.34	0.01
Slovenia	9.28	0.01
South Africa	120.65	0.09
Spain	1,480.97	1.05

Member	$ millions	Percentage of total
Sweden	4,168.64	2.96
Switzerland	2,395.80	1.70
United Arab Emirates	5.58	0.00
United Kingdom	12,373.54	8.79
United States	31,541.78	22.41
Total donors	140,314.77	99.69
Total nondonors	437.97	0.31
Grand Total	140,752.74	100.00

Source: World Bank data as of June 30, 2006.

Note: Numbers may not add to totals because of rounding.

a. Following a referendum in May 2006, Montenegro declared its independence from the union of Serbia and Montenegro, resulting in both states becoming independent countries. Data are for both states prior to independence.

Donor contributions account for more than half of the $33 billion in the 14th replenishment of IDA, known as IDA14, which finances projects over the three-year period ending June 30, 2008.

The United States, the United Kingdom, Japan, Germany, France, Italy, and Canada made the largest pledges to IDA14, but less wealthy nations also contribute to IDA; for example, Turkey, once an IDA borrower, is now a donor. Countries currently eligible to borrow from IBRD but not from IDA, namely, Brazil, the Czech Republic, Hungary, Mexico, Poland, the Russian Federation, the Slovak Republic, and South Africa, are also IDA14 donors. Other contributors include Australia, Austria, Barbados, Belgium, Denmark, Finland, Greece, Iceland, Ireland, Israel, Kuwait, Luxembourg, the Netherlands, New Zealand, Norway, Portugal, Saudi Arabia, Singapore, Slovenia, Spain, Sweden, Switzerland, and the República Bolivariana de Venezuela.

IDA lends to those countries that lack the financial ability to borrow from IBRD and that, in 2005, had an income of less than $1,025 per person. Some blend borrower countries, such as India and Indonesia, are eligible for IDA loans because of their low per person incomes while also being eligible for IBRD loans because they are financially creditworthy. Eighty-two countries are currently eligible to borrow from IDA. Together these countries are home to around 2.6 billion people, almost half the total population of the developing world. Of these people, almost 1 billion survive on incomes of $1 or less a day.

IDA eligibility is a transitional arrangement that gives the poorest countries access to substantial resources before they are capable of obtaining the financing they need from commercial markets. As their economies grow, countries graduate from IDA eligibility. The repayments, or "reflows," that they make on IDA loans are used to help finance new IDA loans to the remaining poor countries. More than 30 countries have graduated from IDA since its founding. Examples include Chile, Costa Rica, the Arab Republic of Egypt, Morocco, Thailand, and Turkey. Some of the graduating countries subsequently "reverse graduated," however, once again becoming IDA eligible.

The International Finance Corporation

IFC is the largest multilateral provider of financing for private enterprise in developing countries. Its mission is to promote sustainable private sector investment in developing countries, thereby helping to reduce poverty and improve people's lives. IFC finances private sector investment, mobilizes capital in international financial markets, facilitates trade, helps clients improve social and environmental sustainability, and provides technical assistance and advice to governments and businesses. Since its founding in 1956, IFC has committed more than $56 billion of its own funds for private sector investment in the developing world; has mobilized an additional $25 billion in syndications; and with funding support from donors, has provided more than $1 billion in technical assistance and advisory services (box 1.5).

Direct lending to businesses is the fundamental contrast between IFC and the World Bank: under their Articles of Agreement, IBRD and IDA can lend only to the governments of member countries. IFC was founded specifically to address this limitation of World Bank lending.

Box 1.5 IFC Basic Facts

Year established:	1956
Number of member countries:	179
Cumulative active portfolio:	$21.6 billion[a] (excluding $5.1 billion in syndicated loans)
Fiscal 2006 commitments:	$6.7 billion for 284 projects in 66 countries
Web:	http://www.ifc.org

a. As of June 30, 2006.

IFC provides equity, long-term loans, loan guarantees, structured finance and risk management products, and advisory services to its clients. It seeks to reach businesses in regions and countries that otherwise would have limited access to capital. It provides financing in markets deemed too risky by commercial investors in the absence of IFC participation.

IFC also supports the projects it finances by providing advice on corporate governance, environmental and social expertise, and advice and technical assistance to businesses and governments. Much of the advisory work is funded by IFC's donor partners, through trust funds, or through facilities with a regional or thematic focus.

IFC continues to seek ways to enhance its development impact. The five key pillars of IFC's strategy are (1) strengthening the focus on frontier markets; (2) building long-term relationships with emerging global companies based in developing countries; (3) leading through environmental and social sustainability; (4) addressing the constraints to private sector growth in infrastructure, health, and education; and (5) developing financial markets through innovative products and institution building.

Project financing

IFC offers an array of financial products and services to companies in its developing member countries, including

- long-term loans in major and local currencies at fixed or variable rates;
- equity investments;
- quasi-equity instruments, such as subordinated loans, preferred stock, income notes, and convertible debt;
- syndicated loans;
- structured finance, such as partial credit guarantees, risk-sharing facilities, and securitizations;
- risk management, such as intermediation of currency and interest rate swaps and provision of hedging facilities;
- intermediary financing;
- subnational financing (for services operated for regional and local governments and government-controlled enterprises);
- trade finance; and
- subnational finance.

IFC can provide financial instruments singly or in whatever combination is necessary to ensure that projects are adequately funded from the outset. It can also help structure financial packages by coordinating financing from foreign and local banks and companies and from export credit agencies.

IFC charges market rates for its products and does not accept government guarantees. Therefore, it carefully reviews the likelihood of success for each enterprise. To be eligible for IFC financing, projects must be profitable for investors, must benefit the economy of the host country, and must comply with IFC's environmental and social standards. IFC finances projects in all types of industries and sectors, including manufacturing, infrastructure, tourism, health and education, and financial services. Financial services projects are the largest component of IFC's portfolio, and they cover the full range of financial institutions, including banks, leasing companies, stock markets, credit rating agencies, venture capital funds, and microfinance institutions. Even though IFC is primarily a financier of private sector projects, it may provide financing for a company with some government ownership provided there is private sector participation and the venture is run on a commercial basis. It can finance companies that are wholly locally owned as well as joint ventures between foreign and local shareholders.

To ensure participation by investors and lenders from the private sector, IFC limits the total amount of own-account debt and equity financing it will provide for any single project. For new projects, the maximum amount is 25 percent of the total estimated project costs or, on an exceptional basis, up to 35 percent for small projects. For expansion projects, IFC may provide up to 50 percent of the total project costs, provided its investments do not exceed 25 percent of the total capitalization of the project company. On average, for every $1 of IFC financing, other investors and lenders provide $3 to $5.

IFC investments typically range from $1 million to $100 million. IFC funds may be used for permanent working capital or for foreign or local expenditures in any IBRD member country to acquire fixed assets. Because IFC operates on commercial terms that target profitability, it has made a profit every year since its inception.

Resource mobilization

Given IFC's record of success and its special standing as a multilateral institution, it is able to act as a catalyst for private investment. Its participation in a project enhances investors' confidence and attracts other lenders and shareholders. IFC mobilizes financing directly for sound companies in developing countries by syndicating loans with international commercial banks. It also helps structure private financing for clients through guarantees, risk-sharing facilities, and securitizations.

Advisory services

IFC advises businesses in developing countries on a wide variety of matters, including physical and financial restructuring; business plans; identification of markets, products, technologies, and financial and technical partners; and corporate governance. IFC can provide such advisory services in the context of an investment or independently for a fee in line with market practice.

IFC also advises governments in developing countries on how to create an enabling business environment, and it provides guidance on attracting foreign direct investment. For example, it helps develop domestic capital markets. It also provides assistance in restructuring and privatizing state-owned enterprises.

The Multilateral Investment Guarantee Agency

Concerns about investment environments and perceptions of political risk often inhibit foreign direct investment, with the majority of flows going to just a handful of countries and leaving the world's poorest economies largely ignored. MIGA addresses these concerns by providing three key services: political risk insurance for foreign investment in developing countries, technical assistance, and dispute mediation services.

MIGA's operational strategy plays to the agency's foremost strength in the marketplace: attracting investors and private insurers into difficult operating environments. The agency's strategy focuses on specific areas where it can make the greatest difference:

- *Infrastructure development,* which is an important priority for MIGA given the estimated need for $230 billion a year solely for new investment to provide infrastructure for rapidly growing urban centers and underserved rural populations in developing countries.
- *Frontier markets,* that is, high-risk or low-income countries and markets, which represent both a challenge and an opportunity for the agency. Such markets typically have the greatest need for, and stand to benefit the most from, foreign investment, but are not well served by the private market.
- *Investment in conflict-affected countries,* which is another operational priority for the agency given that, although such countries tend to attract considerable donor goodwill once the conflict ends, aid flows eventually start to decline, making private investment critical for reconstruction and growth. With many investors wary of potential risks, political risk insurance becomes essential for moving investments forward.
- *Investments between developing countries,* which are contributing a growing proportion of foreign direct investment flows. However, the private

insurance market in these countries is not always sufficiently developed and national export credit agencies often lack the ability and capacity to offer political risk insurance.

Development impact and priorities

Since its creation in 1988, MIGA has issued $16 billion in guarantee coverage in support of 527 projects in 95 member developing countries (box 1.6). MIGA is committed to promoting socially, economically, and environmentally sustainable projects that are, above all, developmentally responsible. Projects supported have widespread benefits; for example, generating jobs and taxes and transferring skills and know-how. In addition, local communities often receive significant secondary benefits through improved infrastructure. Projects encourage similar local investments and spur the growth of local businesses. MIGA ensures that projects are aligned with World Bank Group Country Assistance Strategies and integrate the best environmental, social, and governance practices. (More information about Country Assistance Strategies is provided in chapter 2.)

MIGA's technical assistance services play an integral role in catalyzing foreign direct investment by helping developing countries define and implement strategies to improve their investment climates and promote investment opportunities. MIGA develops and deploys tools and technologies to help disseminate information about investment opportunities, and thousands of users take advantage of the agency's suite of online investment information services.

The agency uses its legal services to protect the investments it supports and remove possible obstacles to future investment by helping governments and investors resolve any differences.

Box 1.6 MIGA Basic Facts

Year established:	1988
Number of member countries:	171
Cumulative guarantees issued:	$16 billion[a]
Fiscal 2006 guarantees issued:	$1.3 billion
Web:	http://www.miga.org

a. As of June 30, 2006. Includes funds leveraged through the Cooperative Underwriting Program.

Added value

MIGA gives private investors the confidence they need to make sustainable investments in developing countries. As part of the World Bank Group, MIGA brings security and credibility to an investment, acting as a potent deterrent against government actions that may adversely affect investments. If disputes do arise, the agency's leverage with host governments frequently enables it to resolve differences to the mutual satisfaction of all parties.

MIGA is a leader in assessing and managing political risks, developing new products and services, and finding innovative ways to meet clients' needs. The agency can also enable complex transactions to go ahead by offering innovative coverage of the nontraditional subsovereign risks that often accompany water and other infrastructure projects. It also provides interest rate hedging instruments and guarantee coverage for capital market transactions.

MIGA complements the activities of other investment insurers and works with partners through its coinsurance and reinsurance programs. By doing so, it expands the capacity of the political risk insurance industry and encourages private sector insurers to enter into transactions they would not otherwise have undertaken.

The International Centre for Settlement of Investment Disputes

ICSID helps encourage foreign investment by providing international facilities for the conciliation and arbitration of investment disputes, thereby helping foster an atmosphere of mutual confidence between states and foreign investors (box 1.7). Many international agreements concerning investment refer to ICSID's arbitration facilities. ICSID also carries out research and publishing in the areas of arbitration law and foreign investment law.

Box 1.7 ICSID Basic Facts

Year established:	1966
Number of member countries:	143
Total cases registered:	210[a]
Fiscal 2006 cases registered:	26
Web:	http://www.worldbank.org/icsid

a. As of June 30, 2006.

ICSID was established under the Convention on the Settlement of Investment Disputes between States and Nationals of Other States. The ICSID Convention came into force in 1966. ICSID has an Administrative Council and a Secretariat. The Administrative Council is chaired by the World Bank's president and consists of one representative of each state that has ratified the ICSID Convention. Annual meetings of the Administrative Council are held in conjunction with the joint Annual Meetings of the Bank Group and the IMF.

ICSID is an autonomous international organization, but it has close links with the World Bank, and all ICSID members are also members of the Bank. Unless a government makes a contrary designation, its governor for the Bank sits ex officio on ICSID's Administrative Council. The expenses of the ICSID Secretariat are financed through the Bank's budget, although the parties involved bear the costs of individual proceedings.

ICSID provides the following three types of services:

- *Facilities for the conciliation and arbitration of disputes between member countries and investors who qualify as nationals of other member countries.* Recourse to ICSID conciliation and arbitration is entirely voluntary; however, after the parties have consented to arbitration under the ICSID Convention, neither can unilaterally withdraw its consent. Moreover, the ICSID Convention requires all ICSID contracting states, whether they are parties to the dispute or not, to recognize and enforce ICSID arbitral awards.
- *Certain types of proceedings between states and foreign nationals that fall outside the scope of the ICSID Convention.* These proceedings include conciliation and arbitration proceedings when either the state party or the home state of the foreign national is not a member of ICSID. "Additional facility" conciliation and arbitration are also available for cases in which the dispute is not an investment dispute, provided it relates to a transaction that has features that distinguish it from an ordinary commercial transaction. The additional facility rules further allow ICSID to administer a type of proceeding not provided for in the ICSID Convention, namely, fact-finding proceedings, to which any states or foreign nationals may have recourse if they wish to institute an inquiry to examine and report on facts.
- *Appointment of arbitrators for ad hoc (that is, noninstitutional) arbitration proceedings.* These appointments are most commonly made in the context of arrangements for arbitration under the arbitration rules of the UN Commission on International Trade Law, which are specially designed for ad hoc proceedings.

Organizing Principles within the World Bank Group

This section explains the basic principles upon which the World Bank Group organizes its work and lists the major organizational units. Later chapters focus on the substance of what the Bank Group does.

Vice Presidential Units

The vice presidential unit (VPU) is the main organizational unit of the World Bank (IBRD and IDA). Such units are commonly referred to as vice presidencies. With a few exceptions that report directly to the president, each of these units reports to a managing director or to the Bank Group's chief financial officer. In general, each vice presidency corresponds to a world region, a thematic network, or a central function (figure 1.3). The network vice presidencies cut across the regional vice presidencies in the form of a matrix. This arrangement helps to ensure an appropriate mix of experience and expertise. Consequently, a staff member may work for a network vice presidency but could be deployed to support work in a specific region or country.

The organizational structures of the other World Bank Group institutions have varying degrees of similarity to the organization of IBRD and IDA, reflecting the unique aspects of each institution's mission. Figures 1.4 and 1.5 show the organization of IFC and MIGA, respectively.

The following subsections provide additional information about the different types of VPUs and other major units within the Bank. For additional information, see http://www.worldbank.org/vpu.

Regional vice presidencies and country offices

Bank Group institutions have long organized much of their work around major world regions and have carried it out through offices in member countries. In recent years, decentralization has been a top priority, with the goal being to bring a higher proportion of Bank Group staff members into closer proximity with their clients. IBRD and IDA, for example, have relocated two-thirds of their country directors from Bank headquarters in Washington, DC, to the field since the mid-1990s. The percentage of staff members who work in the field has also increased significantly. Similarly, IFC is decentralizing key decision-making responsibilities as part of a commitment to transform itself into a client-centered corporation by 2010.

All Bank Group institutions share this increased emphasis on countries and regions, but the World Bank and IFC vary somewhat in how they organize their

Figure 1.3 World Bank Organizational Structure

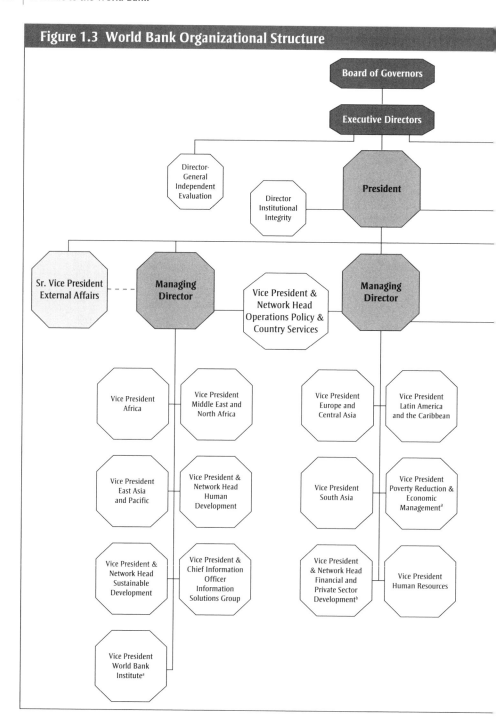

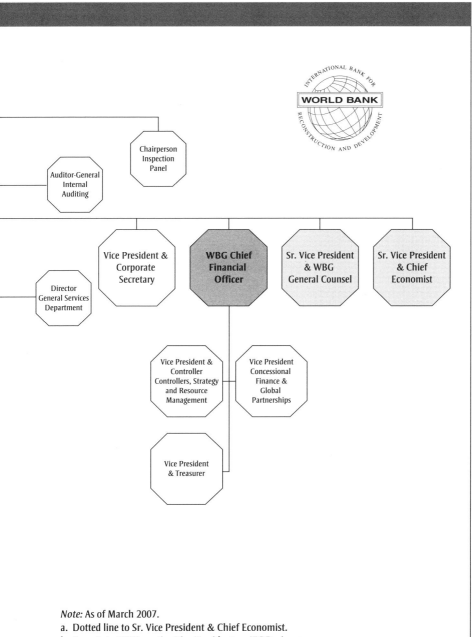

Note: As of March 2007.
a. Dotted line to Sr. Vice President & Chief Economist.
b. Reports to IFC Executive Vice President on IFC Business.

Figure 1.4 IFC Organizational Structure

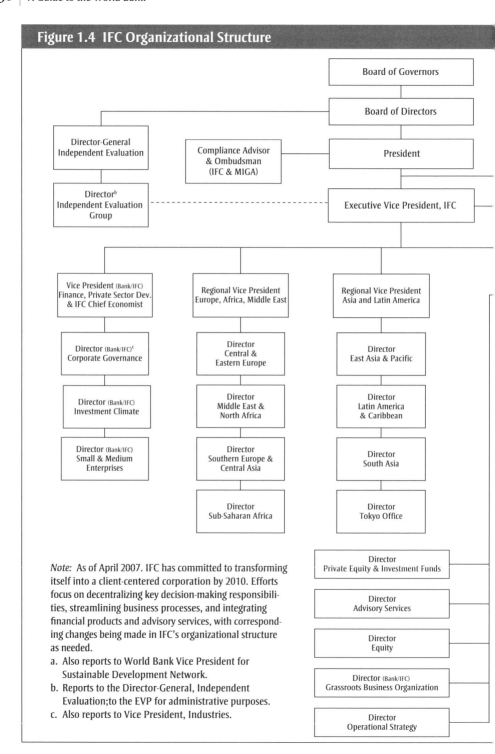

Board of Governors

Board of Directors

Director-General
Independent Evaluation

Compliance Advisor
& Ombudsman
(IFC & MIGA)

President

Director[b]
Independent Evaluation
Group

Executive Vice President, IFC

Vice President (Bank/IFC)
Finance, Private Sector Dev.
& IFC Chief Economist

Regional Vice President
Europe, Africa, Middle East

Regional Vice President
Asia and Latin America

Director (Bank/IFC)[c]
Corporate Governance

Director
Central &
Eastern Europe

Director
East Asia & Pacific

Director (Bank/IFC)
Investment Climate

Director
Middle East &
North Africa

Director
Latin America
& Caribbean

Director (Bank/IFC)
Small & Medium
Enterprises

Director
Southern Europe &
Central Asia

Director
South Asia

Director
Sub-Saharan Africa

Director
Tokyo Office

Director
Private Equity & Investment Funds

Director
Advisory Services

Director
Equity

Director (Bank/IFC)
Grassroots Business Organization

Director
Operational Strategy

Note: As of April 2007. IFC has committed to transforming itself into a client-centered corporation by 2010. Efforts focus on decentralizing key decision-making responsibilities, streamlining business processes, and integrating financial products and advisory services, with corresponding changes being made in IFC's organizational structure as needed.

a. Also reports to World Bank Vice President for Sustainable Development Network.

b. Reports to the Director-General, Independent Evaluation;to the EVP for administrative purposes.

c. Also reports to Vice President, Industries.

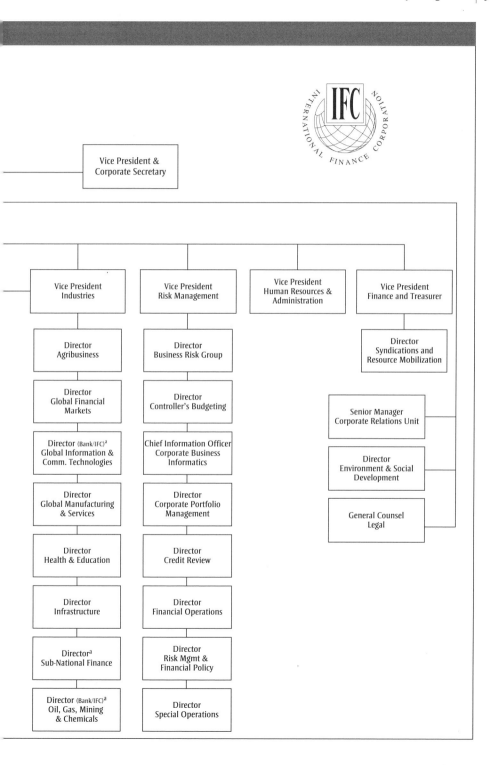

IFC — INTERNATIONAL FINANCE CORPORATION

Vice President &
Corporate Secretary

Vice President
Industries

Vice President
Risk Management

Vice President
Human Resources &
Administration

Vice President
Finance and Treasurer

Director
Agribusiness

Director
Business Risk Group

Director
Syndications and
Resource Mobilization

Director
Global Financial
Markets

Director
Controller's Budgeting

Senior Manager
Corporate Relations Unit

Director (Bank/IFC)[a]
Global Information &
Comm. Technologies

Chief Information Officer
Corporate Business
Informatics

Director
Environment & Social
Development

Director
Global Manufacturing
& Services

Director
Corporate Portfolio
Management

General Counsel
Legal

Director
Health & Education

Director
Credit Review

Director
Infrastructure

Director
Financial Operations

Director[a]
Sub-National Finance

Director
Risk Mgmt &
Financial Policy

Director (Bank/IFC)[a]
Oil, Gas, Mining
& Chemicals

Director
Special Operations

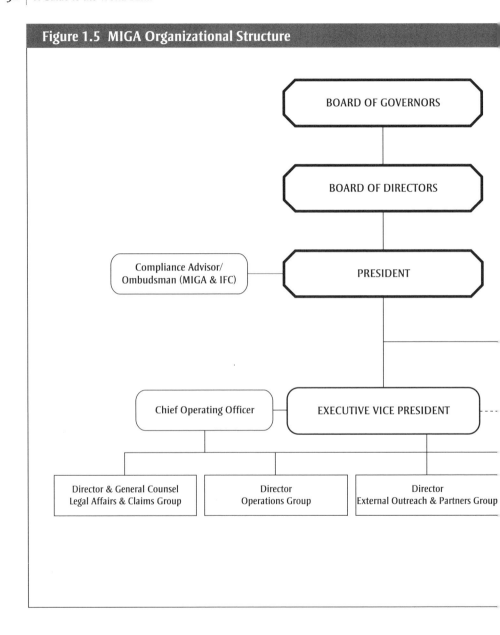

Figure 1.5 MIGA Organizational Structure

BOARD OF GOVERNORS

BOARD OF DIRECTORS

Compliance Advisor/
Ombudsman (MIGA & IFC)

PRESIDENT

Chief Operating Officer

EXECUTIVE VICE PRESIDENT

Director & General Counsel
Legal Affairs & Claims Group

Director
Operations Group

Director
External Outreach & Partners Group

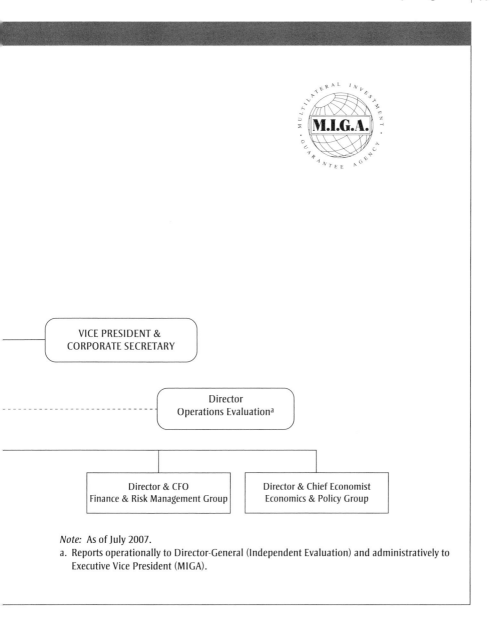

VICE PRESIDENT &
CORPORATE SECRETARY

Director
Operations Evaluation[a]

Director & CFO
Finance & Risk Management Group

Director & Chief Economist
Economics & Policy Group

Note: As of July 2007.

a. Reports operationally to Director-General (Independent Evaluation) and administratively to Executive Vice President (MIGA).

regional and country efforts. The following paragraphs give a brief overview of these organizational units. Chapter 3 summarizes the substance of Bank Group work in the regions, along with the countries covered.

The World Bank has six regional vice presidencies: Africa (Sub-Saharan), East Asia and Pacific, Europe and Central Asia, Latin America and the Caribbean, the Middle East and North Africa, and South Asia. The Bank operates offices in more than 100 member countries, as well as at the UN (New York) and in Europe (Brussels, Geneva, London, Paris, and Rome) and Japan (Tokyo). As part of their work, country offices coordinate and partner with member governments, representatives of civil society, and other international donor agencies operating in the country. Additionally, many country offices, as well as the Paris and Tokyo offices, serve as public information centers (PICS) for the World Bank Group.

IFC defines its regions somewhat differently from the Bank. It assigns directors to the following seven regions: Central and Eastern Europe, East Asia and the Pacific, Latin America and the Caribbean, the Middle East and North Africa, South Asia, Southern Europe and Central Asia, and Sub-Saharan Africa. A few countries are assigned to regions different from those they are assigned to within the Bank. The regional departments are grouped into two vice presidencies, one covering Asia and Latin America and the other covering Europe, Africa, and the Middle East. IFC maintains its own network of more than 60 offices in member countries, which in some cases share quarters with a World Bank office.

MIGA has representatives resident in Africa, Asia, and Europe.

Network vice presidencies and sectors

IBRD and IDA have created thematic networks in order to develop connections among communities of staff members who work in the same fields of development and to link these staff members more effectively with partners outside the Bank. The networks help draw out lessons learned across countries and regions, and they help bring global best practices to bear in meeting country-specific needs.

Each of the thematic networks covers several related sectors of development. In organizational terms, a subunit is generally dedicated to each sector. Each sector has its own board, with representatives drawn from the regions as well as from the network itself. The sector boards are accountable to a network council. Sector boards also identify themes—topics in development that are narrower than the work of the sector itself—on which a small number of staff members will focus, often in partnership with other organizations.

IFC and MIGA are organized along similar lines, with work divided among sectors (or "industry departments" within IFC) and subsectors. A central function of this arrangement is to create coherent sector strategies for all the Bank Group's work in a given aspect of development. Networks and sectors have also created advisory services or help desks to field queries from Bank Group staff members—and, in most cases, from members of the general public—in their areas of expertise.

The sectoral programs correspond broadly to the sections in chapter 4, which provides information on many sector programs within the World Bank and within the corresponding industry departments or other units of IFC. Within the Bank, the thematic networks and the sectors they cover are as follows:

- *Financial and Private Sector Development Network.* The sectors are banking, capital markets, financial services, credit, and regulatory reforms. Some of these sectors are handled by joint World Bank–IFC units.
- *Human Development Network.* The sectors are education; health, nutrition, and population; and social protection.
- *Operations Policy and Country Services.* The sectors are procurement, financial management, operational services, and the Country Services Panel.
- *Poverty Reduction and Economic Management Network.* The sectors are economic policy, gender, governance and public sector reform, and poverty.
- *Sustainable Development Network.* The sectors are water and sanitation, energy and mining, environment, rural development, urban transport, social development, and other infrastructure.

IFC sectors (or industry departments) and subsectors include the following:

- *Agribusiness:* The subsectors are aquaculture; beverages; dairy; fruits and vegetables; grains; livestock processing; oilseed, vegetable fats, and edible oils; processed food; sugar; and other.
- *Global Financial Markets:* The subsectors are Africa MSME finance, banking, business linkages, consumer finance, distressed assets, factoring, financial infrastructure, housing finance, IDA-IFC, insurance, leasing, microfinance, securities markets, and trade finance.
- *Global Manufacturing and Services:* The subsectors are building materials and glass; electronics, machinery, and appliances; forest products; life sciences; metals; retail, hotels, and property development; plastics and fibers; and transport equipment.
- *Health and Education:* The subsectors for health are facilities, pharmaceuticals, e-health, insurance, ancillary services, and education and training.

The subsectors for education are primary and secondary, tertiary, and e-learning.

■ *Infrastructure:* The subsectors are airlines, airports, buses, logistics, ports, ports services, power, railways, shipping, toll services, and water and gas.

■ *Private Equity and Investment Funds*

Additionally, the Global Information and Communication Technologies Department and the Oil, Gas, Mining, and Chemicals Department are joint World Bank and IFC departments.

Sectors within MIGA include the following:

■ Agribusiness, Manufacturing, Services, and Tourism
■ Finance
■ Infrastructure
■ Oil, Gas, and Mining

Other organizational units have adopted certain features of a network. They include the Information Solutions Network, which comprises all staff members working in the field of information technology; CommNet (Communications Network), an association of professionals across Bank Group headquarters and country offices who handle communications, issues management, and constituency relations; and the Administrative and Client Support Network, which comprises all staff members in office support positions.

Other Major World Bank Group Units and Activities

The following paragraphs describe other major units of the World Bank Group. These may be VPUs or the equivalent. Note that a single unit handles some functions for all Bank Group organizations, whereas in other cases each organization has separate units. Note also that this list is not intended to be comprehensive. For more information about World Bank Group organizational units, go to http://www.worldbank.org/about (click on "Organization"), http://www.ifc.org, http://www.miga.org, and http://www.worldbank.org/icsid/.

Corporate Secretariat

This unit supports the day-to-day operations of the Boards of Directors of the World Bank Group. It is responsible for the administration of matters connected with membership, including the Annual Meetings of the Boards of Governors and capital subscriptions. It also provides support to the independent Inspection Panel (see the subsection entitled "Independent Evaluation Group").

Development Economics

The chief economist heads this main research unit of the World Bank. The unit provides data, analyses of development prospects, research findings, analytical tools, and policy advice in support of Bank operations as well as advice to clients. More information on Bank Group research and data appears in chapter 2.

IFC's chief economist is also the World Bank and IFC vice president for the Financial and Private Sector Development VPU.

External Affairs

External Affairs at the World Bank manages communications, issues management, and constituency relations; handles relations with the public, the media and other organizations, governments of donor countries, and the local Washington, DC, community; arranges speaking engagements for Bank representatives; produces and disseminates publications; coordinates the Bank's worldwide network of PICs; and maintains the Bank's external Web site. Programs include Development Communications and CommNet. The Bank's offices in Brussels, Geneva, London, New York, Paris, Rome, and Tokyo are part of this unit.

IFC and MIGA each maintain a corporate relations unit.

Financial Management

The Bank Group's chief financial officer is responsible for the finance and risk management functions for the World Bank Group. Three vice presidencies within IBRD and IDA report directly to the Bank Group chief financial officer:

- *Concessional Finance and Global Partnerships,* which oversees the mobilization of funds for IDA and key environmental and debt relief initiatives; manages trust funds and development grants; and is responsible for interaction with bilateral partners, multilateral development banks, and foundations.
- *Controllers, Strategy, and Resource Management,* which oversees the Accounting and Loan departments as well as the strategic allocation of resources across the Bank.

▪ *Treasury,* which oversees capital markets and financial engineering, asset and liability management, technical assistance to borrowing countries, financial products and services, and investment management.

Two departments within IBRD and IDA also report directly to the Bank Group's chief financial officer: Corporate Finance and Credit Risk.

In addition, the Bank Group's chief financial officer is responsible for signing off on the financial policies of the finance and risk management functions within IFC and MIGA.

IFC groups the following units under its Risk Management Vice Presidency: Business Risk Group, Controller's Budgeting, Corporate Business Informatics, Corporate Portfolio Management, Credit Review, Financial Operations, Risk Management and Financial Policy, and Special Operations.

In MIGA, the following units report directly to the executive vice president: Operations, Legal, Finance and Risk Management, Economics and Policy, and External Outreach and Partnerships.

General Services

This unit is responsible for the design and maintenance of office space; procurement of goods and services; translation and interpretation; security; travel and shipping support; printing and graphic design; and mail, messenger, and food services. IFC and MIGA handle some of these responsibilities through their own offices for facilities management and administration.

Human Resources

This unit manages all personnel issues, including providing information on job opportunities and internships. The World Bank and IFC have separate human resources VPUs, and in MIGA, the Office of Central Administration handles human resources. The World Bank human resources VPU conducts orientations for all new Bank Group staff members and operates a staff exchange program. This program arranges temporary secondment of Bank Group staff members and staff members of participating companies and organizations. The program enhances the professional and technical skills of participating individuals and promotes cultural exchange, fresh perspectives, and diversity for the institutions involved. Separate from these human resources units is the Bank Group's Conflict Resolution System, a group of independent offices that address problems in the workplace, such as ethical issues and disputes regarding staff rules, pay, career advancement, and benefits. In addition to these units, the World Bank Group Staff Association, an independent, voluntary organization, advocates for the rights and welfare of staff members.

Independent Evaluation Group

The Independent Evaluation Group is an independent unit that reports directly to the Board of Executive Directors. Led by the Independent Evaluation Group's director general, the unit is tasked with assessing the results of all of the Bank Group's work and offering relevant recommendations. Separate units of the Independent Evaluation Group work with the Bank, IFC, and MIGA. The group undertakes its work during the evaluation phase of all World Bank Group projects, as outlined in chapter 2. The unit also supports the development of evaluation capacity in recipient countries.

Other units with related missions include the Compliance Advisor/Ombudsman for IFC and MIGA; the Office of Ethics and Business Conduct, which deals with joint Bank and IFC units; and the Quality Assurance Group at the World Bank.

In addition, the World Bank has set up the independent Inspection Panel, a three-member body to whom citizens of developing countries can bring their concerns if they believe that they or their interests have been or could be directly harmed by a project financed by the World Bank.

Information Solutions Group

This unit builds and operates the Bank Group's infrastructure for information and communications technologies. It falls under the direction of the chief information officer, who is also responsible for library oversight. IFC has a separate unit to provide support in this area.

Institutional Integrity Department

The Institutional Integrity Department investigates allegations of fraud, corruption, coercion, and collusion related to Bank-financed projects and Bank Group operations. It also investigates allegations of serious staff misconduct. In addition to investigations, the department also helps improve compliance with World Bank policies and prevent corruption by a variety of means, including training staff to detect and deter fraud and corruption in Bank Group projects and to improve control and compliance systems. As of February 2007, the Institutional Integrity Department had investigated and closed more than

2,400 cases since 1999. It has also sanctioned 355 firms and individuals for fraud and corruption in Bank-financed projects since 1999. The department publishes an annual integrity report with aggregate data, outcomes, and generic descriptions of significant cases. To ensure the independence of its activities, the director of the Institutional Integrity Department reports directly to the president of the World Bank Group.

Legal

The World Bank, IFC, and MIGA have separate legal VPUs, each headed by its own general counsel. Each of these units provides legal services for its respective institution and helps ensure that all activities comport with the institution's charter, policies, and rules. The focus includes legal and judicial reform in developing countries.

Office of the President

This office provides support to the World Bank Group president and maintains information on the president's speeches, interviews, and travels.

World Bank Institute

The World Bank Institute (WBI) is the main capacity development unit of the World Bank. WBI helps Bank clients develop capacity through thematic learning events, technical assistance, and economic and sector work. Its activities include holding training courses, offering policy consultations, and supporting knowledge networks related to international development. WBI's focus includes distance learning and other innovative uses of technology for education and training. WBI works in close collaboration with Bank operations staff and other partners to design and deliver customized country programs, to provide global and regional activities that address key sectoral issues that go beyond country boundaries, and to develop diagnostic tools to assess countries' capacity needs.

Relationship to the IMF and the UN

The World Bank Group is an independent specialized agency of the UN and works in particularly close cooperation with another independent specialized UN agency, the IMF. This section explains these relationships (see also the history timeline in appendix B).

The Bretton Woods Institutions

The World Bank and the IMF were both created in 1944 at a conference of world leaders in Bretton Woods, New Hampshire, with the aim of placing the international economy on a sound footing after World War II. As a result of their shared origin, the two entities—the IMF and the expanded World Bank Group—are sometimes referred to collectively as the Bretton Woods institutions. The Bank Group and the IMF—which came into formal existence in 1945—work closely together, have similar governance structures, have a similar relationship with the UN, and are headquartered in close proximity in Washington, DC. Indeed, membership in the Bank Group organizations is open only to countries that are already members of the IMF. However, the Bank Group and the IMF remain separate institutions. Their work is complementary, but their individual roles are quite different.

Key differences between the work of the World Bank Group and that of the IMF include the following:

- The Bank Group lends only to developing or transition economies, whereas all member countries, rich or poor, can draw on the IMF's services and resources.
- The IMF's loans address short-term economic problems: they provide general support for a country's balance of payments and international reserves while the country takes policy action to address its difficulties. The Bank Group is concerned mainly with longer-term issues: it seeks to integrate countries into the wider world economy and to promote economic growth that reduces poverty.
- The IMF focuses on the macroeconomic performance of economies, as well as on macroeconomic and financial sector policy. The Bank Group's focus extends further into the particular sectors of a country's economy and its work includes specific development projects as well as broader policy issues.

There are a few joint Bank Group and IMF units, including the Library Network; Health Services; and the Bank/Fund Conferences Office, which plans and coordinates the Annual and Spring Meetings. The staff members of the two institutions have formed the joint Bank-Fund Staff Federal Credit Union, but this entity is independent of the institutions themselves.

The Development Committee and the International Monetary and Financial Committee

The Development Committee is a forum of the Bank Group and the IMF that facilitates intergovernmental consensus building on development issues.

Known formally as the Joint Ministerial Committee of the Boards of the Bank and Fund on the Transfer of Real Resources to Developing Countries, the committee was established in 1974.

The committee's mandate is to advise the Boards of Governors of the two institutions on critical development issues and on the financial resources required to promote economic development in developing countries. Over time, the committee has interpreted this mandate to include trade and global environmental issues in addition to traditional development matters.

The committee has 24 members, usually ministers of finance and development, who represent the full membership of the Bank Group and the IMF. They are appointed by each of the countries—or groups of countries—represented on the Boards of Executive Directors of the two institutions. The chair is selected from among the committee's members and is assisted by an executive secretary elected by the committee. The Development Committee meets twice a year. For more information see http://www.worldbank.org/devcom.

The International Monetary and Financial Committee has a similar structure, selection process for members, and schedule for meetings. It serves in an advisory role to the IMF Board of Governors; however, unlike the Development Committee, the International Monetary and Financial Committee is solely an IMF entity.

Annual and Spring Meetings

Each September or October, the Boards of Governors of the World Bank Group and the IMF hold joint Annual Meetings to discuss a range of issues related to poverty reduction, international economic development, and finance. These meetings provide a forum for international cooperation and enable the two institutions to serve their member countries more effectively. In addition, the Development Committee and the International Monetary and Financial Committee are officially convened.

These meetings have traditionally been held in Washington, DC, two years out of three and in a different member country every third year. Recent meetings outside Washington, DC, have taken place in Prague, the Czech Republic (2000); Dubai, the United Arab Emirates (2003); and Singapore (2006). The Bank Group and the IMF organize a number of forums around these meetings to facilitate interaction by government officials and Bank Group and IMF staff members with CSO and private sector representatives and with journalists.

The Development Committee and the International Monetary and Financial Committee also meet in March or April of each year to discuss progress on the work of the Bank Group and the IMF. As with the Annual Meetings, a number of activities are organized at these Spring Meetings to involve the press, CSOs, and the private sector. However, plenary sessions of the two institutions' Boards of Governors are scheduled only during the Annual Meetings in September or October.

Specialized Agency of the United Nations

Cooperation between the Bank Group and the UN has been in place since the founding of the two organizations (in 1944 and 1945, respectively) and focuses on economic and social areas of mutual concern, such as reducing poverty, promoting sustainable development, and investing in people. In addition to a shared agenda, the Bank Group and the UN have almost the same membership: only a handful of UN member countries are not members of IBRD.

The World Bank's formal relationship with the UN is defined by a 1947 agreement that recognizes the Bank (now the Bank Group) as an independent specialized agency of the UN and as an observer in many UN bodies, including the General Assembly. As an independent specialized agency, the Bank Group officially falls under the purview of the Economic and Social Council. In recent years, the Economic and Social Council has conducted a special high-level meeting with the Bretton Woods institutions immediately after the Spring Meetings of the Bank Group and the IMF. The Bank Group president is also a member of the UN System Chief Executives Board for Coordination, which meets twice annually. In addition, the Bank Group plays a key role in supporting UN-led processes, such as the International Conference on Financing for Development and the World Summit on Sustainable Development. It also provides knowledge about country-level challenges and helps formulate international policy recommendations.

In terms of operations, the Bank Group works with other UN funds and programs to coordinate policies, aid, and project implementation. It also helps prepare for and participates in most of the UN's global conferences and plays an important role in follow-up, especially in relation to the implementation of goals at the country level.

Further information on the Bank Group's collaboration with UN agencies can be found under "Partnerships" in chapter 2.

The World Bank Treasury trading room in Washington, DC. IBRD, which facilitates more than half of the World Bank's annual lending, raises money primarily by selling bonds in international financial markets.

2 How the World Bank Group Operates

This chapter covers the basics of Bank Group operations, many aspects of which are interconnected. The chapter is organized as follows:

- *Strategies.* This section explains the Bank Group's overall framework for its fight against poverty as well as strategies that are pertinent to individual countries and specific sectors of development.
- *Policies and Procedures.* This section provides an overview of the policies and procedures that the Bank Group has established for its operations to help ensure quality and fairness in its projects.
- *The Bank Group's Finances.* This section offers a quick primer on how the Bank Group institutions are funded and what they do with their money.
- *Financial Products and Services.* This section describes the financial products and services offered by World Bank Group institutions.
- Knowledge Sharing. This section describes the knowledge-sharing services that the Bank Group provides in support of development and poverty reduction activities.
- *World Bank Project Cycle.* This section covers the typical phases of a World Bank project, the documentation that each phase creates, and the resources for locating detailed information about Bank projects.
- *IFC Project Cycle.* This section covers the typical phases of an IFC project.
- *Partnerships.* This section provides an overview of the types of partners the Bank Group works with, including affiliates whose secretariats are located at Bank Group headquarters.
- *Staff, Consultants, and Vendors.* This section provides details about the Bank Group's staff and related opportunities: job openings, internships, and scholarships. It also provides links to basic information on doing business with the Bank Group.

Strategies

This section covers the main strategies guiding the work of the Bank Group. More information on strategies can be found online at http://www.developmentgoals.org.

Millennium Development Goals

The MDGs (box 2.1) identify—and quantify—specific gains that could be made to improve the lives of the world's poor people. Their aim is to reduce poverty while improving health, education, and the environment. These goals were endorsed by 189 countries at the September 2000 UN Millennium General Assembly in New York. They focus on significant, measurable improvements for the efforts of the World Bank Group, other multilateral organizations, governments, and other partners in the development community.

The MDGs grew out of the agreements and resolutions that have resulted from world conferences organized by the UN in the past 10–15 years. Each goal is to be achieved by 2015, with progress to be measured by comparison with 1990 levels. Although the goals are sometimes numbered, the numbers are not intended to indicate any differences of priority or urgency.

The goals establish yardsticks for measuring results, not just for developing countries but also for the high-income countries that help fund development programs and for the multilateral institutions that help countries implement these programs. The first seven goals are mutually reinforcing and are directed at reducing poverty in all its forms. The last goal—to develop a global partnership for development—is directed at the means to achieve the first seven.

Many of the poorest countries will need assistance if the MDGs are to be achieved, and countries that are both poor and heavily indebted will need further help in order to reduce their debt burdens. But providing assistance isn't limited to providing financial aid. Developing countries may also benefit if trade barriers are lowered, thereby allowing a freer exchange of goods and services.

Achieving the goals is an enormous challenge. Partnerships between the Bank Group, the UN Development Group (UNDG), and other organizations, as well as between donors and developing countries, are the only way to ensure coordinated and complementary efforts. The UNDG consists of the many UN programs, funds, and agencies engaged in development assistance and related activities. The Bank Group participates in the UNDG and supports its framework for greater coherence and cooperation in UN development operations.

Box 2.1 Millennium Development Goals (MDGs)

Goals and Targets from the Millennium Declaration

GOAL 1	**ERADICATE EXTREME POVERTY AND HUNGER**
TARGET 1	Halve, between 1990 and 2015, the proportion of people whose income is less than $1 a day
TARGET 2	Halve, between 1990 and 2015, the proportion of people who suffer from hunger
GOAL 2	**ACHIEVE UNIVERSAL PRIMARY EDUCATION**
TARGET 3	Ensure that by 2015, children everywhere, boys and girls alike, will be able to complete a full course of primary schooling
GOAL 3	**PROMOTE GENDER EQUALITY AND EMPOWER WOMEN**
TARGET 4	Eliminate gender disparity in primary and secondary education, preferably by 2005, and at all levels of education no later than 2015
GOAL 4	**REDUCE CHILD MORTALITY**
TARGET 5	Reduce by two-thirds, between 1990 and 2015, the under-five mortality rate
GOAL 5	**IMPROVE MATERNAL HEALTH**
TARGET 6	Reduce by three-quarters, between 1990 and 2015, the maternal mortality ratio
GOAL 6	**COMBAT HIV/AIDS, MALARIA, AND OTHER DISEASES**
TARGET 7	Have halted by 2015 and begun to reverse the spread of HIV/AIDS
TARGET 8	Have halted by 2015 and begun to reverse the incidence of malaria and other major diseases
GOAL 7	**ENSURE ENVIRONMENTAL SUSTAINABILITY**
TARGET 9	Integrate the principles of sustainable development into country policies and programs and reverse the loss of environmental resources
TARGET 10	Halve by 2015 the proportion of people without sustainable access to safe drinking water and basic sanitation
TARGET 11	Have achieved a significant improvement by 2020 in the lives of at least 100 million slum dwellers

(continued)

Box 2.1 *continued*

GOAL 8	DEVELOP A GLOBAL PARTNERSHIP FOR DEVELOPMENT
TARGET 12	Develop further an open, rule-based, predictable, nondiscriminatory trading and financial system (including a commitment to good governance, development, and poverty reduction, nationally and internationally)
TARGET 13	Address the special needs of the least developed countries (including tariff- and quota-free access for exports of the least developed countries; enhanced debt relief for heavily indebted poor countries and cancellation of official bilateral debt; and more generous official development assistance for countries committed to reducing poverty)
TARGET 14	Address the special needs of landlocked countries and small island developing states (through the Programme of Action for the Sustainable Development of Small Island Developing States and the outcome of the 22nd special session of the General Assembly)
TARGET 15	Deal comprehensively with the debt problems of developing countries through national and international measures to make debt sustainable in the long term
TARGET 16	In cooperation with developing countries, develop and implement strategies for decent and productive work for youth
TARGET 17	In cooperation with pharmaceutical companies, provide access to affordable, essential drugs in developing countries
TARGET 18	In cooperation with the private sector, make available the benefits of new technologies, especially information and communication

Source: United Nations 2000, 2001.

Note: The Millennium Development Goals and targets come from the *Millennium Declaration* signed by 189 countries, including 147 heads of state, in September 2000. The goals and targets are related and should be seen as a whole. They represent a partnership of countries determined, as the Declaration states, "to create an environment—at the national and global levels alike—which is conducive to development and the elimination of poverty."

Since 2004, the World Bank—in partnership with the IMF—has published the *Global Monitoring Report,* which monitors the performance of donor countries, developing countries, and international financial institutions in delivering on their commitments to support achievement of the MDGs. The report reviews key developments in the previous year, discusses priority emerging issues, and assesses performance. For more information about this report, go to http://www.worldbank.org/globalmonitoring.

In 2007, the World Bank launched the Online Atlas of Millennium Development Goals, which includes a complete set of indicators for the MDGs, interactive world maps, graphs, and links to related Web sites. It contains a range of data for more than 200 economies. Visit http://devdata.worldbank.org/atlas-mdg.

For the Bank Group, as for other agencies, the challenge of implementing the MDGs provides a starting point for all operations. The Web site of the MDGs is http://www.developmentgoals.org.

Strategic Framework

The Bank Group's strategic framework concentrates on the twin pillars of (1) building an appropriate climate for investment, jobs, and sustainable growth so that economies will grow and of (2) investing in and empowering poor people to participate in development. In recent years, the executive directors have underscored the continued relevance of these priorities, have reaffirmed the need for selectivity in the Bank Group's work, and have called for greater collaboration with development partners. The executive directors have reviewed a number of progress reports on ongoing efforts to harmonize operational policies, procedures, and practices among donors; on meeting the needs of low-income countries, including heavily indebted poor countries and fragile states; and on strengthening partnerships with middle-income countries. They have also stressed the need for the Bank Group to intensify its efforts in implementing the strategic framework by refining the tools and procedures for meeting the development challenges set forth in the MDGs.

Thematic and Sector Strategies

Thematic and sector strategies address cross-cutting facets of poverty reduction, such as HIV/AIDS, the environment, and participation in and decentralization of government. In addition, these strategies serve as a guide for future work in a given sector, and they help in assessing the appropriateness and impact of related Bank Group policies. The strategies are revised on a rolling basis through extensive consultation with a wide variety of stakeholders. The process helps to build consensus within the Bank Group and to strengthen relationships with external partners. Figures 2.1 and 2.2 present overall shares of lending by theme and sector for the World Bank, figure 2.3 presents IFC investment projects by industry, and figure 2.4 presents overall shares of MIGA guarantees by sector.

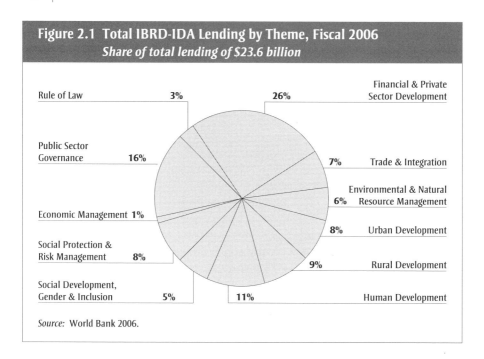

Figure 2.1 Total IBRD-IDA Lending by Theme, Fiscal 2006
Share of total lending of $23.6 billion

Rule of Law — 3%

26% — Financial & Private Sector Development

Public Sector Governance — 16%

7% — Trade & Integration

6% — Environmental & Natural Resource Management

Economic Management — 1%

8% — Urban Development

Social Protection & Risk Management — 8%

9% — Rural Development

Social Development, Gender & Inclusion — 5%

11% — Human Development

Source: World Bank 2006.

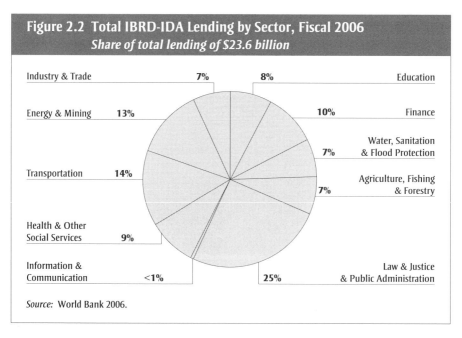

Figure 2.2 Total IBRD-IDA Lending by Sector, Fiscal 2006
Share of total lending of $23.6 billion

Industry & Trade — 7%

8% — Education

Energy & Mining — 13%

10% — Finance

7% — Water, Sanitation & Flood Protection

Transportation — 14%

7% — Agriculture, Fishing & Forestry

Health & Other Social Services — 9%

Information & Communication — <1%

25% — Law & Justice & Public Administration

Source: World Bank 2006.

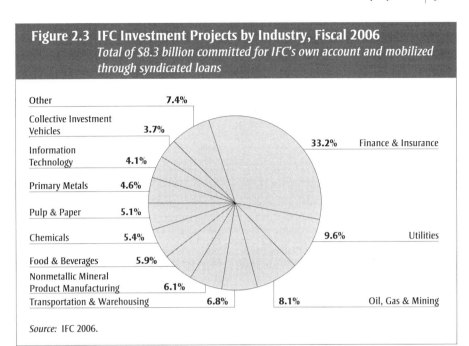

Figure 2.3 IFC Investment Projects by Industry, Fiscal 2006
Total of $8.3 billion committed for IFC's own account and mobilized through syndicated loans

Other — **7.4%**

Collective Investment Vehicles — **3.7%**

Information Technology — **4.1%**

Primary Metals — **4.6%**

Pulp & Paper — **5.1%**

Chemicals — **5.4%**

Food & Beverages — **5.9%**

Nonmetallic Mineral Product Manufacturing — **6.1%**

Transportation & Warehousing — **6.8%**

33.2% Finance & Insurance

9.6% Utilities

8.1% Oil, Gas & Mining

6.8%

Source: IFC 2006.

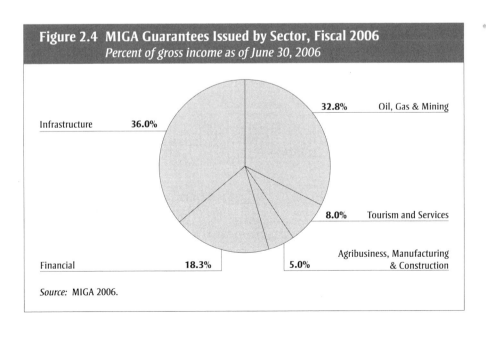

Figure 2.4 MIGA Guarantees Issued by Sector, Fiscal 2006
Percent of gross income as of June 30, 2006

Infrastructure — **36.0%**

Financial — **18.3%**

32.8% Oil, Gas & Mining

8.0% Tourism and Services

5.0% Agribusiness, Manufacturing & Construction

Source: MIGA 2006.

Many sector strategies are posted on the World Bank's Web sites and some of the published findings are available for purchase online (http://publications. worldbank.org/ecommerce/).

Comprehensive Development Framework

The Comprehensive Development Framework, adopted in January 1999, is an approach to development whereby countries become the leaders and owners of their own development and poverty reduction policies. It emphasizes the interdependence of all aspects of development: social, structural, human, governance related, environmental, economic, and financial. It also aims to correct the historical shortcomings of many aid programs, which often were implemented with a limited focus and with little support in the affected countries.

Specifically, the Comprehensive Development Framework advocates

- a holistic, long-term strategy with the country taking the lead, both owning and directing the development agenda, while the Bank Group and other partners each define their support in their respective business plans;
- the development of stronger partnerships between governments, donors, civil society, the private sector, and other development stakeholders in implementing the country strategy; and
- a transparent focus on accountability for development results to ensure better practical success in reducing poverty.

The Comprehensive Development Framework is not a blueprint to be applied to all countries in a uniform manner, but a new way of doing business to make development efforts more effective in a world challenged by poverty and distress. The related Web site is http://www.worldbank.org/cdf.

Poverty Reduction Strategies

Poverty reduction strategies represent the tangible outcomes of the approach defined by the Comprehensive Development Framework. In contrast to past approaches, which were applied to countries by donor organizations, developing countries now write their own strategies for reducing poverty (box 2.2). The resulting Poverty Reduction Strategy Papers (PRSPs) then become the basis for IDA lending from the World Bank, for comparable lending from the IMF's Poverty Reduction and Growth Facility, and for debt relief under the Heavily Indebted Poor Countries (HIPC) Initiative.

A PRSP is an annually updated document that a country prepares in collaboration with the Bank and the IMF. The PRSP is expected to be comprehensive in scope and partnership oriented, with civil society and the private sector participating in its preparation. The PRSP describes the country's plans to foster growth and reduce poverty through three-year economic adjustment programs that include macroeconomic, structural, and social policies. In addition, it describes associated external financing needs and major sources of financing. The World Bank has produced *A Sourcebook for Poverty Reduction Strategies,* with chapters that address the various sectors of development, as a resource to help countries prepare their PRSPs. A PDF version of this volume is available for free online (http://www.worldbank.org/prsp), as well as in book form for purchase (http://publications.worldbank.org/ecommerce/).

When preparing its PRSP, a country can submit an interim PRSP to avoid delays in receiving assistance. The interim document must take stock of a coun-

---

Box 2.2 Poverty Reduction Strategies: Key Steps

No blueprint is available for building all countries' poverty reduction strategies. Rather, the process reflects countries' individual circumstances and characteristics. Recommended features of PRSPs include the following:

- *Description of the participatory process.* The PRSP will describe the format, frequency, and location of consultations; summarize the main issues raised and the views of participants; provide an account of the impact of the consultations on the design of the strategy; and discuss the role of civil society in future monitoring and implementation.
- *Comprehensive poverty diagnostics.* A good understanding of the poor and where they live allows the PRSP to analyze the macroeconomic, social, structural, and institutional constraints to faster growth and poverty reduction.
- *Clearly presented and costed priorities for macroeconomic, structural, and social policies.* In light of a deeper understanding of poverty and its causes, the PRSP will set out the macroeconomic, structural, and social policies that together comprise a comprehensive strategy for achieving poverty-reducing outcomes. Policies will be costed and prioritized as far as possible so that they do not become just a "wish list."
- *Appropriate targets, indicators, and systems for monitoring and evaluating progress.* The PRSP will define medium- and long-term goals for poverty reduction outcomes (monetary and nonmonetary), establish indicators of progress, and set annual and medium-term targets. The indicators and targets will be consistent with the assessment of poverty, the institutional capacity to monitor, and the strategy's policy choices.

try's current poverty reduction strategy and must lay out a road map of how the country is going to develop its complete PRSP. On receiving the interim or final document, the World Bank and IMF conduct a joint staff assessment, which helps the boards of the institutions judge whether the document provides a sound basis on which to proceed with assistance and debt relief.

Country Assistance Strategies

Country Assistance Strategies (CASs) identify the key areas in which Bank Group support can best assist a country in achieving sustainable development and poverty reduction. They are the central vehicle used by the executive directors to review and guide the Bank Group's support for borrowers from IBRD and IDA. Each CAS includes a comprehensive diagnosis—drawing on analytic work by the Bank Group, the government, and other partners—of the development challenges facing the country, including the incidence, trends, and causes of poverty. From this assessment, the level and composition of Bank Group financial, advisory, and technical support to the country is determined. So that implementation of the CAS program can be tracked, CASs are increasingly results focused. Thus, each CAS includes a framework of clear targets and indicators that are used to monitor Bank Group and country performance in achieving stated outcomes.

The key elements of the CAS are discussed with the country's government and often with civil society representatives before the CAS is considered by the Board; however, it is not a negotiated document. Any differences between the country's own agenda and the strategy advocated by the Bank Group are highlighted in the CAS. Even though the country owns its development strategy as outlined in the PRSP, the Bank Group provides the CAS to its shareholders specifically to account for its diagnosis of a country's development situation and for the programs it supports.

Some CASs are publicly available. More information on the purpose, process, and content of CASs—as well as a CAS calendar—can be found at http://www.worldbank.org/cas.

IFC and Private Sector Development Strategies

IFC's Operational Strategy Department produces an annual Strategic Directions Paper, which reviews IFC's external environment, assesses the progress it has made in implementing its strategic priorities, and sets out goals to be achieved in order to increase development impact. The paper is available at http://www.ifc.org/disclosure.

The World Bank Group also has a private sector development strategy that includes activities undertaken by IFC, MIGA, and some World Bank units. The lead unit in this area is the joint World Bank and IFC Financial and Private Sector Development Vice Presidency.

Policies and Procedures

The World Bank Group has established policies and procedures to help ensure that its operations are economically, financially, socially, and environmentally sound. Each operation must follow these policies and procedures to ensure quality, integrity, and adherence to the Bank Group's mission, corporate priorities, and strategic goals. These policies and procedures—including rigorous safeguard policies on projects affecting, for example, women, the environment, and indigenous peoples—are codified in the World Bank's "Operational Manual." They are subject to extensive review while being formulated and to compliance monitoring after being approved.

Operational Manual

The World Bank's "Operational Manual" is available online at http://www.worldbank.org/opmanual. Volume I deals with the Bank's core development objectives and goals and the instruments for pursuing them. Volume II covers the requirements applicable to Bank-financed lending operations. The manual includes several different kinds of operational statements: operational policies, Bank procedures, good practices, and operational directives.

Policy definitions and documentation

Operational Policies are short, focused statements that follow from the Bank's Articles of Agreement and the general conditions and policies approved by the Board of Executive Directors. They establish the parameters for conducting operations, describe the circumstances in which exceptions to policy are admissible, and spell out who authorizes exceptions. *Bank Procedures* explain how staff members carry out the operational policies by describing the procedures and documentation required to ensure consistency and quality across the Bank. *Good Practices* are statements that contain advice and guidance on policy implementation, such as the history of an issue, the sectoral context, and the analytical framework, along with examples of good practice. Although they may be included in the manual, good practices are generally maintained and made available by the Bank units responsible for specific policies. *Operational Directives* contain a mixture of policies, procedures, and guidance; however, they are gradually being replaced by the operational policies, Bank procedures, and good practices.

Environmental and social safeguard policies

Environmental and social safeguard policies help to ensure that Bank operations assist, rather than harm, people and the environment. The Bank has 10 environmental and social safeguard policies, which consist of a policy on environmental assessments followed by 9 related policies that fall within the scope of the first. These 9 policies cover natural habitats, pest management, involuntary resettlement, indigenous peoples, forests, cultural resources, dam safety, international waterways, and disputed areas.

The Bank conducts environmental screening of each proposed project to determine the appropriate extent and type of environmental assessment to be undertaken and to ascertain whether the project may trigger other safeguard policies. The Bank classifies the proposed project into one of four categories (A, B, C, and FI) depending on the type, location, sensitivity, and scale of the project and the nature and magnitude of its potential environmental impact. Category A requires the project to undergo the most comprehensive environmental assessment, category B requires a narrower assessment, and category C requires no environmental assessment. A project classified as A, B, or C can trigger other safeguard policies, in which case additional assessments related to those specific policies are required. Category FI identifies subprojects that are funded by the Bank through financial intermediaries and that may affect the environment adversely.

Assessments provide mechanisms for public review and scrutiny. The borrower is responsible for any assessment required by the safeguard policies, with general assistance provided by Bank staff members. The Bank's Legal Vice Presidency monitors compliance with the policies addressing international waterways and disputed areas.

Policy formulation and review

The Bank's Operations Policy and Country Services Vice Presidency reviews, updates, and formulates policies and procedures that govern the Bank's operations. Proposals for policy revisions or new policies respond to the strategic priorities set by the Bank's management and Board. Formulation or review of a policy entails bringing together experienced regional and network staff members, legal experts, and policy writers. If the policy or proposed revision is complex, the task may entail an iterative process of consultation inside and outside the Bank (including with internal experts, clients, external experts and partners such as CSOs, and the public). Following the consultation process, a final draft, usually accompanied by an explanatory paper, is submitted for comment and approval to the appropriate management group, the Bank's managing directors, and the Board of Executive Directors.

Recent policy and procedural reforms have included revisions of the Bank's audit policy, the policy on the eligibility of expenditures, the procurement guidelines, and the Bank's policy on development policy lending, and a new policy on additional financing for investment lending.

Compliance monitoring

The Bank's credibility rests on effective implementation of its policies. The mission of Operations Policy and Country Services is to enhance the Bank's operational effectiveness. Operations Policy and Country Services supports and advises World Bank staff and management on a wide range of operational areas, from preparing and implementing lending and nonlending programs to applying policies and procedures in Bank priority areas. It works in collaboration with the Bank's other vice presidencies and with other World Bank Group organizations.

The Bank has also set up the Inspection Panel, an independent forum for private citizens who believe that their rights or interests have been or could be directly harmed by a Bank-financed project. If people living in a project area believe that harm has resulted from, or will result from, a failure by the Bank to follow its policies and procedures, they or a representative may request a review of the project by the Inspection Panel. The panel's Web site is at http://www.worldbank.org/inspectionpanel.

Disclosure of information

The Bank has established its disclosure policy to support important goals: to be open about its activities, to explain its work to the widest possible audience, and to promote overall accountability and transparency in the development process. The Bank seeks to provide balanced information, reporting, and learning drawn from both operational failures or disappointments and successes.

Recent extensions of the disclosure policy include the release of a greater number of project-related documents, the disclosure of the chair's summaries of Board discussions regarding CASs and Sector Strategy Papers, and the development of a more systematic approach to accessing Bank archives. Country Policy and Institutional Assessment scores—which assess the quality of a country's policy and institutional framework—have been publicly disclosed since the summer of 2006. The Bank continues to review the provisions and implementation of its disclosure policy on a regular basis. More about disclosure is available at http://www.worldbank.org/disclosure.

Fiduciary policies

The Bank's fiduciary policies, set forth in volume II of the "Operational Manual," govern the use and flow of Bank funds, including procurement. The Operations Policy and Country Services Vice Presidency provides guidelines for the procurement of goods and services in Bank projects. The guidelines help ensure that funds are used for their intended purposes and with economy, efficiency, and transparency. They also ensure competitive bidding and help protect Bank-funded projects from fraud and corruption (box 2.3). The procurement policy Web site is at http://www.worldbank.org/procure.

Independent firms periodically audit Bank projects to ensure that the procurement rules are being followed. Any allegations of fraud or corruption that surface are referred to the Oversight Committee for follow-up, including investigations where appropriate. If the allegations prove to be true, the Bank may terminate the employment of a staff member, debar the firms implicated, and cancel the funds allocated to the contract in question.

IFC, MIGA, and ICSID Policies

The policies and procedures of the World Bank Group apply also to IFC and to MIGA, with some specific variations in guidelines as appropriate to their clients:

- For links to IFC's disclosure policy and its environmental and social policy and standards, see http://www.ifc.org/disclosure.
- For a list of MIGA policies, click on "About MIGA" at http://www.miga.org and see "Environmental and Disclosure Policies."
- ICSID's policies are set forth in its basic documents, additional facility documents, and other documents available at http://www.worldbank.org/icsid.

Box 2.3 Reporting Fraud or Corruption

The Bank's Department of Institutional Integrity investigates allegations of fraud or corruption in World Bank Group–financed operations, as well as allegations of staff misconduct within the Bank Group.

Examples of issues that should be reported to the Department of Institutional Integrity for further review include suspected contract irregularities and violations of the Bank's procurement guidelines; bid manipulation; bid collusion; coercive practices; fraudulent bids; fraud in contract performance; fraud in an audit inquiry; product substitution; price manipulation; use of substandard or inferior parts or materials; cost or labor mischarges; kickbacks, bribery, or acceptance of gratuities; abuse of authority; misuse of Bank Group funds or of funds entrusted to the Bank Group; travel-related fraud; theft and embezzlement; benefits and allowances fraud; conflict of interest; misrepresentation; and forgery and the involvement of Bank Group staff in any of the aforementioned activities.

The Department of Institutional Integrity can be contacted via several means:

- Directly at World Bank headquarters:
  Telephone: 1-202-458-7677
  Fax: 1-202-522-7140
  Email: investigations_hotline@worldbank.org
  Web site: http://www.worldbank.org/integrity
- Through a fraud and corruption hotline hired by the department for this purpose that is accessible 24 hours a day with translation services available:
  Toll-free: 1-800-831-0463
  Collect calls: 1-704-556-7046
  Mail: PMB 3767
  13950 Ballantyne Corporate Place
  Charlotte, NC 28277
  USA
- Anonymous calls are also accepted.

The Bank Group's Finances

This section provides an overview of how the Bank Group institutions are financed, how they provide assistance in developing countries, and how they report on their finances. More details about Bank Group loans and other assistance follow in the next sections, "Financial Products and Services" and "Knowledge Sharing."

IBRD and IDA Funding and Lending

The World Bank finances its development programs by tapping the world's capital markets (in the case of IBRD) and by receiving contributions from wealthier member governments (in the case of IDA). Additionally, specific activities can be funded by donors through trust funds managed by the World Bank.

IBRD, which facilitates more than half of the Bank's annual lending, raises money primarily by selling bonds in international financial markets. It sells AAA-rated bonds and other debt securities to pension funds, insurance companies, corporations, other banks, and individuals around the world. Additionally, IBRD charges interest to its borrowers at rates that reflect its cost of borrowing. Loans must be repaid in 15 to 20 years, and there is a 3- to 5-year grace period before repayment of principal begins.

Less than 5 percent of IBRD's funds are paid in by countries when they join the Bank. Member governments purchase shares, the number of which is based on their relative economic strength, but pay in only a small portion of the value of those shares. The unpaid balance is "on call" in case the Bank should suffer losses so grave that it could no longer pay its creditors—something that, to date, has never happened. This guaranteed capital can be used only to pay bondholders, not to cover administrative costs or to make loans. IBRD's rules require that the sum of all loans outstanding and disbursed not exceed the combined total of capital and reserves.

The income that IBRD earns each year from the return on its equity and from the small margin it makes on lending pays for its operating expenses, goes into reserves to strengthen the balance sheet, and is used to fund annual transfers to IDA. Because it is a cooperative institution, IBRD seeks not to maximize profit but to earn enough income to ensure its financial strength and to sustain its development activities.

IDA, the world's largest source of interest-free loans and grant assistance to the poorest countries, is replenished every three years by donor countries. Additional funds are regenerated through repayments of loan principal on its 35- to 40-year no-interest loans, and these funds are then available for relending. IDA accounts for nearly 40 percent of World Bank lending. Forty countries contribute to IDA's funding. Donor nations include not only industrial member countries such as France, Germany, Japan, the United Kingdom, and the United States, but also developing countries such as Botswana, Brazil, Hungary, the Republic of Korea, the Russian Federation, and Turkey, some of which were once IDA borrowers. As with IBRD, to date there has never been a default on an IDA credit.

Cumulative lending by IBRD and IDA as of June 30, 2006, amounted to more than $589 billion (table 2.1). More information on IBRD and IDA product lines and lending instruments follows in the next section, "Financial Products and Services." Grants and loans obtained from cofinanciers and partnerships often complement government funds and World Bank lending to make up the total package of assistance to a country.

Funding of IFC, MIGA, and ICSID

IFC and MIGA each have share capital that is paid in by member countries, which vote in proportion to the number of shares they hold.

IFC makes loans and equity investments. The corporation's equity and quasi-equity investments are funded out of paid-in capital and retained earnings from these investments. Strong shareholder support, AAA ratings, and the substantial paid-in capital base have allowed IFC to raise funds for its lending activities on favorable terms in the international capital markets.

In addition to its share capital, MIGA receives funding for some of its operating expenses from the World Bank. MIGA also charges fees for the services it provides.

The operating expenses of the ICSID Secretariat are funded through the World Bank's budget, although the parties involved bear the costs of individual proceedings.

Financial Reporting: Bank Group Annual Reports

Each Bank Group institution provides detailed financial statements in its annual report. The fiscal year for these institutions runs from July 1 of a given year to June 30 of the following calendar year. The reports catalog financial performance and new activities. They also include comparative information on the regions and development sectors in which the institutions have provided assistance. These reports are available for free to the public, both in print and on the Internet. The reports are published in multiple languages, and the Web sites include past editions. For Web links to the Bank Group's annual reports, see appendix A.

Financial Products and Services

The World Bank Group is known best for its financial services. The sections below describe the financial products and services provided by World Bank Group institutions.

Table 2.1 IBRD-IDA Cumulative Lending by Country/Region

Country/region	IBRD loans Number	IBRD loans Amount ($ millions)	IDA Loans Number	IDA Loans Amount ($ millions)	Total Number	Total Amount ($ millions)
Afghanistan			42	1,353.3	42	1,353.3
Africa	11	259.8	18	1,155.4	29	1,415.2
Albania			59	854.8	59	854.8
Algeria	71	5,765.8			71	5,765.8
Angola			16	487.1	16	487.1
Argentina	130	22,728.2			130	22,728.2
Armenia	1	12.0	41	915.0	42	927.0
Australia	7	417.7			7	417.7
Austria	9	106.4			9	106.4
Azerbaijan	2	248.0	29	779.5	31	1,027.5
Bahamas, The	5	42.8			5	42.8
Bangladesh	1	46.1	189	12,027.1	190	12,073.2
Barbados	12	118.4			12	118.4
Belarus	5	242.8			5	242.8
Belgium	4	76.0			4	76.0
Belize	9	86.2			9	86.2
Benin			59	1,005.5	59	1,005.5
Bhutan			13	123.1	13	123.1
Bolivia	15	314.3	72	1,929.6	87	2,243.9
Bosnia and Herzegovina	0		50	1,039.3	50	1,039.3
Botswana	19	280.7	6	15.8	25	296.5
Brazil	312	37,898.2			312	37,898.2
Bulgaria	32	2,060.5			32	2,060.5
Burkina Faso	0	1.9	70	1,792.6	70	1,794.5
Burundi	1	4.8	56	1,078.2	57	1,083.0
Cambodia			27	659.2	27	659.2
Cameroon	45	1,347.8	33	1,301.7	78	2,649.5
Cape Verde			21	237.9	21	237.9
Caribbean	4	83.0	3	52.0	7	135.0
Central African Republic			27	448.5	27	448.5
Central America			2	42.0	2	42.0
Central Asia			1	25.0	1	25.0
Chad	1	39.5	47	1,041.6	48	1,081.1
Chile	69	4,016.3		19.0	69	4,035.3
China	203	30,976.8	71	9,946.7	274	40,923.5
Colombia	187	13,384.5		19.5	187	13,404.0
Comoros			19	132.4	19	132.4
Congo, Democratic Republic of	7	330.0	70	3,322.5	77	3,652.5
Congo, Republic of	10	216.7	18	383.3	28	600.0
Costa Rica	42	998.5		5.5	42	1,004.0

Country	IBRD loans Number	IBRD loans Amount ($ millions)	IDA Loans Number	IDA Loans Amount ($ millions)	Total Number	Total Amount ($ millions)
Côte d'Ivoire	62	2,887.9	25	2,042.5	87	4,930.4
Croatia	31	1,701.2			31	1,701.2
Cyprus	29	404.8			29	404.8
Czech Republic	3	776.0			3	776.0
Denmark	3	85.0			3	85.0
Djibouti			19	172.1	19	172.1
Dominica	3	6.6	4	21.1	7	27.7
Dominican Republic	38	1,263.5	3	22.0	41	1,285.5
Eastern Africa			1	45.0	1	45.0
Ecuador	78	3,113.7	5	36.9	83	3,150.6
Egypt, Arab Republic of	71	5,770.0	41	1,984.0	112	7,754.0
El Salvador	40	1,332.6	2	25.6	42	1,358.2
Equatorial Guinea			9	45.0	9	45.0
Eritrea			14	519.4	14	519.4
Estonia	8	150.7			8	150.7
Ethiopia	12	108.6	88	5,458.1	100	5,566.7
Fiji	12	152.9			12	152.9
Finland	18	316.8			18	316.8
France	1	250.0			1	250.0
Gabon	16	267.0			16	267.0
Gambia, The			29	271.2	29	271.2
Georgia			39	830.8	39	830.8
Ghana	9	187.0	116	5,065.4	125	5,252.4
Greece	17	490.8			17	490.8
Grenada	6	22.0	2	32.0	8	54.1
Guatemala	43	1,583.8			43	1,583.8
Guinea	3	75.2	61	1,388.0	64	1,463.2
Guinea-Bissau			26	314.9	26	314.9
Guyana	12	80.0	22	355.3	34	435.3
Haiti	1	2.6	42	757.5	43	760.1
Honduras	33	717.3	43	1,590.3	76	2,307.6
Hungary	40	4,247.6			40	4,247.6
Iceland	10	47.1			10	47.1
India	202	33,580.4	262	32,097.9	464	65,678.3
Indonesia	264	29,313.9	51	2,110.3	315	31,424.2
Iran, Islamic Republic of	48	3,413.1			48	3,413.1
Iraq	6	156.2	2	235.0	8	391.2
Ireland	8	152.5			8	152.5
Israel	10	254.5			10	254.5
Italy	8	399.6			8	399.6

(continued)

Table 2.1 *continued*

Country	IBRD loans Number	IBRD loans Amount ($ millions)	IDA Loans Number	IDA Loans Amount ($ millions)	Total Number	Total Amount ($ millions)
Jamaica	70	1,690.1			70	1,690.1
Japan	31	862.9			31	862.9
Jordan	57	2,334.7	15	85.3	72	2,420.0
Kazakhstan	27	2,113.0			27	2,113.0
Kenya	45	1,180.7	89	3,757.7	134	4,938.4
Korea, Republic of	112	15,472.0	6	110.8	118	15,582.8
Kosovo			8	35.5	8	35.5
Kyrgyz Republic			36	756.3	36	756.3
Lao People's Democratic Republic			43	835.9	43	835.9
Latvia	19	416.0			19	416.0
Lebanon	21	1,085.4			21	1,085.4
Lesotho	2	155.0	33	378.4	35	533.4
Liberia	19	156.0	15	144.5	34	300.5
Lithuania	17	490.9			17	490.9
Luxembourg	1	12.0			1	12.0
Macedonia, former Yugoslav Republic of	21	442.9	15	378.7	36	821.6
Madagascar	5	32.9	91	2,989.3	96	3,022.2
Malawi	9	124.1	83	2,366.7	92	2,490.8
Malaysia	87	4,145.6			87	4,145.6
Maldives			9	101.5	9	101.5
Mali	0	1.9	74	1,893.2	74	1,895.1
Malta	1	7.5			1	7.5
Mauritania	3	146.0	55	876.0	58	1,022.0
Mauritius	33	459.7	4	20.2	37	479.9
Mexico	205	38,039.8			205	38,039.8
Moldova	9	302.8	20	343.6	29	646.4
Mongolia			24	370.3	24	370.3
Morocco	138	9,378.1	3	50.8	141	9,428.9
Mozambique			55	3,080.5	55	3,080.5
Myanmar	3	33.4	30	804.0	33	837.4
Nepal			83	2,051.9	83	2,051.9
Netherlands	8	244.0			8	244.0
New Zealand	6	126.8			6	126.8
Nicaragua	27	233.6	41	1,322.7	68	1,556.3
Niger			58	1,325.7	58	1,325.7
Nigeria	84	6,248.2	36	2,888.0	120	9,136.2
OECS countries	3	11.8		8.5	3	20.2
Oman	11	157.1			11	157.1
Norway	6	145.0			6	145.0

Country	IBRD loans		IDA Loans		Total	
	Number	Amount ($ millions)	Number	Amount ($ millions)	Number	Amount ($ millions)
Pakistan	90	7,326.6	133	9,353.6	223	16,680.2
Panama	45	1,273.2			45	1,273.2
Papua New Guinea	35	786.6	9	113.2	44	899.8
Paraguay	43	921.1	6	45.5	49	966.6
Peru	107	6,629.5			107	6,629.5
Philippines	169	11,913.2	5	294.2	174	12,207.4
Poland	43	6,210.2			43	6,210.2
Portugal	32	1,338.8			32	1,338.8
Romania	83	7,248.5			83	7,248.5
Russian Federation	61	13,596.1			61	13,596.1
Rwanda			62	1,393.5	62	1,393.5
Samoa			13	87.8	13	87.8
São Tomé and Principe			12	80.4	12	80.4
Senegal	19	164.9	92	2,501.7	111	2,666.6
Serbia and Montenegro[a]			26	725.0	26	725.0
Seychelles	2	10.7			2	10.7
Sierra Leone	4	18.7	35	815.1	39	833.8
Singapore	14	181.3			14	181.3
Slovak Republic	9	424.6			9	424.6
Slovenia	5	177.7			5	177.7
Solomon Islands			8	49.9	8	49.9
Somalia			39	492.1	39	492.1
South Africa	13	302.8			13	302.8
Spain	12	478.7			12	478.7
Sri Lanka	12	210.7	90	3,200.1	102	3,410.8
St. Kitts and Nevis	5	23.5		1.5	5	25.0
St. Lucia	11	32.9		38.3	11	71.2
St. Vincent and the Grenadines	5	12.0	1	18.2	6	30.1
Sudan	8	166.0	47	1,352.9	55	1,518.9
Swaziland	12	104.8	2	7.8	14	112.6
Syrian Arab Republic	16	579.6	3	47.3	19	626.9
Taiwan, China	14	329.4	4	15.3	18	344.7
Tajikistan			26	404.9	26	404.9
Tanzania	17	318.9	122	5,718.5	139	6,037.4
Thailand	118	8,027.4	6	125.1	124	8,152.5
Timor-Leste			4	16.5	4	16.5
Togo	1	20.0	41	733.5	42	753.5
Tonga			5	22.8	5	22.8
Trinidad and Tobago	22	333.6			22	333.6

(continued)

Table 2.1 *continued*

Country	IBRD loans Number	IBRD loans Amount ($ millions)	IDA Loans Number	IDA Loans Amount ($ millions)	Total Number	Total Amount ($ millions)
Tunisia	123	5,509.8	5	69.8	128	5,579.6
Turkey	153	25,079.6	10	178.5	163	25,258.1
Turkmenistan	3	89.5			3	89.5
Uganda	1	9.1	94	4,560.1	95	4,569.2
Ukraine	33	4,498.1			33	4,498.1
Uruguay	56	2,546.0			56	2,546.0
Uzbekistan	13	554.1	1	85.0	14	639.1
Vanuatu			5	18.9	5	18.9
Venezuela, República Bolivariana de	40	3,328.4			40	3,328.4
Vietnam			60	6,327.7	60	6,327.7
Western Africa	1	6.1	3	52.5	4	58.6
Yemen, Republic of			135	2,498.3	135	2,498.3
Yugoslavia, former Yugoslav Republic	89	6,090.7			89	6,090.7
Zambia	27	679.1	60	2,847.2	87	3,526.3
Zimbabwe	24	983.2	12	662.0	36	1,645.2
Total	5,029	420,200.0	4,067	169,543.6	9,096	589,743.6

Source: World Bank 2006.
Note: OECS = Organization of Eastern Caribbean States. Joint IBRD and IDA operations are counted only once as IBRD operations. When more than one loan is made for a single project, the operation is counted only once. Amounts may not add to totals because of rounding.
a. Following a referendum in May 2006, Montenegro declared its independence from the union of Serbia and Montenegro, resulting in both states becoming independent countries. Data are for both states prior to independence.

World Bank

Lending instruments

The World Bank offers two basic types of lending instruments to its client governments: investment loans and development policy loans. Depending on its eligibility, a member country will draw on loans from either IBRD or IDA to support a lending project. Whether the money is lent through IBRD or IDA determines the terms of the loan (box 2.4 presents key terms and rates).

Loans are made as part of the comprehensive lending program set out in the CASs, which tailor Bank assistance (both lending and services) to each borrower's development needs. Lending operations are developed in several phases, as outlined in the "World Bank Project Cycle" section later in this chapter. Complete descriptions of the Bank's various lending instruments are available by clicking on "Financing Instruments" at http://www.worldbank.org/projects.

The Bank has a searchable online database of all projects: visit http://www.worldbank.org and click on "Projects and Operations." In addition, the Bank posts information on loans and credits most recently approved by its Board of Executive Directors under "News" on the Bank's Web site. For more information, see the later subsection on "Project Information."

Investment lending. Investment loans provide long-term financing for a range of activities aimed at creating the physical and social infrastructure necessary for poverty reduction and sustainable development. Over the past two decades, investment lending has, on average, accounted for 75 to 80 percent of all Bank lending.

Box 2.4 Financial Terms and Rates

IBRD

Front-end fee: 1 percent of the loan amount, payable on loan effectiveness

Lending rate: product specific; for some products, also currency specific

Commitment fee: varies by product, but 0.75 percent on undisbursed balance for most loans; a partial waiver may apply

Maturity: 15 to 20 years, with a 3- to 8-year grace period, for standard country terms

IDA

Service charge: 0.75 percent

Commitment fee: 0.0 to 0.5 percent on undisbursed balance (set annually, 0.2 percent for fiscal 2007)

Maturity: 20, 30, and 40 years, with a 10-year grace period

Interest rate: 4 percent for hard-term credits approved in fiscal 2007

CONTACT INFORMATION

Financial Products and Services Group

World Bank

1818 H Street, NW

MS MC7-708

Washington, DC, 20433, USA

Tel: 1-202-458-1122

Fax: 1-202-522-2102

E-mail: fps@worldbank.org

The nature of investment lending has evolved over time. Originally focused on hardware, engineering services, and bricks and mortar, investment lending has come to focus more on institution building, social development, and the public policy infrastructure needed to facilitate private sector activity. Examples of areas in which recent projects have been funded include

- urban poverty reduction (involving private contractors in new housing construction),
- rural development (formalizing land tenure to increase the security of small farmers),
- water and sanitation (improving the efficiency of water utilities),
- natural resource management (providing training in sustainable forestry and farming),
- postconflict reconstruction (reintegrating soldiers into communities),
- education (promoting the education of girls), and
- health (establishing rural clinics and training health care workers).

Development policy lending. Development policy loans provide quick-disbursing assistance to countries to support structural reforms in a sector or in the economy as a whole. They support the policy and institutional changes needed to create an environment conducive to sustained and equitable growth. Over the past two decades, development policy lending—previously called adjustment lending—has accounted, on average, for 20 to 25 percent of total Bank lending.

Development policy loans were originally designed to provide support for macroeconomic policy reforms, such as in trade policy and agriculture. However, they have evolved over time, and now they generally aim to promote competitive market structures (for example, legal and regulatory reform), correct distortions in incentive regimes (taxation and trade reform), establish appropriate monitoring and safeguards (financial sector reform), create an environment conducive to private sector investment (judicial reform, adoption of a modern investment code), encourage private sector activity (privatization and public-private partnerships), promote good governance (civil service reform), and mitigate the short-term adverse effects of development policy (establishment of social protection funds).

Grants

A limited number of grants are available through the Bank, funded either directly or through partnerships. Most are designed as seed money for pilot projects with innovative approaches and technologies. They also foster collaboration with other organizations and encourage broader participation in development projects. The Development Grant Facility provides overall strategy, allocations, and management for Bank grant-making activities. It has supported programs in such sectors as economic policy, education, environment, health, private sector development, and rural development. For more information go to http://worldbank.org/dgf/.

Cofinancing

The World Bank often cofinances its projects with governments, commercial banks, export credit agencies, multilateral institutions, and private sector investors. Cofinancing is any arrangement under which funds from the Bank are associated with funds provided by sources from outside the recipient country for a specific lending project or program. Official cofinancing—through either donor government agencies or multilateral financial institutions—constitutes the largest source of cofinancing for Bank-assisted operations.

Trust funds

Trust funds are financial arrangements between the World Bank and a donor or a group of donors under which the donor entrusts the Bank with funds for a specific development-related activity. They enable the Bank, along with bilateral and multilateral donors, to mobilize funds for investment operations as well as for debt relief, emergency reconstruction, technical assistance, and advisory services. Bank-administered trust funds support poverty reduction activities across a wide range of sectors and regions, thereby supporting clients in achieving development results at the global, regional, and country levels.

Much of the recent growth in these funds reflects the international community's desire for the Bank to help manage broad global initiatives through multilateral partnerships, such as the Global Fund to Fight AIDS, Tuberculosis, and Malaria; the Global Environment Facility; and the HIPC Initiative. Trust funds also support the World Bank's own development operations and work programs. Contributions from donors in fiscal 2006 totaled $5.3 billion, an increase of 9.5 percent over fiscal 2005. The main Web page for Bank trust funds is at http://www.worldbank.org/cfp.

Trust funds are also used by IFC. Refer to the "IFC" section for more information.

Guarantees and risk management

Guarantees promote private financing by covering risks that the private sector is not normally ready to absorb or manage. All World Bank guarantees are partial guarantees of private debt, so that risks are shared by the Bank and private lenders. The Bank's objective is to cover risks that it is in a unique position to bear given its experience in developing countries and its relationships with governments.

IBRD also offers hedging products, which can transform the risk characteristics of a borrower's IBRD obligations even though the negotiated terms of particular loan contracts themselves may be fixed. These products give borrowers improved risk management capability in the context of projects, lending programs, or sovereign asset-liability management. IBRD hedging products include interest rate swaps, interest rate caps and collars, currency swaps, and—on a case-by-case basis—commodity swaps.

Additional information on guarantees and risk management services follows in the sections on IFC and MIGA financial products and services. See also "Guarantees and Risk Management" at http://worldbank.org/businesscenter.

International Finance Corporation

IFC invests primarily in enterprises majority-owned by the private sector in almost all developing countries. For details of the corporation's products and services, click "About IFC" or "Products and Services" at http://www.ifc.org. For a printed copy of the brochure *IFC's Products and Services,* contact IFC Corporate Relations by telephone at (202) 473-3800 or e-mail at Webmaster@ IFC.org.

Lending and investments

IFC's investments in emerging market companies and financial institutions create jobs, build economies, and generate tax revenues. IFC brings its extensive knowledge of social and environmental issues and corporate governance to each investment to strengthen the financial health of the enterprise and ensure its long-term sustainability.

IFC offers clients a variety of lending instruments, including senior, subordinated, and convertible loans, as well as a choice of interest rates, namely, fixed- and variable-rate loans and, on occasion, loans indexed to the price of a commodity. Loans are issued at market rates. Most are denominated in major currencies, but an increasing number are in local currencies. IFC lending includes credit lines for on-lending to intermediary banks, leasing companies, and other financial institutions, particularly those that serve small businesses or microenterprises.

IFC also makes equity investments, risking its own capital by buying and holding shares in companies, other project entities, financial institutions, and portfolio or private equity funds. IFC is always a minority shareholder, generally limiting its shareholding to 20 percent or less of a company's equity, and will not normally be the largest shareholder in a project. In addition, IFC invests through quasi-equity instruments, products that have both debt and equity characteristics.

IFC offers clients risk management products that provide them with access to long-term derivatives markets. Instruments such as swaps and options help clients manage their currency, interest rate, and commodity price risks.

Working closely with the World Bank, IFC has also begun making new financial products and services and access to capital markets available to subnational entities—states, municipalities, and municipally controlled institutions—in developing countries. The goal is to help such local public entities deliver key infrastructure services and improve their efficiency and accountability. As with the corporation's other investments, subnational transactions do not require sovereign guarantees.

Resource mobilization

IFC serves as a catalyst for private capital through all of its investments, but it also offers products and services aimed specifically at resource mobilization.

IFC's structured finance products enable clients with strong, sustainable projects to access capital that otherwise might not be available to them. Products include credit enhancement structures for bonds and loans through partial credit guarantees, participation in securitizations, and risk-sharing facilities.

Through the syndicated loan or "B-loan" program, IFC offers commercial banks and other financial institutions the chance to lend to projects and companies they might not otherwise consider.

IFC also mobilizes financing through investment funds, a commercial sector that it has helped develop in emerging markets.

Trust funds

IFC uses donor-supported trust funds to help with technical assistance for various projects. IFC initiated the Technical Assistance Trust Funds Program in 1988 in an effort to identify and support viable business projects in developing countries at an early stage. These trust funds allow IFC to offer integrated solutions that combine commercial investments and donor-supported technical assistance. In addition, they catalyze innovative business approaches and facilitate pilot projects, which often develop into long-term technical assistance. The program is currently sponsored by 23 donor countries that collectively contribute $15 million to $20 million a year to support 100 to 150 new projects. IFC issues an annual report on trust funds that is available at http://www.ifc.org/tatf.

For details of IFC's advisory activities, see chapters 3 and 4 or select "Advisory Services" under "Products & Services" at http://www.ifc.org.

Multilateral Investment Guarantee Agency

Investment guarantees

MIGA provides investment guarantees against certain noncommercial risks (that is, political risk insurance) to eligible foreign investors for qualified investments in developing member countries. MIGA's investment guarantees cover the following risks: transfer restrictions, expropriation, breach of contract, and war and civil disturbance. MIGA makes a preliminary application for guarantee available on its Web site.

Knowledge Sharing

The Bank Group's development mission has always included analytic and advisory services as well as relevant training and publishing. Since the mid-1990s, however, the Bank Group has made knowledge sharing an explicit objective and has increased its efforts to organize its knowledge-sharing activities in a systematic way so that information can have the broadest possible impact.

Analytic and Advisory Services

World Bank

Most of the Bank's analytic and advisory services consist of economic and sector work and technical assistance. Economic and sector work examines a country's economic prospects—including, for example, its banking or financial sectors—and trade, poverty, and social safety net issues. The results often form the basis for assistance strategies, government investment programs, and projects supported by IBRD and IDA lending. Much of this economic research output is available through the World Bank research Web site at http://econ.worldbank.org.

The Bank's advisory services correspond with its thematic networks and sectors. They provide information on such topics as environmentally and socially sustainable development; the financial sector; health, nutrition, and population; and law and justice. Advisory services serve the Bank's clients and staff members, other development organizations, and the general public. More information can be found at http://www.worldbank.org/askus, which provides contacts for numerous specific aspects of the Bank's work.

Some of the Bank's networks and sectors have also prepared topical tool kits for development practitioners. These tool kits cover, for example, food and nutrition; gender; legal, financial, and procurement requirements; management and monitoring; project design; and resettlement safeguards.

International Finance Corporation

IFC's expertise in technical assistance focuses on five business lines: business-enabling environment, access to finance, environmental and social sustainability, infrastructure and public-private partnerships, and value addition to firms. These initiatives, funded mainly through IFC's partnerships with donors, complement its investments and nurture entrepreneurial growth. IFC delivers these services through a network of donor-funded facilities, each of which focuses on a developing region or a specific aspect of development, and through trust funds supported by individual countries or other donors.

Capacity Development

World Bank

The World Bank Institute (WBI) provides client countries with a capacity development program that comprises technical assistance, thematic learning programs, cabinet-level retreats, and other leadership development programs. Its activities include organizing training courses, undertaking policy consultations, entering into partnerships with training and research institutions worldwide, and supporting knowledge networks related to international development. WBI places special emphasis on distance learning and other innovative uses of technology. Many of its initiatives are described in chapter 4. WBI's Web site is http://www.worldbank.org/wbi.

The Global Development Learning Network is a fully interactive, multichannel network that harnesses video, Internet, and satellite communications to build local capacity, learning, and knowledge in the developing world and to develop a global community dedicated to fighting poverty. Its vision is for decision makers to have affordable and regular access to a global network of peers, experts, and practitioners with whom they may share ideas and experiences regarding the fight against poverty. The network operates through the facilities of Global Development Learning Network partners around the world. The Web site is at http://www.gdln.org.

Multilateral Investment Guarantee Agency

MIGA's Investment Marketing Services Department works to equip investment promotion intermediaries with leading-edge knowledge, tools, and techniques to strengthen their capacity to attract and retain foreign direct investment. To this end, MIGA provides both hands-on operational assistance to promotion intermediaries and a range of investment information services to member countries and firms that are contemplating direct investments in the developing world. These core services and products fall into three broad areas: capacity building, information dissemination, and investment facilitation.

Research

The World Bank's Development Economics Vice Presidency supports studies on the implications of a range of development issues such as the environment, poverty, trade, and globalization. The resultant findings facilitate a deeper understanding of development challenges and can be used to influence policy, thereby leading to better outcomes for poor people.

Legal Counsel

MIGA provides a broad range of legal support, both internally and for client countries. Its activities include supporting other MIGA departments and the Board of Directors with legal advice, advising countries on membership in MIGA, negotiating agreements with developing member countries in support of underwriting and salvage, providing technical assistance and advice to member countries on issues affecting the attraction of foreign investment, researching and disseminating information, mediating investment disputes, administering claims, and advising on increasing guarantee capacity. MIGA also cooperates with other entities of the World Bank Group and with other international and national agencies or institutions on legal aspects of investment protection and guarantee.

Conciliation and Arbitration

ICSID provides facilities for and coordination of the conciliation and arbitration of investment disputes between contracting states and nationals of other contracting states. ICSID's objective in making such facilities available is to promote an atmosphere of mutual confidence between states and foreign investors—an atmosphere that is conducive to increasing the flow of private international investment.

Publications, Data, and Statistics

In addition to issuing annual reports and providing project information, the Bank Group produces and distributes about 200 formal publications a year in print and in electronic format. Major annual titles include the *World Development Report, World Development Indicators, African Development Indicators, Global Development Finance, Global Economic Prospects, Global Monitoring Report, Doing Business,* and the *Atlas of Global Development.* All formal publications are distributed to World Bank country offices and a network of depository libraries in developing countries. Commercial sales offer significant discounts for customers in developing countries (see box 2.5 or for a list of country-specific distributors go to http://www.worldbank.org/reference/ and select "Book Distributors" in the "Finding Publications" box). In addition, the World Bank's e-library offers an online, fully cross-searchable portal to more than 4,000 World Bank documents. The collection consists of more than 1,600 World Bank publications and 2,400 policy research working papers, plus all new books and papers as they are published. For more information, go to http://www.worldbank.org/elibrary.

Working in close cooperation with the official statistical systems that national governments organize and finance, the Bank Group generates comprehensive data and statistics on many aspects of development. It also works to improve the coverage and effectiveness of national systems. Much of this information is available online, some for free and some by subscription. The key resource is the data and statistics Web site at http://www.worldbank.org/data. Many other specific datasets are available on Bank Group Web sites.

Events: Conferences, Forums, and Summits

The Bank Group sponsors, hosts, or participates in numerous conferences, both on its own and in conjunction with other organizations. Among the best known is the Annual World Bank Conference on Development Economics. Two of these conferences are held each year, one global and one regional. For major

---

Box 2.5 Obtaining World Bank Group Publications

World Bank Group Publications
P.O. Box 960
Herndon, VA 20172-0960, USA
Tel: 1-800-645-7247 or 1-703-661-1580
Fax: 1-703-661-1501
E-mail: books@worldbank.org
Web: http://www.worldbank.org/publications
E-library: http://www.worldbank.org/elibrary

World Bank events, see the "Events Calendar" at http://www.worldbank.org/events. Many of the Web sites of specific Bank Group units also list upcoming events.

World Bank Project Cycle

Each year the World Bank lends between $15 billion and $20 billion for projects in the more than 100 countries it works with. Projects range across the economic and social spectrum in these countries, from infrastructure, to education, to health, to government financial management.

The projects the Bank finances are conceived and supervised according to a well-documented project cycle (figure 2.5). Documents produced as part of the project cycle can be valuable sources of information for interested stakeholders wanting to keep abreast of the work the Bank is financing and for businesses wishing to participate in Bank-financed projects. The following text provides a step-by-step guide to the project cycle and the documents that are produced as part of the process. Most of this information is specific to World Bank projects, and information about IFC's project cycle follows in the next section. Information about how to access information about World Bank projects appears at the end of this section.

How the Process Begins: Poverty Reduction and Country Assistance Strategies

The Bank recognizes that many past assistance efforts, including some of its own, failed because donors, rather than the governments they were trying to assist, drove the agenda. Under its current development policy, the Bank helps governments take the lead in preparing and implementing development

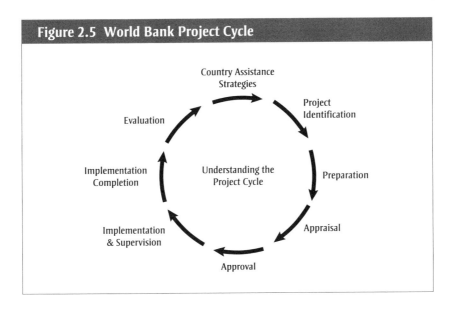

Figure 2.5 World Bank Project Cycle

Country Assistance Strategies

Project Identification

Evaluation

Preparation

Implementation Completion

Understanding the Project Cycle

Appraisal

Implementation & Supervision

Approval

strategies in the belief that programs that the country owns and that have widespread stakeholder support have a greater chance of success.

In low-income countries, the Bank uses the poverty reduction strategy approach, which involves widespread consultation and consensus building on how to boost development. Under this process, the country devises a national poverty reduction strategy, thereby creating a framework that enables donors to better coordinate their programs and align them with national priorities. The government consults a wide cross-section of local groups and combines such consultations with an extensive analysis of poverty in the country and of the country's economic situation. The government determines its own priorities from this process and produces targets for reducing poverty over a three- to five-year period. These priorities and targets are outlined in a PRSP. The Bank and other aid agencies then align their assistance efforts with the country's own strategy—a proven way of improving development effectiveness.

The Bank's blueprint for its work with a country is based on a CAS that, in the case of low-income countries, is derived from the priorities contained in the countries' PRSPs. The CAS is produced in cooperation with the government and interested stakeholders. The preparation of the CAS may draw on analytical work conducted by the Bank or other parties on a wide range of sectors, such as agriculture, education, fiscal management, health, public expenditure and budgeting, and procurement.

The Identification Phase

The Bank's CAS forms the blueprint for its assistance to a country and, as noted, in low-income countries, the CAS is based on the priorities identified in the country's PRSP. The goals outlined in the CAS guide priorities for the Bank's lending program and are a useful source of information for interested stakeholders and businesses wishing to identify potential future areas of Bank lending. During the identification phase, Bank teams work with the government to identify projects that can be funded as part of the agreed-on development objectives. Once a project has been identified, the Bank team prepares a project concept note, which is an internal document that outlines the basic elements of the project, the proposed objective, the likely risks, the alternative scenarios to conducting the project, and a likely timetable for the project approval process.

The following project documentation is required at this stage:

- Project information document
- Integrated safeguards data sheet

The Preparation Phase

The preparation phase is driven by the country that the Bank is working with, and it can take from a few months to as long as three years, depending on the complexity of the project being proposed. The Bank plays a supporting role, offering analysis and advice when requested. During this period, the technical, institutional, economic, environmental, and financial issues facing the project will be studied and addressed, including a review of whether alternative methods are available for achieving the same objectives. The Bank requires an assessment of projects proposed for Bank financing to help ensure that they are environmentally sound and sustainable. The scope of the environmental assessment depends on the project's scope, scale, and potential impact.

Project documentation at this stage includes the following:

- Environmental assessment report
- Indigenous peoples development plan
- Environmental action plan

The Appraisal Phase

The Bank is responsible for the appraisal phase. Bank staff review the work done during identification and preparation, often spending three to four weeks in the client country. They prepare either project appraisal documents (for investment projects) or program documents (for adjustment operations) for review by Bank management, and the Financial Management team assesses the project's financial aspects. The project information document is updated during this phase. The documents prepared during this stage are released to the public after the project has been approved (see below).

The Negotiation and Approval Phase

After Bank staff members have appraised the proposed project, the Bank and the country that is seeking to borrow the funds negotiate its final shape. Both sides come to agreement on the terms and conditions of the loan. Then the project appraisal document or the program document, along with the memorandum of the president and legal documents, are submitted to the Bank's Board of Executive Directors for approval. The appropriate documents are also submitted to the borrowing government for final clearance, which may involve ratification by a council of ministers or the country's legislature. Following approval by both parties, the loan agreement is formally signed by both parties' representatives. Once this has occurred, the loan or credit is declared effective—or ready for disbursement—after the relevant conditions have been met, and the agreement is made available to the public.

Project documentation at this stage includes the following:

- Project appraisal document, which presents all the information that the Board needs to approve Bank financing of the proposal. Before 1999, this document was called the staff appraisal report. The program document describes adjustment lending operations and sets out the Bank's appraisal and assessment of the feasibility and justification for the program.
- Technical annex, which supplements a memorandum and recommendation of the president for freestanding technical assistance loans. Such loans do not require project appraisal documents.

The Implementation and Supervision Phase

The borrowing country is responsible for implementing the project, while the Bank is responsible for supervision. Once the loan has been approved, the borrowing government, with technical assistance from the Bank, prepares specifications and evaluates bids for the procurement of goods and services for the project. The Bank reviews this activity to ensure that its procurement guidelines have been followed. If they have, the funds will be disbursed. The Bank's Financial Management team oversees the financial management of the project, which includes a requirement for periodic submissions of audited financial statements.

The Evaluation Phase

Following the completion of a project, the Bank's Independent Evaluation Group conducts an audit to measure the project's outcome against the original objectives. The audit entails a review of the project completion report and the preparation of a separate report. Both reports are then submitted to the executive directors and to the borrower. They are not released to the public.

Project documentation at this stage includes the following:

- Project performance assessment reports
- Impact evaluation reports
- Inspection Panel reports

Projects may be dropped at any point in the project cycle from preparation to approval. For projects that never achieve active status, the project information document is effectively the final document.

Other Monitoring

The Quality Assurance Group monitors the quality of the Bank's activities during implementation to facilitate better management. It examines project quality both for loans (shortly after project approval by the Board) and for advisory services (after delivery to country clients). It also monitors the quality of project supervision and reports to the Board of Executive Directors on the overall health of the portfolio of ongoing projects through the *Annual Report on Portfolio Performance.* For more information, see "Measuring Results" at http://go.worldbank.org/J4OO0PFYM0.

Another independent body within the World Bank, the Inspection Panel, provides a forum for citizens who believe they have been or could be harmed by a Bank-financed project. For details, go to http://www.worldbank.org/inspectionpanel.

Project Information

Several major resources are available in relation to project documents, which are also referred to as operational documents, and in relation to other project information (see box 2.6 for additional Web links):

- *Projects database.* Available online at http://www.worldbank.org/projects, this database enables users to search the entire World Bank project port-

Box 2.6 Web Links for Project Information, Disclosure, and Evaluation

WORLD BANK
Loans and credits: http://www.worldbank.org/loansandcredits
Projects, policies, and strategies: http://www.worldbank.org/projects
Project cycle: http://www.worldbank.org/projectcycle
Operational procedures: http://www.worldbank.org.operations
Country assistance strategies: http://www.worldbank.org/cas
Operational documents: http://www.worldbank.org/infoshop
PRSPs: http://www.worldbank.org/prsp
PICs: http://www.worldbank.org/pics
Policy on disclosure of information: http://www.worldbank.org/disclosure
Independent Evaluation Group: http://www.worldbank.org/ieg
Inspection Panel: http://www.worldbank.org/inspectionpanel

IFC
Projects: http://www.ifc.org/projects
Project cycle: http://www.ifc.org/ifcext/proserv.nsf/content/IFCprojectcycle
Policy on disclosure of information: see "Disclosure Policy Review" at
    http://www.ifc.org/policyreview
Environment and social review (monitoring of projects):
    http://www.ifcext/enviro.nsf/content/ESRP
Independent Evaluation Group: http://www.ifc.org/ieg

IFC AND MIGA
Office of the Compliance Advisor/Ombudsman:
    http://www.cao-ombudsman.org

MIGA
Projects insured by MIGA: http://www.miga.org
Disclosure policies: see "Environment and Disclosure Policies" at
    http://www.miga.org

ICSID
Cases: http://www.worldbank.org/icsid/cases/cases.htm

folio from the founding of IBRD to the present. Users can search in the projects database or in project documents, contract awards, or documents on analytical and advisory work. The search can be defined by any combination of the following: keyword, region, country or area, theme, sector, project status, product line, lending instrument, year approved, and environmental category. Results show the basic project information with links to available project documents.

■ *Recent loans, credits, and grants.* The World Bank also posts information on loans, credits, and grants most recently approved by the Board of Executive Directors under "News" on the Bank's Web site (http://www.worldbank.org/loansandcredits). Here, users can view information by date, by topic (sector), by region, or by country. The listings generally include the names of contacts who can provide additional information.

■ *Documents and reports.* This feature of the World Bank's Web site, available at http://www-wds.worldbank.org, provides more than 14,000 World Bank documents—the full range of material that is made available to the public under its disclosure policy. This approach to accessing project documents is an alternative to searching the projects database. This site also includes documents created through the Bank's country economic and sector work, as well as various working papers and informal series from departments around the Bank. Users of the site can access documents in both text and in PDF. Printed copies can be ordered from the InfoShop.

■ *InfoShop.* The InfoShop is the World Bank Group's bookstore and is located at Bank headquarters. It provides printed copies of project documents and also sells the Bank Group's formal publications, books on development topics by other publishers, souvenirs, and gifts. For more information, see "How to Order" at http://www.worldbank.org/infoshop.

■ *Public Information Centers (PICs).* These centers, which are maintained at World Bank country offices, make Bank information available to the public and disseminate its work to the widest possible audience. PIC Europe in Paris and PIC Tokyo offer the complete range of project documents for all member countries and maintain libraries of recent World Bank publications. Other country office PICs and libraries worldwide have project documents specific to the country in which the office is located and often offer a library of recent Bank publications. Each PIC serves as the central contact in the country for people seeking to obtain Bank documents and information on the Bank's operations. The InfoShop coordinates with all PICs to ensure broad dissemination of information in compliance with the Bank's disclosure policy. For more information, see appendix F.

IFC Project Cycle

IFC offers a wide variety of financial products to private sector projects in developing countries. The project cycle, outlined below, illustrates the stages a business idea goes through as it becomes an IFC-financed project.

- *Application for IFC financing.* IFC does not have a standard application form for financing. A company or entrepreneur, foreign or domestic, seeking to establish a new venture or to expand an existing enterprise can approach IFC directly. This is best done by reading "How to Apply for IFC Financing" (available on IFC's Web site, http://www.ifc.org/) and by submitting an investment proposal. After these initial contacts and a preliminary review, IFC may proceed by requesting a detailed feasibility study or business plan to determine whether to appraise the project.
- *Project appraisal.* Typically, an appraisal team consists of an investment officer with financial expertise and knowledge of the country in which the project is located, an engineer with relevant technical expertise, and an environmental specialist. The team is responsible for evaluating the technical, financial, economic, and environmental aspects of the project. This process entails visits to the proposed site of the project and extensive discussions with the project sponsors. After returning to headquarters, the team submits its recommendations to the senior management of the relevant IFC department. If financing of the project is approved at the department level, IFC's Legal Department drafts appropriate documents with assistance from outside counsel as necessary. Outstanding issues are negotiated with the company and other involved parties, such as governments or financial institutions.
- *Public notification.* Before the proposed investment is submitted to IFC's Board of Directors for review, the public is notified of the main elements of the project. Environmental review documents are also made available to the public.
- *Board review and approval.* The project is submitted to IFC's Board of Directors, which reviews the proposed investment and approves it if it sees fit.
- *Resource mobilization.* After Board approval, IFC seeks to mobilize additional financing by encouraging other institutions to make investments in the project.
- *Legal commitment.* If the investment is approved by the Board—and if stipulations from earlier negotiations are fulfilled—IFC and the company will sign the deal, entering into a legal commitment.
- *Disbursement of funds.* Funds are disbursed under the terms of the legal commitment signed by all parties.
- *Project supervision and evaluation.* After funds have been disbursed, IFC monitors its investments closely. It consults periodically with project managers and sends field missions to visit the enterprise. It also requires quarterly progress reports and information on factors that might materially

affect the enterprise in which it has invested, including annual financial statements audited by independent public accountants. IFC's basic instrument of evaluation is the expanded project supervision report. These self-evaluative reports are prepared by IFC's investment departments on a randomly selected, representative sample of investment operations (numbering about 70 a year) that have reached early operating maturity (generally five years after Board approval). IFC's Independent Evaluation Group reviews each of these reports.

▪ *Closing.* When an investment is repaid in full—or when IFC exits an investment by selling its equity stake—IFC closes its books on the project.

▪ *Project information.* IFC produces a summary of project information for each project it undertakes. It also publishes its environmental documents for each project. All project information is posted on the Web at http://www.ifc.org/projects. Users can narrow their searches by document type, project country, sector, IFC region, environmental category, or keywords.

Partnerships

The World Bank Group has a large array of partners in the global fight against poverty. As discussed under "Strategies" earlier in this chapter, the most important partnership is with the developing countries themselves, not only with the many government agencies, but also with the whole range of civil society, especially the poor, who are most affected by Bank Group activities.

The Bank Group also partners with other international institutions and donors, the private sector, civil society, and professional and academic associations to improve the coordination of aid policies at the country, regional, and global levels. Partnerships for financing, such as trust funds and cofinancing arrangements, are described in the earlier sections on Bank Group financial products and services. See also "Partners" at http://www.worldbank.org/about.

Partnerships with International Institutions

In addition to the IMF, the UN, and the UN's many agencies and programs (see chapter 1), the Bank Group works with many other organizations whose membership is made up of country governments. Major examples include the following:

▪ The European Union.
▪ The World Trade Organization.

- Multilateral development banks and other multilateral financial institutions. These institutions provide financial support and professional advice for economic and social development activities in developing countries. The term "multilateral development bank" typically refers to the World Bank Group and four regional development banks: the African Development Bank, the Asian Development Bank, the European Bank for Reconstruction and Development, and the Inter-American Development Bank. The Bank Group also works with several other banks and funds—the "multilateral financial institutions"—that lend to developing countries but have a narrower membership and focus. These include, among others, the European Commission and the Islamic Development Bank. Subregional banks owned by groups of countries and established for development purposes also work with the Bank Group. Among these are the Caribbean Development Bank, the Central American Bank for Economic Integration, the East African Development Bank, and the West African Development Bank.

Partnerships with Bilateral Development Agencies

The World Bank Group works with the development agencies of individual countries to coordinate aid and achieve development goals, sometimes formally through trust funds, and often with such countries' representatives in the field. Work is coordinated by various committees and through consultations that take place throughout the year.

Programmatic Partnerships

The World Bank hosts the secretariats of several closely affiliated organizations at its headquarters, including the following:

- *Consultative Group on International Agricultural Research.* This is an association of 62 members that supports agricultural research and related activities carried out by 16 autonomous research centers. Priorities include increasing productivity, protecting the environment, saving biodiversity, improving policies, and strengthening research at the national level. Members of the Consultative Group on Agricultural Research include industrial and developing countries, foundations, and international and regional organizations. The group's Web site is at http://www.cgiar.org.
- *Consultative Group to Assist the Poor.* This is a consortium of 33 public and private development agencies that seeks to improve the capacity of microfinance institutions (specialized institutions that provide financial services to very poor people). The Consultative Group to Assist the Poor supports

the development of these institutions and works to increase their commercial viability and the legal and regulatory framework for them in poor countries. The group's Web site is at http://www.cgap.org.

■ *Development Gateway.* The Development Gateway is an Internet portal for information and knowledge sharing on sustainable development and poverty reduction. Features include AiDA (Accessible Information on Development Activities), a comprehensive database of development projects; dgMarket, an international procurement marketplace; and Country Gateways, a network of 41 locally owned and managed public-private partnerships, each of which promotes innovative and effective use of the Internet and other information and communication technologies in a country to reduce poverty and promote sustainable development. The Development Gateway Web site is at http://www.developmentgateway.org.

■ *Education for All.* This is a global commitment to provide quality basic education for all children, youth, and adults. The movement was launched at the World Conference on Education for All in 1990.

■ *GAVI Alliance.* The GAVI Alliance (formerly known as the Global Alliance for Vaccines and Immunisation) is a public-private partnership focused on increasing children's access to vaccines in poor countries. Partners include the GAVI Fund, national governments, the United Nations Children's Fund, the World Health Organization, the World Bank, the Bill & Melinda Gates Foundation, the vaccine industry, public health institutions, and NGOs. The GAVI Fund provides resources for the GAVI Alliance's programs. The latter provides a forum where partners can agree on mutual goals, share strategies, and coordinate efforts. Its Web site is at http://www.gavialliance.org.

■ *Global Environment Facility.* This entity provides grants and concessional loans to help developing countries meet the costs of measures designed to achieve global environmental benefits. The focus is on climate change, biological diversity, international waters, and ozone layer depletion. The World Bank, the UN Development Programme, and the UN Environment Programme are the three implementing agencies of the Global Environment Facility, which is supported administratively by the World Bank but remains functionally independent. Each agency finances the facility's activities within its respective areas of competence. Its Web site is at http://www/worldbank.org/gef.

NGOs and Civil Society

Most development projects approved by the Bank Group involve active participation by NGOs in their implementation, and most of the Bank Group's country strategies benefit from consultations with civil society organizations. The Bank Group uses the term "civil society organizations" to refer to the wide array of nongovernmental and not-for-profit organizations that have a presence in public life, expressing the interests and values of their members, or other organizations that are based on ethical, cultural, political, scientific, religious, or philanthropic considerations.

The Bank Group's outreach in this area encompasses trade unions, community-based organizations, social movements, faith-based institutions, charitable organizations, research centers, foundations, student organizations, professional associations, and many other entities. Staff members working in 70 country offices around the world reach out to and collaborate with NGOs in a variety of areas, ranging from education and HIV/AIDS to the environment. The home pages of the Bank Group's civil society efforts are at http://www.worldbank.org/civilsociety (for the World Bank) and http://www.ifc.org/ngo (for IFC). For NGO correspondence with MIGA, see "NGOs and Civil Society" at http://www.miga.org.

Staff, Consultants, and Vendors

World Bank Group Staff

The institutions of the World Bank Group together have a full-time staff of about 12,500 professionals and support personnel (as of May 2007). Of these, 40 percent are located in country offices. The proportion of field personnel has grown in recent years, reflecting the Bank Group's commitment to operating in close partnership with its clients. Staff members are drawn from most member countries and typically have strong academic backgrounds, a broad understanding of development issues, and international work experience. Most have specializations appropriate to their particular unit.

Staff salaries and benefits are intended to be competitive and are based on data from comparable organizations in the public sector as well as from the private industrial and financial sectors. According to a treaty signed by the U.S. government when the Bank's headquarters was established in Washington, DC, in 1945, foreign nationals are exempt from federal and state taxes on World Bank Group income, but U.S. citizens working at the Bank Group are required to pay both federal and state income taxes on their salaries. Thus, to keep after-tax income in line for all staff members, the Bank Group pays salaries on a net-of-tax basis and gives an additional allowance to staff members who are liable for income taxes. All staff members also pay local property, sales, and other taxes. These tax arrangements are comparable to those of other international organizations.

Over the past several years, the Bank Group has made considerable progress in mobilizing the diversity of its staff members as a strategic business asset. The business case for diversity—that it enriches the organization's talent base, reflects the Group's global membership, and brings a wider range of perspectives to bear on the organization's poverty reduction work—increasingly is recognized. The Bank Group has changed the face of senior management with a record number of women, developing-country nationals, and individuals of Sub-Saharan African origin. The diversity focus has been expanded beyond nationality, gender, and race to address areas including disabilities and sexual orientation as well as education and previous experience. Diversity has also been integrated into managerial training.

Job Openings, Internships, and Scholarships

The Bank Group provides information on its job openings, special job opportunities for younger professionals, and internships through a careers Web site maintained by Human Resources. The Web address is http://www.worldbank.org/careers. For information specific to MIGA, see "About Us" at http://www.miga.org.

In addition, the Bank Group offers scholarship and fellowship programs, information about which is available at http://www.worldbank.org/wbi/scholarships. Specific programs include the following:

- The *Young Professionals Program,* which is for highly qualified and motivated people younger than 32 who are skilled in areas relevant to the World Bank's operations. Candidates must hold the equivalent of a master's degree and have significant work experience or continued academic study at the doctoral level. Initial appointments are for two years and often lead to a career in the Bank.
- The *Junior Professional Associates Program,* which is for recent graduates younger than 29 who have superior academic records and an interest in international work. Candidates must hold the equivalent of a bachelor's or master's degree or must be a doctoral candidate. This is a two-year, entry-level program. Associates are not eligible for employment with the World Bank for two years following the end of their appointments.
- The *Bank Internship Program,* which is for nationals of a World Bank member country who are enrolled full time in a master's or doctoral program. Interns work either in the winter (November–January) or the sum-

mer (May–September), although dates may vary according to university schedules. Interns in this program receive a salary.

- The *Joint Japan–World Bank Graduate Scholarship Program,* which covers up to two years of study toward a master's degree. Candidates must be nationals of a World Bank member country, must have been accepted at a university outside their country, must study in a field related to development, must be younger than 45, and must have at least two years of professional experience. The program is funded by the Japanese government but it does not require study in Japan.
- The *Robert S. McNamara Fellowships Program,* which is part of the Woodrow Wilson School of Public Affairs at Princeton University. This program provides a full tuition scholarship, a travel allowance, and a stipend for living expenses. The student must be a national of a World Bank member country and have at least seven years of professional experience. Candidates apply directly to the Master's in Public Policy program at Princeton and indicate that they are applying for admission as a McNamara Fellow.

Procurement Opportunities in Projects Financed by IBRD and IDA

Every year, investment projects financed by the World Bank generate billions of dollars in opportunities for suppliers of goods and services. Government agencies from the Bank's borrowing countries are responsible for the purchase of goods and services to support these projects. Bank procedures have been established to ensure that procurement is conducted efficiently and in an open, competitive, and transparent manner.

The procurement policies and procedures in Bank-financed projects are explained in "Guidelines: Procurement under IBRD Loans and IDA Credits" and "Guidelines: Selection and Employment of Consultants by World Bank Borrowers," which are available at http://www.worldbank.org/procure. On the same page, under the "Bidding / Consulting Opportunities" tab, the "Resource Guide to Consulting, Supply, and Contracting Opportunities in Projects Financed by the World Bank" provides detailed guidance on how to identify and track business opportunities.

Supplying Directly to the World Bank Group

The Bank Group regularly seeks qualified vendors for assistance in running its operations in Washington, DC, and its offices around the world. Opportunities range from supplying printer toner cartridges to managing complex communications systems. For information on how to sell goods and services to the Bank Group, including vendor registration, the key Web site is the vendor kiosk at http://info.worldbank.org/vendorkiosk/. Another Web site at http://www.worldbank.org/corporateprocurement lists current business opportunities with the Bank Group.

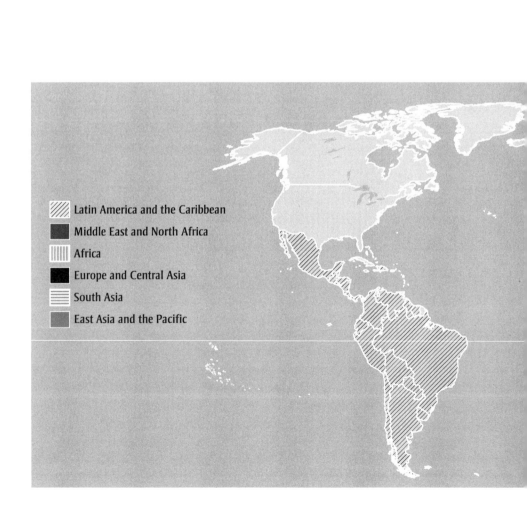

Latin America and the Caribbean
Middle East and North Africa
Africa
Europe and Central Asia
South Asia
East Asia and the Pacific

3 World Bank Group Countries and Regions

This chapter provides information on the countries of the Bank Group: the mechanics of membership, the ways that countries are classified, and the initiatives focusing on groups of countries with shared characteristics or concerns. It then provides a review of each of the regions into which the Bank Group organizes its member countries as it provides development assistance.

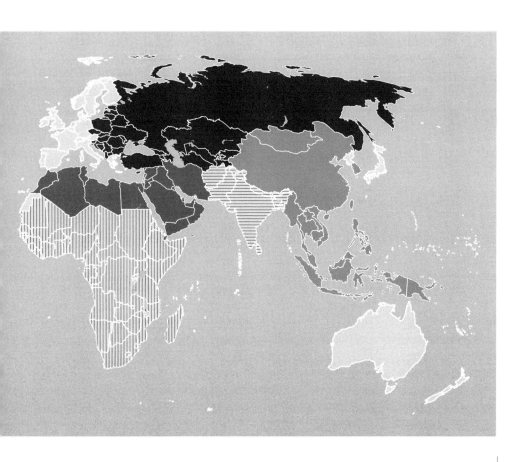

Member Countries

Membership

The five institutions of the Bank Group are owned by their member countries (see box 3.1 for Web links). To become a member of IBRD, a country must first join the IMF. Similarly, membership in IDA, IFC, and MIGA is contingent upon membership in IBRD. In each of these cases, member countries buy shares in the institution, thereby helping build the institution's capital and borrowing power. This arrangement is known as "capital subscriptions." Member countries also sign the founding document of each institution: the Articles of Agreement for IBRD, IDA, and IFC and the MIGA Convention. Membership in ICSID entails signing and ratifying the ICSID Convention and also involves capital subscriptions. Links to the founding documents for each institution can be found at http://www.worldbank.org/articles.

As of April 2007, IBRD had 185 members, IDA had 166, IFC had 179, MIGA had 171, and ICSID had 143. The Bank Group's Corporate Secretariat keeps up-to-date lists of membership, handles official country names used by the Bank Group, and deals with communications regarding membership status and capital subscriptions. In its maps and publications, the Bank Group sometimes indicates contested boundaries or territorial claims between member countries, but it does not endorse any member country's position where such disputes exist.

As covered in chapter 1, member countries govern the Bank Group through the Boards of Governors and the Boards of Directors. The voting power of each executive director is determined by the value of the capital subscriptions held by the countries that he or she represents. For each of the four shareholding institutions—IBRD, IDA, IFC, and MIGA—the executive director for the United States has the greatest voting power, followed by the executive director for Japan.

Member countries can withdraw from Bank Group institutions at any time by giving notice. A member may also be suspended and, after a year, expelled

---

Box 3.1 Web Links for Country Membership Information

- IBRD and IDA member countries:
  see "Members" at http://www.worldbank.org/about
- IFC member countries:
  see "Member Countries" at http://www.ifc.org/about
- MIGA member countries:
  see "About MIGA" and click on "Member Countries" at http://www.miga.org
- ICSID contracting states:
  see "List of Contracting States" at http://www.worldbank.org/icsid

if it fails to fulfill any of its obligations to a Bank Group institution. A country that ceases to be a member of the IMF automatically ceases to be a member of the Bank Group unless, within three months, the Bank Group decides by a special majority to allow the country to remain a member. When a country ceases to be a member, it continues to be liable for its contractual obligations, such as servicing its loans. It also continues to be liable for calls on its unpaid subscription resulting from losses sustained by a Bank Group institution on guarantees or loans outstanding on the date of withdrawal.

Member countries are listed by geographic region later in this chapter. A master list—with dates of membership and each country's voting power is provided in appendix D.

Ways of Classifying Countries

Several designations for member countries are commonly used at the Bank Group. These designations reflect important distinctions among the member countries. Although the meanings of the terms overlap—and they are all based on wealth—they are not interchangeable.

Low-income, middle-income, and high-income countries

In its analytical and operational work, the Bank Group characterizes country economies as low-income, middle-income (subdivided into lower-middle-income and upper-middle-income), and high-income. It makes these classifications for most nonsovereign territories as well as for independent countries. Low-income and middle-income economies are sometimes referred to as "developing economies." On the basis of gross national income in 2005, low-income countries are those with average annual per capita incomes of $875 or less. For lower-middle-income countries, the figures are $876 to $3,465; for upper-middle-income countries, $3,466 to $10,725; and for high-income countries, $10,726 or more. Classification by income does not necessarily reflect development status.

Developing and industrial countries

In general, the term "developing" refers to countries whose economies are classified as low-income or middle-income. The terms "industrial" or "developed" refer to countries whose economies are high-income. The use of these terms is not intended to imply that all economies in the group are experiencing similar development or that other economies have reached a preferred or final stage of development.

Part I and Part II countries

Countries choose whether they are Part I or Part II primarily on the basis of their economic standing. Part I countries are almost all industrial countries and donors to IDA, and they pay their contributions in freely convertible currency. Part II countries are almost all developing countries, some of which are donors to IDA. Part II countries are entitled to pay most of their contributions to IDA in local currency.

MIGA makes a similar distinction between Category I and Category II member countries. The breakdown of countries into these categories differs slightly from the breakdown within IDA.

Donors and borrowers

In general, the term "donor" refers to a country that makes contributions specifically to IDA. In contrast, the term "borrower" refers to a country that borrows from IDA or IBRD or both. Note, however, that all member countries pay capital subscriptions, and this payment is distinct from a given country's lending and borrowing.

IBRD, IDA, and blend countries and graduates

The distinctions between IBRD and IDA borrowers—and the circumstances in which a country may be eligible to receive a blend of IBRD loans and IDA credits and grants—are based on per capita income and the country's creditworthiness. These distinctions are discussed in detail in chapter 1 (see also "Country Eligibility for Borrowing" in *The World Bank Annual Report*). Note that, as a country's per capita income increases, it can graduate out of eligibility for IDA credits and grants and, in turn, out of eligibility for IBRD loans (box 3.2). However, wealthier countries remain members of Bank Group organizations even if they or the enterprises operating within their borders do not draw upon Bank Group services.

Country Activities and Operations

As indicated in chapter 2, the Bank Group's project databases enable users to search for information on individual institutions' activities in a given country. The Bank Group's key resource for comparative data on countries is *World Development Indicators,* published each year in April and available in both print and online formats. In addition, the World Bank maintains numerous country-specific Web sites, some maintained by the regional vice presi-

Box 3.2 IBRD Graduates

1947: France
1948: Luxembourg
1957: Netherlands
1958: Belgium
1962: Australia and Austria
1964: Denmark, Malta,
and Norway
1965: Italy
1967: Japan
1971: Taiwan, China
1972: New Zealand

1974: Iceland
1975: Finland, Israel,
and Singapore
1976: Ireland
1977: Spain
1979: Greece
1987: Oman
1989: Portugal and
The Bahamas
1992: Cyprus

1994: Barbados and
the Slovak
Republic
2004: Slovenia
2005: Czech
Republic
2006: Estonia and
Lithuania
2007: Hungary and
Latvia

Graduates That Have Returned to Borrower Status

Country	Last Year Borrowed (before relapse)	Year of Reinitiated Borrowing
Costa Rica	1994	2000
Malaysia	1994	1998
Korea, Rep. of	1995	1998
Chile	1996	1999

dencies and some by the country offices. The Web site showing World Bank information on countries and regions is at http://www.worldbank.org/countries. Country information for IFC is accessible through the Web sites of the investment regions; links to these sites are at http://www.ifc.org/sitemap.

The appendixes to this book provide a number of resources covering both borrower and donor countries:

- A comprehensive table of member countries, including their memberships in the various Bank Group institutions, the years they joined, and their individual voting power (appendix D).
- A list of country groupings that form the constituencies of the 24 executive directors with the total voting power that each director represents (appendix E).
- A description of additional country resources and where information about them can be found (appendix F). These resources include country offices and Web sites, PICs, depository libraries, and distributors of World Bank publications.

Initiatives for Groups of Countries

Some Bank Group initiatives target groups of countries with key features in common, for example, their income level, their degree of indebtedness, or the strength of their institutions.

Multilateral Debt Relief Initiative (MDRI)

September 2006 marked the tenth anniversary of the Heavily Indebted Poor Countries (HIPC) Initiative. Established by the World Bank, the IMF, and member countries in 1996 and significantly expanded in 1999, the HIPC Initiative is a comprehensive approach to reducing the external debt of the world's poorest, most heavily indebted countries. Its goals are to help countries move from endless restructuring of debt to lasting debt relief, to reduce multilateral debt, and to free up resources for countries that pursue economic and social reforms targeted at measurable poverty reduction.

The Multilateral Debt Relief Initiative (MDRI), introduced in 2006 following the Group of Eight (G-8) Gleneagles Summit of 2005, has built on the HIPC Initiative to cut the debt burdens of many of the world's poorest countries to acceptable levels. At the 2005 summit, the leaders of the G-8 nations proposed 100 percent cancellation of debt owed to IDA, the IMF, and the African Development Fund by some of the world's poorest countries, most of them in Africa and Latin America. The MDRI was endorsed by the Bank-Fund Development Committee in September 2005. Total debt relief under the MDRI is estimated at about $50 billion, including $37 billion from IDA alone, which is equivalent to more than a quarter of IDA's total resources. Debt relief will be provided up front and irrevocably once a HIPC country becomes MDRI-eligible. The Board of Executive Directors of IDA approved the MDRI on March 28, 2006; IDA's Board of Governors adopted the MDRI on April 21, 2006. IDA began implementing the MDRI at the start of fiscal 2007. For more information about the MDRI, including a list of eligible countries, visit www.worldbank.org/debt.

Fragile states: The LICUS Initiative

Recent thinking about development models and internal reflection on past development failures in difficult environments has brought the concept of the fragile state to the fore. In November 2001, the World Bank set up the Task Force on Low-Income Countries Under Stress (LICUS), which recommended ways to help countries with particularly weak policies and institutions get onto a path of sustained growth and poverty reduction by improving the effectiveness of development aid. Many low-income countries under stress are affected by ongoing armed conflicts.

The Low-Income Countries Under Stress Unit was established at the end of 2002 to help coordinate this Bank-wide effort. The Bank is working with development partners to create an analytic framework and assemble the right tools to help countries in difficult circumstances. Working with low-income countries under stress is about catalyzing forces of change from within, even in the most difficult environments.

Analytic work suggests that there is a need to increase fragile states' capacity and accountability; to forge peace, security, and development links; to harmonize donor assistance; and to develop strong and flexible institutional responses. In February 2007, the Bank's Board approved a reform package for fragile states that aims to reduce the average time to first disbursement of reconstruction funds from nine to three months, to place 30 more staff in the field, to strengthen incentives for staff, and to increase work across the Bank on tools and good practice for this client segment. Implementation of the new framework for rapid response is supported by new organizational and staffing measures designed to ensure that experienced people from all parts of the Bank are mobilized to work on rapid response operations in fragile states. For more information, see http://www.worldbank.org/licus.

Education for All Fast-Track Initiative

Launched in 2002 by the World Bank and all major education donors, the Education for All Fast-Track Initiative is a global partnership between donor and developing countries. The initiative's goal is to accelerate progress toward achievement of the MDGs for education. It is open to all low-income countries that demonstrate a serious commitment to achieving universal primary education. As of April 2006, the Fast-Track Initiative compact included 20 developing countries: Burkina Faso, Djibouti, Ethiopia, The Gambia, Ghana, Guinea, Guyana, Honduras, Kenya, Lesotho, Madagascar, Mauritania, Moldova, Mozambique, Nicaragua, Niger, Tajikistan, Timor-Leste, Vietnam, and the Republic of Yemen. Since 2000, the World Bank has more than doubled its annual new lending for education: total education lending increased from $728 million in 2000 to almost $2 billion in 2006.

Middle-income countries

Middle-income countries continue to face substantial development challenges: achieving sustained growth that provides productive employment; reducing poverty and inequality; reducing volatility, particularly in their access to private financial markets; and strengthening the institutional and governance structures that underpin viable, market-based economies. The Bank Group is uniquely placed to help these countries craft institutional reforms, attract infrastructure investment across the public-private spectrum, improve social service delivery, and cope with volatility.

To support the development efforts of middle-income countries, in 2005 the Bank Group began implementing an action plan designed to strengthen the ability of its staff to respond to these countries' borrowing needs. Initiatives include piloting the use of countries' own environmental and social safeguards and fiduciary systems, where applicable; streamlining policy conditionality; and making greater use of the flexibility of Country Assistance Strategies to customize support to countries' circumstances, respond quickly to emerging opportunities, and realign investment lending instruments and disbursement mechanisms with clients' evolving needs. The plan leverages Bank Group resources and skills to provide timely, relevant, and high-quality knowledge services that draw on Bank Group synergies and partnerships with bilateral and multilateral agencies.

Small states

"Small states" is a term applied to a diverse group of sovereign developing countries—some quite wealthy, some very poor, some islands or groups of islands, some landlocked, and many with populations of 1.5 million or less. Forty-five developing countries have populations of 1.5 million or less and 41 of these are members of the World Bank.

A 1999 report by the Commonwealth Secretariat/World Bank Joint Task Force on Small States identified a number of characteristics that developing small states share and that shape their development challenges. For instance, many are especially vulnerable to external events, including natural disasters, that cause high volatility in national incomes; many suffer from limited capacity in the public and private sectors; and many currently face an uncertain and difficult economic transition under a changing world trade regime. For more information, see http://www.worldbank.org/smallstates.

Regional groupings

Most Bank Group institutions approach their work by grouping developing countries into geographic regions. As discussed in chapter 1, these regions are one dimension of an organizational matrix, the other dimension being the thematic network or sector aspects of development that cut across regions. The following sections provide a brief overview of Bank Group regions: which countries they include, a few essential facts, and some information on the Bank Group's activities and priorities. They also offer information on major regional initiatives, which in most cases are partnership initiatives between the Bank Group and other organizations or governments.

Additional issue briefs for world regions can be found at http://www. worldbank.org/issuebriefs. More comprehensive information on regions can be found in the annual reports of the Bank Group institutions.

The regional sections hereafter follow the organization of the World Bank's regional vice presidencies (see figure 3.1 for the share of total lending provided to each region). These vice presidencies largely correspond to IFC's regional departments, except that IFC has two separate but closely coordinated departments within Europe and Central Asia. Additionally, IFC assigns a few countries to different regions than the Bank (see figure 3.2 for the share of total investments provided to each region). A small number of IFC investment projects are classified as global because they involve private enterprises that are active in more than one developing region.

In its annual report, MIGA reports on East Asia and the Pacific and South Asia as a single region (see figure 3.3 for MIGA's outstanding portfolio distribution by region). ICSID does not organize its work by regions.

Note that, strictly speaking, Bank Group regions refer only to the countries that are eligible for borrowing or other services. Wealthier member countries that lie within these geographic areas—for example, Barbados, Oman, and Singapore—are not normally included in lists of countries within these regions. The Bank Group gathers economic information on all countries, however, and operates offices in a number of donor countries.

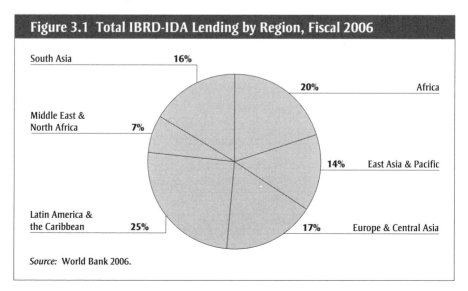

Figure 3.1 Total IBRD-IDA Lending by Region, Fiscal 2006

South Asia 16%

Africa 20%

Middle East & North Africa 7%

East Asia & Pacific 14%

Latin America & the Caribbean 25%

Europe & Central Asia 17%

Source: World Bank 2006.

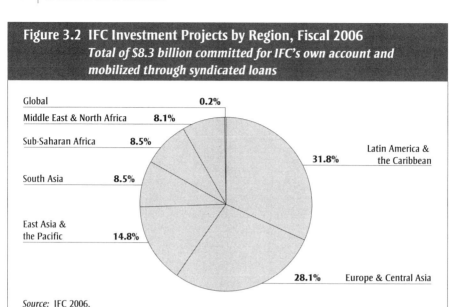

Figure 3.2 IFC Investment Projects by Region, Fiscal 2006
Total of $8.3 billion committed for IFC's own account and mobilized through syndicated loans

Global 0.2%
Middle East & North Africa 8.1%
Sub-Saharan Africa 8.5%
South Asia 8.5%
East Asia & the Pacific 14.8%
Latin America & the Caribbean 31.8%
Europe & Central Asia 28.1%

Source: IFC 2006.
Note: Some amounts include regional shares of investments that are officially classified as global projects.

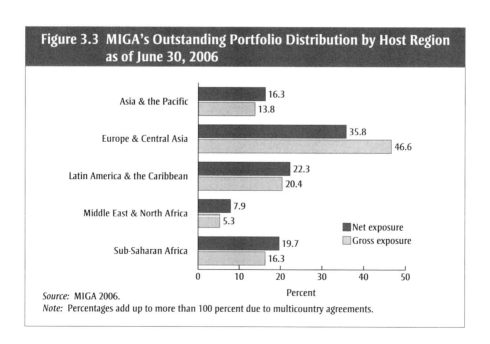

Figure 3.3 MIGA's Outstanding Portfolio Distribution by Host Region as of June 30, 2006

Asia & the Pacific — 16.3 / 13.8
Europe & Central Asia — 35.8 / 46.6
Latin America & the Caribbean — 22.3 / 20.4
Middle East & North Africa — 7.9 / 5.3
Sub-Saharan Africa — 19.7 / 16.3

■ Net exposure
☐ Gross exposure

Percent

Source: MIGA 2006.
Note: Percentages add up to more than 100 percent due to multicountry agreements.

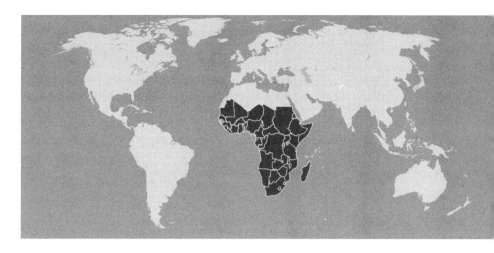

Africa (Sub-Saharan)

This World Bank region includes the following countries that are eligible for borrowing:

Angola	Ethiopia	Niger
Benin	Gabon	Nigeria
Botswana	The Gambia	Rwanda
Burkina Faso	Ghana	São Tomé and Principe
Burundi	Guinea	Senegal
Cameroon	Guinea-Bissau	Seychelles
Cape Verde	Kenya	Sierra Leone
Central African Republic	Lesotho	Somalia
Chad	Liberia	South Africa
Comoros	Madagascar	Sudan
Democratic Republic of Congo	Malawi	Swaziland
	Mali	Tanzania
Republic of Congo	Mauritania	Togo
Côte d'Ivoire	Mauritius	Uganda
Equatorial Guinea	Mozambique	Zambia
Eritrea	Namibia	Zimbabwe

All these countries are members of IBRD. As for the other institutions,

- Namibia and the Seychelles are not members of IDA;
- Djibouti is included in IFC's Africa region; São Tomé and Principe is not a member of IFC;
- The Comoros, Niger, São Tomé and Principe, and Somalia are not members of MIGA; and

- Angola, Cape Verde, Eritrea, Ethiopia, Guinea-Bissau, Namibia, São Tomé and Principe, and South Africa are not members of ICSID.

The World Bank in Sub-Saharan Africa

Sub-Saharan Africa is a priority for the development community and the World Bank Group. It is the Bank Group's largest region with the greatest number of client countries and the highest volume of IDA lending, and it presents some of the greatest challenges to the development community. (Box 3.3 presents key regional facts.) In 2006, the region's leaders reaffirmed their commitment to achieving the MDGs by improving governance, accelerating and sustaining economic growth and job creation, delivering human services, and fighting poverty. The UN Millennium Project and Millennium+5 Summit, the U.K. Commission for Africa, and the Gleneagles Summit all focused global attention on the continent, and the international community committed itself to doubling Africa's development assistance to $50 billion a year by 2010.

To support Africa's development, the World Bank Group implemented the Africa Action Plan. The plan sets out the Bank Group's priorities for supporting strategies to achieve broadly shared economic growth, accelerate progress toward the MDGs, and build capable states. It also defines priorities for the Bank Group's efforts to strengthen the Development Partnership for Africa through more, and more effective, aid. The action plan has eight focus areas:

- Strengthen the African private sector
- Increase the economic empowerment of women
- Build skills for competitiveness in the global economy

Box 3.3 Africa Fast Facts

0.7 billion	Total population
2.1 percent	Population growth
46 years	Life expectancy at birth
100	Infant mortality per 1,000 births
77 percent	Female youth literacy
$750	2005 gross national income per capita
24.8 million	Number of people living with HIV/AIDS

Source: World Bank 2006.

■ Raise agricultural productivity
■ Improve access to and reliability of clean energy
■ Expand and upgrade road networks and transit corridors
■ Increase access to safe water and sanitation
■ Strengthen national health systems and combat malaria and HIV/AIDS

The World Bank is the largest provider of development assistance to Africa, and it has increased its support dramatically since 2001 (figures 3.4 and 3.5 present thematic and sectoral breakdowns of lending for fiscal 2006). The portfolio of projects under implementation in Africa as of June 2006 amounted to $18.4 billion. IDA funding in fiscal 2006 of $1.1 billion in grants and $3.5 billion in credits represented a doubling of aid from fiscal 2000, and disbursements of $4 billion represented an increase of more than 100 percent. Through the recently approved Multilateral Debt Relief Initiative, Africa will also benefit from a total of $28.9 billion of relief.

The Bank's strategic objectives for Africa are outlined in the report titled *Strategic Framework for Assistance to Africa*, which draws on the report *Can Africa Claim the 21st Century?* The framework focuses on reducing conflict, improving governance, investing in people, improving aid effectiveness, and increasing economic growth through enhanced competitiveness and trade.

For more information, visit the Region's Web site at http://www.worldbank.org/africa.

IFC in Sub-Saharan Africa

IFC is the largest multilateral source of loan and equity financing for private sector projects in Africa. The corporation's investments in the region are growing rapidly and cover a wide range of sectors, including microfinance and other financial sector projects, telecommunications, infrastructure, and education. The region is also a focus of many trade finance transactions through IFC's new Global Trade Finance Program.

IFC's strategy for the region calls for an increase in advisory services, which are being delivered through the new Private Enterprise Partnership for Africa, a joint program with IDA, and other initiatives. The focus includes expanding the use of leasing, promoting exports, reforming business regulation, and helping companies respond to the challenges of HIV/AIDS. IFC is also advising on projects to bring private sector participation into infrastructure, with a key recent example being a successful private concession for a port in Madagascar.

The Sub-Saharan Africa Department is managed from IFC's regional hub in Johannesburg. Its Web site is at http://www.ifc.org/africa.

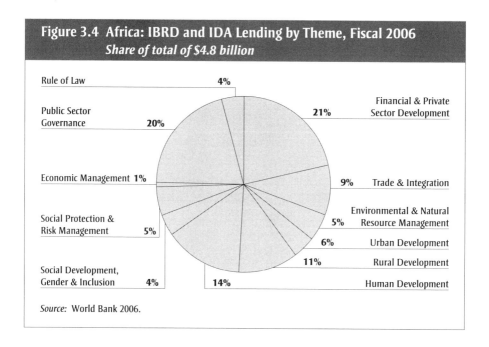

Figure 3.4 Africa: IBRD and IDA Lending by Theme, Fiscal 2006
Share of total of $4.8 billion

Rule of Law — 4%

Public Sector Governance — 20%

Financial & Private Sector Development — 21%

Economic Management — 1%

Trade & Integration — 9%

Social Protection & Risk Management — 5%

Environmental & Natural Resource Management — 5%

Urban Development — 6%

Rural Development — 11%

Social Development, Gender & Inclusion — 4%

Human Development — 14%

Source: World Bank 2006.

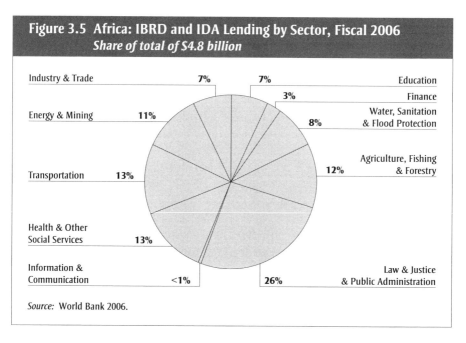

Figure 3.5 Africa: IBRD and IDA Lending by Sector, Fiscal 2006
Share of total of $4.8 billion

Industry & Trade — 7%

Education — 7%

Finance — 3%

Energy & Mining — 11%

Water, Sanitation & Flood Protection — 8%

Transportation — 13%

Agriculture, Fishing & Forestry — 12%

Health & Other Social Services — 13%

Information & Communication — <1%

Law & Justice & Public Administration — 26%

Source: World Bank 2006.

MIGA in Sub-Saharan Africa

Sub-Saharan Africa is a priority area for MIGA, which works to attract new investment and build greater institutional capacity in the region. MIGA has established a regional field office in Johannesburg and also works through some 30 field missions and mobile offices. The agency pursues new investment project guarantees and undertakes numerous technical assistance activities in the region. Its efforts are focused on the need for infrastructure investment in southern Africa and on how best to support privatization efforts involving public-private partnerships.

Regional Initiatives

Regional initiatives in Sub-Saharan Africa include the following:

- *Africa Action Plan.* The Africa Action Plan promotes the expansion of public-private partnerships and innovative financing approaches. The Bank, IFC, and MIGA are working to combine the complementary skills of the World Bank Group to support additional private participation in priority infrastructure projects.
- *Africa Capacity Development Operational Task Force.* Capacity development remains a binding constraint to development despite substantial donor support and concerted efforts by developing countries. Implementing poverty reduction strategy programs successfully and achieving the MDGs underscores the need for stronger institutions in Africa. See "Regional Initiatives" at http://www.worldbank.org/africa.
- *Chad-Cameroon Pipeline Project.* The objective of this project is to develop the oil fields in southern Chad and construct a pipeline to offshore oil-loading facilities on Cameroon's Atlantic coast. The unprecedented framework for this project will transform oil wealth into direct benefits for the poor, the vulnerable, and the environment. The World Bank and the government of Chad signed a memorandum of understanding in July 2006 under which Chad has committed 70 percent of its 2007 budget spending to priority poverty reduction programs. See "Regional Initiatives" at http://www.worldbank.org/africa.
- *Global Partnership for Eliminating River Blindness.* This global partnership's mission is to wipe out river blindness (onchocerciasis) in the whole of Africa by 2010. River blindness, caused by the *Onchocerca volvulus* parasite, poses a serious public health problem and creates an obstacle to socioeconomic development in Africa, where it is endemic in 30 countries. See "Regional Initiatives" at http://www.worldbank.org/africa.

- *Knowledge Partnerships for Africa.* A major area of focus and activity for this partnership is sharing knowledge and learning from clients and partners to improve the quality and impact of the World Bank's assistance. See "Regional Initiatives" at http://www.worldbank.org/africa.

- *Multi-Country HIV/AIDS Program.* This initiative is helping a growing number of African countries, almost 30 as of January 2007, to provide increased access to HIV/AIDS prevention, care, and treatment programs, with an emphasis on vulnerable groups. See "Regional Initiatives" at http://www.worldbank.org/africa.

- *Nile Basin Initiative.* Launched in February 1999, the initiative is a regional partnership in which countries of the Nile Basin have united in common pursuit of the long-term development and management of Nile waters. See "Regional Initiatives" at http://www.worldbank.org/africa.

- *Regional integration.* Most African countries have already recognized the benefits of regional integration and participate in at least one regional arrangement. While past performance has been mixed, there is renewed momentum for a more pragmatic approach to regional integration. See "Regional Initiatives" at http://www.worldbank.org/africa.

- *Regional Program on Enterprise Development.* This is an ongoing research project aimed at generating business knowledge and policy advice useful to the development of private sector manufacturing in Sub-Saharan Africa. See "Regional Initiatives" at http://www.worldbank.org/africa.

- *Roll Back Malaria.* This global initiative, made up of more than 90 partners, is a coordinated international approach to fighting malaria. The disease kills more than 1 million people each year, most of them children. The partnership's goal is to halve the burden of malaria by 2010. The Web site is http://www.rbm.who.int.

- *Strategic Partnership with Africa.* This is an informal association of donors and African partners whose goal is to support poverty reduction in Africa by working to improve the quality and increase the quantity of assistance to Africa. The partnership's Web site is http://www.spa.synisys.com/main.html.

- *Sub-Saharan Africa Transport Policy Program.* This international partnership facilitates policy development and related capacity building in the transport sector. The objective is to ensure that safe, reliable, and cost-effective transport plays its full part in achieving the development objectives of Sub-Saharan Africa (poverty reduction, pro-poor growth, and regional integration) and to help countries compete internationally. See "Regional Initiatives" at http://www.worldbank.org/africa.

▨ *TerrAfrica.* This is a partnership between Sub-Saharan African countries, donor countries and agencies, civil society, and the research community with the collective goal of scaling up harmonized support of effective and efficient land management approaches that are sustainable and country driven. The Web site is http://www.terrafrica.org.

Key Publications

The following publications address issues in Sub-Saharan Africa:

▨ *Africa Development Indicators*
▨ *Africa's Silk Road: China and India's New Economic Frontier*
▨ *Attacking Africa's Poverty: Experience from the Ground*
▨ *Challenges of African Growth: Opportunities, Constraints, and Strategic Directions*
▨ *Down to Earth: Agriculture and Poverty Reduction in Africa*
▨ *Disease and Mortality in Sub-Saharan Africa,* second edition
▨ *Facing the Challenges of African Growth: Opportunities, Constraints, and Strategic Directions*
▨ *Improving Health, Nutrition, and Population Outcomes in Sub-Saharan Africa: The Role of the World Bank*
▨ *Making Finance Work for Africa*
▨ *A Model for Calculating Interconnection Costs in Telecommunications*
▨ *A Sourcebook of HIV/AIDS Prevention Programs*
▨ *A Strategic Framework for Assistance to Africa: IDA and the Emerging Partnership Model*

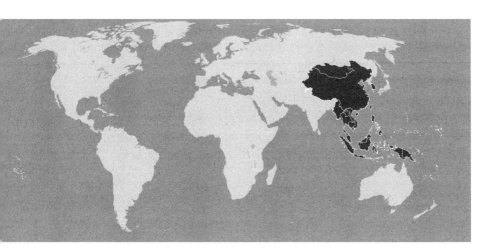

East Asia and the Pacific

This World Bank region includes the following countries that are eligible for borrowing:

Cambodia	Malaysia	Philippines
China	Marshall Islands	Samoa
Fiji	Federated States of	Solomon Islands
Indonesia	Micronesia	Thailand
Kiribati	Mongolia	Timor-Leste
Republic of Korea	Myanmar	Tonga
Lao People's Democratic	Palau	Vanuatu
Republic	Papua New Guinea	Vietnam

All these countries are members of the IBRD, IDA, and IFC. As for the other institutions,

- Kiribati, the Marshall Islands, Myanmar, and Tonga are not members of MIGA; and
- Kiribati, the Lao People's Democratic Republic, the Marshall Islands, Myanmar, Palau, Thailand, Vanuatu, and Vietnam are not members of ICSID.

The World Bank in East Asia and the Pacific

From 1965 to 2000, East Asian economies grew faster than all others in the world. The top eight economies grew twice as fast as the rest of East Asia, three

Box 3.4 East Asia and the Pacific Fast Facts

1.9 billion	Total population
0.8 percent	Population growth
70 years	Life expectancy at birth
29	Infant mortality per 1,000 births
97 percent	Female youth literacy
$1,630	2005 gross national income per capita
2.4 million	Number of people living with HIV/AIDS

Source: World Bank 2006.

times as fast as Latin America and South Asia, and 25 times as fast as Sub-Saharan Africa. As a result of this growth, human welfare improved dramatically. Life expectancy increased from almost 40 years in 1960 to 70 years in 2006. With just 8 percent of the population living below $1 a day in 2006, the region has the chance to reduce absolute poverty significantly by 2010. Much of the region's poverty reduction has resulted from rapid growth in China, which in turn has increased exports from China's neighbors. The region's exports have almost doubled since 2003.

Box 3.4 presents key regional facts.

Progress on structural and institutional reforms remains a key focus for the World Bank in the region. These reforms include accelerating financial and corporate restructuring; improving competitiveness; tackling impediments that under- mine the investment climate; ensuring adequate social protection; pursuing public sector governance reforms in such areas as public expenditure management, public financial accountability and transparency, civil service reform, and decentralization; and preventing countries from retreating into environmental neglect.

To reduce vulnerability and to ensure that poor people benefit from growth, the Bank's strategy has evolved from supporting safety nets and crisis assessment to focusing on the policies and institutions that help households manage social risks, that build an effective social policy framework, and that enable the poor to participate in the benefits of growth. Social programs have increasingly emphasized community empowerment and demand-driven approaches to promote efficiency, transparency, and effectiveness. Figures 3.6 and 3.7 present thematic and sectoral breakdowns of lending for fiscal 2006. The region's Web site is at http://www.worldbank.org/eap.

Figure 3.6 East Asia and the Pacific: IBRD and IDA Lending by Theme, Fiscal 2006
Share of total of $3.4 billion

22%	Financial & Private Sector Development
3%	Trade & Integration
12%	Environmental & Natural Resource Management
Rule of Law <1%	
Public Sector Governance 11%	
	13% Urban Development
Economic Management 2%	
Social Protection & Risk Management 4%	14% Rural Development
Social Development, Gender & Inclusion 2%	
17%	Human Development

Source: World Bank 2006.

Figure 3.7 East Asia and the Pacific: IBRD and IDA Lending by Sector, Fiscal 2006
Share of total of $3.4 billion

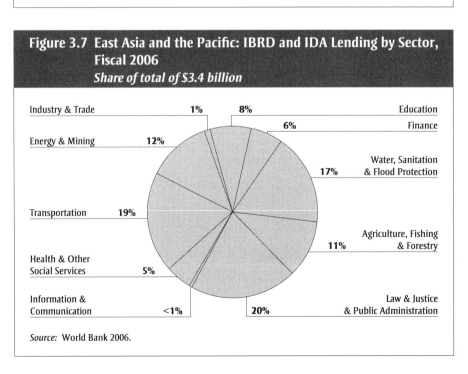

Industry & Trade 1%	8% Education
	6% Finance
Energy & Mining 12%	
	17% Water, Sanitation & Flood Protection
Transportation 19%	
	11% Agriculture, Fishing & Forestry
Health & Other Social Services 5%	
Information & Communication <1%	20% Law & Justice & Public Administration

Source: World Bank 2006.

IFC in East Asia and the Pacific

IFC is helping economies deepen and diversify their financial systems, strengthen corporate governance and other responsible business practices, and improve the environment for private investment in infrastructure. IFC's focus in the region includes strengthening the sustainability of private sector development by building financial sector institutions; developing model transactions that will further catalyze private investment in a variety of sectors; and setting standards for corporate governance, international accounting, environmental technologies, best practices, and efficiency of operations.

IFC also operates multidonor advisory services facilities in places throughout the region where support for private sector development, including small and medium enterprises, is especially crucial, namely, the Mekong region; the Pacific islands; and less developed areas of China, Indonesia, and the Philippines.

The East Asia and the Pacific Department is managed from IFC's regional hub in Hong Kong, China. Its Web site is at http://www.ifc.org/eastasia.

MIGA in East Asia and the Pacific

MIGA supports projects in East Asia and the Pacific through its guarantee program as well as through technical assistance activities in the region. Technical assistance goals for the region include developing and implementing targeting strategies to mobilize and promote investment opportunities, identifying and fostering sectors with solid potential for investment promotion, and devising targeted work programs. Other key objectives involve assisting in the development and implementation of information technology tools and promotional materials.

Regional Initiatives

The following initiatives are in place in East Asia and the Pacific:

- *Asia Alternative Energy Program.* This is a partnership between the World Bank and key bilateral donors to incorporate alternative energy options into the design of energy sector strategies and lending operations for all the Bank's client countries in Asia. The Web site is at http://www.worldbank.org/astae.
- *Asia Development Forum.* This is a regional forum to strengthen links and policy dialogues within the development community of the Asia and Pacific region. It is sponsored by the Asian Development Bank, the Korea Development Institute, the Korea Institute for International Economic

Policy, and the World Bank. The Web site is at http://www.adb.org/ Documents/Events/2002/ADF.

■ *InfoCity: Connecting Cities to Global Knowledge and Resources.* The Info-City initiative, funded by the Cities Alliance, seeks to facilitate the exchange of experience, ideas, and knowledge and to provide a repository for this type of information among participating cities in East Asia. The Web site is at http://infocity.org.

Key Publications

The following publications deal with East Asia and the Pacific:

■ *Connecting East Asia: A New Framework for Infrastructure*
■ *Dancing with Giants: China, India, and the Global Economy*
■ *East Asia Decentralizes: Making Local Government Work*
■ *East Asia Integrates: A Trade Policy Agenda for Shared Growth*
■ *East Asian Finance: The Road to Robust Markets*
■ *An East Asian Renaissance: Ideas for Economic Growth*
■ *East Asian Visions: Perspectives on Economic Development*
■ *Global Change and East Asian Policy Initiatives*
■ *Global Production Networking and Technological Change in East Asia*
■ *Postindustrial East Asian Cities*
■ *Sustainable Energy in China: The Closing Window of Opportunity*
■ *Under New Ownership: China's State-Owned Enterprises*

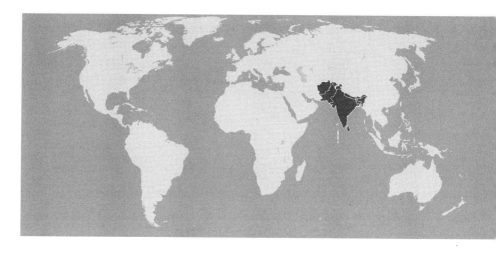

South Asia

This World Bank region includes the following countries that are eligible for borrowing:

Afghanistan	India	Pakistan
Bangladesh	Maldives	Sri Lanka
Bhutan	Nepal	

All these countries are members of IBRD and IDA. As for the other institutions,

- Afghanistan and Pakistan are included in IFC's Middle East and North Africa region;
- Bhutan is not a member of MIGA; and
- Bhutan, India, and the Maldives are not members of ICSID.

The World Bank in South Asia

South Asia entered the 21st century having experienced a decade of rapid economic growth: growth rates for the region averaged 5.9 percent annually during the 1990s. In recent years, many nations in the region have reduced tariffs, removed trade barriers, dismantled restrictions on domestic and foreign private investment, and reformed their financial systems. However, South Asia still attracts the lowest rate of foreign direct investment in the world, just 0.5 percent

Box 3.5 South Asia Fast Facts

1.5 billion	Total population
1.6 percent	Population growth
63 years	Life expectancy at birth
66	Infant mortality per 1,000 births
65 percent	Female youth literacy
$680	2005 gross national income per capita
6.2 million	Number of people living with HIV/AIDS

Source: World Bank 2006.

of gross domestic product. Some economies are still highly protected, and intra-regional trade is still far below its potential. Box 3.5 presents key regional facts.

Despite recent gains, the region remains one of the most disadvantaged in the world: more than one-third of its 1.5 billion people live on less than $1 a day, making South Asia home to nearly half the world's poor. This pervasive poverty is both a cause and a consequence of its low level of human development. Despite improvements in education and health services, the region still has the world's highest youth illiteracy rate and one-third of the world's maternal deaths. Nearly half of children under five years of age are malnourished. Environmental degradation, inadequate infrastructure, and social exclusion are also among the many obstacles to growth and poverty reduction.

South Asia's long-term economic prospects will hinge on much needed reforms in the key sectors of banking, power, and infrastructure, as well as on commitments to improve public spending and reform state enterprises. Improved governance, including stronger regulatory reforms and increased transparency, is a critical challenge for the region.

The World Bank's strategy for the South Asia region has two pillars: accelerated growth and faster human development. Accelerating growth will require addressing the region's vast urban and rural infrastructure needs, which have been ignored because of a lack of resources and effective policy frameworks that could promote public-private partnerships. Despite having five megacities with populations of more than 10 million people, South Asia is the least urbanized region in the world and is the only region that has no city that can provide piped water 24 hours a day. In India, private investment in infrastructure has remained well under the projected 2 percent of gross domestic product. Deficiencies in the region's overall investment climate that need to be addressed include corruption and excessive red tape.

More rapid human development has different meanings for different parts of South Asia. In Bangladesh, the Maldives, Sri Lanka, and parts of India, such as Kerala, which have achieved such basic goals as universal enrollment in primary education, the focus is on improving quality, whereas in other parts of the region, such as Pakistan, concerted efforts are needed to attain these basic goals, especially for women. In all cases, in supporting public expenditures for faster human development, the strategy emphasizes increasing the accountability of service providers and policy makers to poor people.

Figures 3.8 and 3.9 provide thematic and sectoral breakdowns of lending for fiscal 2006. The region's Web site is at http://www.worldbank.org/sar.

IFC in South Asia

South Asia has been one of the world's fastest-growing regions in recent years, with particularly strong growth in India. IFC's strategic priorities in the region include increasing private investment in infrastructure, developing local financial markets, supporting the restructuring and modernization of domestic manufacturing enterprises, and promoting the growth of small businesses. Through investments that have a high development impact, IFC is helping companies in the region improve their international competitiveness and pursue new investment opportunities in South Asia and beyond.

Through its South Asia Enterprise Development Facility, IFC provides advisory services to improve the business environment, strengthen providers of business services, and increase financial services for smaller businesses. This multidonor facility focuses on Bangladesh, Bhutan, Nepal, and northeast India and is currently expanding to serve the Maldives and Sri Lanka.

The South Asia Department is managed from IFC's regional hub in New Delhi. Its Web site is at http://www.ifc.org/southasia.

MIGA in South Asia

MIGA supports projects in South Asia through guarantees and technical assistance. Recent guarantee activity has occurred in the power sector in Nepal and the software and telecommunications industries in Pakistan.

Regional Initiatives

Regional initiatives include the following:

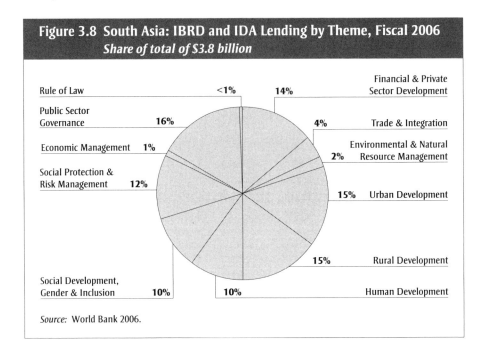

Figure 3.8 South Asia: IBRD and IDA Lending by Theme, Fiscal 2006
Share of total of $3.8 billion

Rule of Law <1%

Public Sector Governance 16%

Economic Management 1%

Social Protection & Risk Management 12%

Social Development, Gender & Inclusion 10%

14% Financial & Private Sector Development

4% Trade & Integration

2% Environmental & Natural Resource Management

15% Urban Development

15% Rural Development

10% Human Development

Source: World Bank 2006.

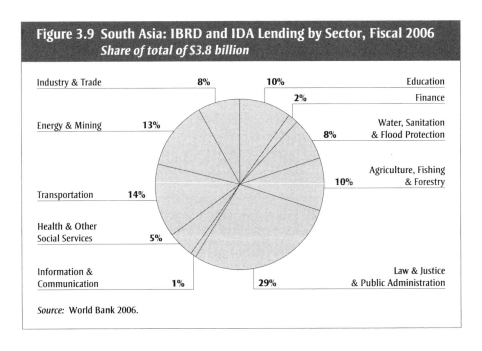

Figure 3.9 South Asia: IBRD and IDA Lending by Sector, Fiscal 2006
Share of total of $3.8 billion

Industry & Trade 8%

Energy & Mining 13%

Transportation 14%

Health & Other Social Services 5%

Information & Communication 1%

10% Education

2% Finance

8% Water, Sanitation & Flood Protection

10% Agriculture, Fishing & Forestry

29% Law & Justice & Public Administration

Source: World Bank 2006.

■ *Immunization Efforts in India and South Asia.* The World Bank is the largest external financier of immunization programs in South Asia. It is actively working with countries to strengthen their routine immunization programs for major childhood diseases and, more recently, to accelerate polio eradication. In agreement with national governments, the goal is to reach all children with effective and high quality vaccinations. Over the next few years, the Bank will collaborate with governments in South Asia to help strengthen routine immunization services, eradicate polio, and introduce "new" vaccines. Strengthening the vaccine delivery system to ensure that all children are immunized with the basic six vaccines remains the top priority.

■ *HIV/AIDS and South Asia.* Between 5.5 and 6 million people in South Asia are living with HIV and AIDS. The World Bank has focused on mobilizing South Asian countries to improve and accelerate their responses to HIV and AIDS. It has supported national efforts to slow the spread of HIV since the first India project in 1992, and has committed $380 million to support national programs to date. The main components of these projects are surveillance, monitoring and evaluation, targeted interventions for vulnerable populations, blood safety, efforts aimed at reducing stigma among the general population, and strengthening public and private institutions for a multisector response.

■ *Tuberculosis in South Asia.* Three of the 10 countries with the largest number of tuberculosis (TB) patients are in South Asia. India carries the world's greatest burden of tuberculosis cases, so advances in India's TB programs are critical to global TB control. In India, the World Bank supports a revised national TB control program, which treated 1.1 million patients in 1999, with that number increasing in 2000 under DOTS (Directly-Observed Treatment, Short-course—a cost-effective strategy that reduces illness, deaths, and transmission). Treatment success rates in India are at 84 percent. In Bangladesh, the World Bank has supported TB control efforts through two consecutive health projects that aim to implement priority public health interventions and ensure sustainability through systems reform and integration. In these countries, the challenges ahead are expanding DOTS coverage, involving the private sector, and improving program management at all levels of government.

■ *Child Labor and South Asia.* Despite the fact that legislation banning child labor has been enacted in all South Asian countries, South Asia remains home to the largest number of working children in the world. The long-term solution to child labor problems lies in reducing poverty, improving the quality of education, and expanding access to schooling to disadvantaged social groups. These are central objectives of the Bank's assistance programs in the South Asian countries.

- *Urban Air Quality Management.* The majority of South Asian cities suffer from extremely high levels of urban air pollution, particularly in the form of small particles. Regionwide, urban air pollution is estimated to cause over 250,000 deaths and billions of cases of respiratory illnesses every year. The World Bank, with support from the United Nations Development Programme, has initiated a regional program to address this issue. It draws lessons from international experience, identifies where more data are needed to arrive at viable policy recommendations, and assists governments, civil society, and the media as they work to improve urban air quality.

Key Publications

The following publications deal with South Asia:

- *Dancing with Giants: China, India, and the Global Economy*
- *Ending Poverty in South Asia: Ideas that Work*
- *Explaining South Asia's Development Performance: The Role of Good Policies*
- *Improving Access to Finance for India's Rural Poor*
- *India and the WTO*
- *India's Undernourished Children: A Call for Reform and Action*
- *Local Organizations in Decentralized Development: Their Functions and Their Performance in India*
- *Overcoming Drought: Adaptation Strategies for Andhra Pradesh*

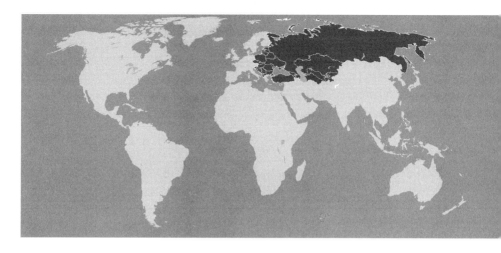

Europe and Central Asia

This World Bank region includes the following countries that are eligible for borrowing:

Albania
Armenia
Azerbaijan
Belarus
Bosnia and Herzegovina
Bulgaria
Croatia
Georgia
Kazakhstan

Kyrgyz Republic
Former Yugoslav
  Republic of
  Macedonia
Moldova
Montenegro
Poland
Romania
Russian Federation

Serbia
Slovak Republic
Tajikistan
Turkey
Turkmenistan
Ukraine
Uzbekistan

All the countries listed are members of IBRD, IFC, and MIGA. As for the other institutions,

- Belarus, Bulgaria, Estonia, Lithuania, Romania, and Turkmenistan are not members of IDA;
- The Czech Republic, Estonia, Lithuania, and Slovenia are included in IFC's Central and Eastern Europe Region; and
- The Kyrgyz Republic, Moldova, Montenegro, Poland, Russia, Serbia, and Tajikistan are not members of ICSID.

Box 3.6 Europe and Central Asia Fast Facts

0.5 billion	Total population
0.1 percent	Population growth
69 years	Life expectancy at birth
28	Infant mortality per 1,000 births
98 percent	Female youth literacy
$4,110	2005 gross national income per capita
1.5 million	Number of people living with HIV/AIDS

Source: World Bank 2006.

The World Bank in Europe and Central Asia

Most countries in the region have established the basic institutions and framework of open market economies. Poverty has declined significantly: overall, 40 million people moved out of poverty between 1999 and 2003, but poverty remains widespread in Central Asia and the South Caucasus. Box 3.6 presents key regional facts.

At the other end of the spectrum, middle-income countries in the region face the same challenge as such countries everywhere—convergence with upper-income countries. Per capita income in the eight newest members of the European Union is 40 to 60 percent that of the countries they joined, and convergence is expected to take 20 to 30 years. Countries such as Azerbaijan, Kazakhstan, and Russia struggle with policy issues similar to those other resource-rich countries face, including the need to ensure good governance of their revenues and reduce their dependence on extractive industries.

The legacy of central planning remains throughout the region, with the stage of transition varying from country to country. On the positive side, human development indicators in education and health are relatively good. On the negative side, many towns are located in far-flung and unviable locations, especially in Russia; state bureaucracies are bloated and overextended; and serious environmental issues remain. Less than full recovery from the recession that was in effect at the onset of transition and the emergence of new challenges mean that countries in the region face an uphill task in meeting the MDGs, especially those related to health and the environment. Another particularly worrisome issue is the rapid spread of tuberculosis and HIV/AIDS throughout the region.

The Bank's Country Assistance Strategies are tailored to meet the needs of each subregion. They are organized around two broad themes: fostering growth and competitiveness by building a climate for investment, and promoting social inclusion. The Bank is also addressing global issues such as HIV/AIDS—which goes hand in hand with youth issues in Europe and Central Asia—and key environmental challenges pertaining to biodiversity, water, carbon emissions, and renewable energy, among others. Figures 3.10 and 3.11 present thematic and sectoral breakdowns of lending for fiscal 2006. The region's Web site is at http://www.worldbank.org/eca.

IFC in Europe and Central Asia

IFC pursues its work in Europe and Central Asia through two departments: the Central and Eastern Europe Department, managed from a regional hub in Moscow, and the Southern Europe and Central Asia Department, managed from a regional hub in Istanbul. Growth is strong in the region, with most countries at varying stages of transition to market economies and integration with Western private capital. IFC activity is led by the financial sector, where IFC's investments, expertise in structuring transactions, and advice to firms and governments are helping to build capital markets and expand access to finance. Other key sectors include infrastructure and manufacturing, and IFC continues to assist with privatization in many industries.

IFC provides advisory services through multidonor operations, the Private Enterprise Partnership in Russia and the former Soviet republics, and a similar partnership in South East Europe. Efforts are tailored to the specific needs of economies, which range from new or prospective members of the European Union to frontier markets where opportunities for investment remain severely constrained. Country and regional programs focus on leasing, housing and mortgage finance, microfinance, corporate governance, and supply chain links between small and large companies.

IFC's Europe and Central Asia Web site, covering countries served by both regional departments, is at http://www.ifc.org/eca.

MIGA in Europe and Central Asia

Guarantees in the energy, agribusiness, manufacturing, and finance sectors, as well as strong capacity-building assistance, highlight MIGA's current efforts in Europe and Central Asia. For more information, see "Regions" at http://www.miga.org.

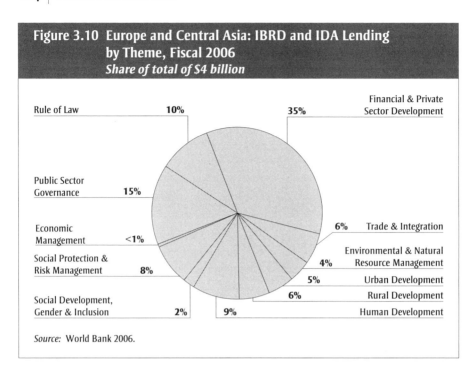

Figure 3.10 Europe and Central Asia: IBRD and IDA Lending by Theme, Fiscal 2006
Share of total of $4 billion

Rule of Law **10%**

Public Sector Governance **15%**

Economic Management **<1%**

Social Protection & Risk Management **8%**

Social Development, Gender & Inclusion **2%**

Financial & Private Sector Development **35%**

Trade & Integration **6%**

Environmental & Natural Resource Management **4%**

Urban Development **5%**

Rural Development **6%**

Human Development **9%**

Source: World Bank 2006.

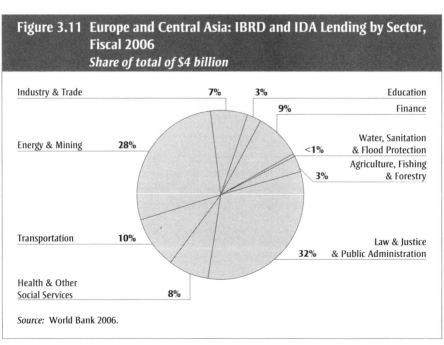

Figure 3.11 Europe and Central Asia: IBRD and IDA Lending by Sector, Fiscal 2006
Share of total of $4 billion

Industry & Trade **7%**

Energy & Mining **28%**

Transportation **10%**

Health & Other Social Services **8%**

Education **3%**

Finance **9%**

Water, Sanitation & Flood Protection **<1%**

Agriculture, Fishing & Forestry **3%**

Law & Justice & Public Administration **32%**

Source: World Bank 2006.

Regional Initiatives

Regional initiatives include the following:

- *Black Sea and Danube Basin Initiative.* The Black Sea and Danube Basin have become polluted over the past four decades, causing significant losses through reduced revenues from tourism and fisheries, loss of biodiversity, and increased prevalence of water-borne diseases. This initiative aims to promote investment and capacity building to return the environment to its condition in the 1960s. See "Regional Initiatives" at http://www.worldbank.org/eca.

- *European Union integration.* In recent years, the World Bank has actively partnered with the accession candidate countries and the European Commission in relation to the European Union's enlargement process. See "Regional Initiatives" at http://www.worldbank.org/eca.

- *Forest law enforcement and governance in Europe and North Asia.* In November 2005, 48 countries committed to cracking down on illegal logging by improving forest law enforcement and governance. To this end, they signed the St. Petersburg Declaration. See "Regional Initiatives" at http://www.worldbank.org/eca.

- *Program of Accounting Reform and Institutional Strengthening.* This regional program seeks to create a transparent policy environment and effective institutional framework for corporate reporting within South Central and South East Europe. See "Regional Initiatives" at http://www.worldbank.org/eca.

- *South Caucasus regional initiatives.* The Caucasus region has been a major trade and transport corridor since ancient times, but during the last decade it has lost this role because transport costs are prohibitively high. See "Regional Initiatives" at http://www.worldbank.org/eca.

- *South East Europe Social Development Initiative.* This regional initiative aims to provide the governments of South East Europe and the donor community involved in the region (in particular, the World Bank) with the capacity to carry out social analyses, promote institution building, and launch pilot projects to address interethnic tensions and social cohesion issues. See "Regional Initiatives" at http://www.worldbank.org/eca.

- *Trade and Transport Facilitation in South East Europe Program.* This initiative aims to foster trade in the subregion. It promotes more efficient and less costly trade flows across the countries of South East Europe and provides customs standards compatible with those of the European Union. The Web site is http://www.seerecon.org/ttfse.

Key Publications

The following publications deal with Europe and Central Asia:

- *Anticorruption in Transition: Who Is Succeeding and Why?*
- *The Caucasian Tiger: Sustaining Economic Growth in Armenia*
- *Enhancing Job Opportunities: Eastern Europe and the Former Soviet Union*
- *Fiscal Policy and Economic Growth: Lessons for Transition Economies*
- *From Disintegration to Reintegration: Eastern Europe and the Former Soviet Union in International Trade*
- *From Red to Gray: The Third Transition of Aging Populations in Eastern Europe and the Former Soviet Union*
- *Growth, Poverty, and Inequality: Eastern Europe and the Former Soviet Union*
- *Judicial Systems in Transition Economies: Assessing the Past, Looking to the Future*
- *Migration and Remittances in Eastern Europe and the Former Soviet Union*
- *Pension Reform in Europe: Process and Progress*
- *Reducing Poverty through Growth and Social Policy Reform in Russia*

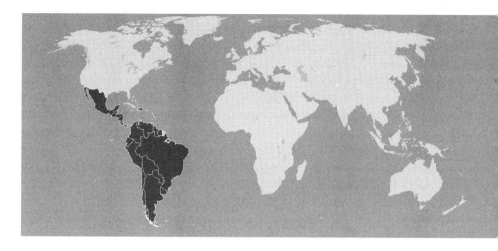

Latin America and the Caribbean

This World Bank region includes the following countries that are eligible for borrowing:

Antigua and Barbuda	El Salvador	Peru
Argentina	Grenada	St. Kitts and Nevis
Belize	Guatemala	St. Lucia
Bolivia	Guyana	St. Vincent and the
Brazil	Haiti	Grenadines
Chile	Honduras	Suriname
Colombia	Jamaica	Trinidad and Tobago
Costa Rica	Mexico	Uruguay
Dominica	Nicaragua	República Bolivariana de
Dominican Republic	Panama	Venezuela
Ecuador	Paraguay	

All these countries are members of IBRD. As for the other institutions,

- Jamaica, Suriname, Trinidad and Tobago, and República Bolivariana de Venezuela are not members of IDA;
- The Bahamas and Barbados are included in IFC's Latin America and the Caribbean region; St. Vincent and the Grenadines and Suriname are not members of IFC;
- Mexico is not a member of MIGA; and
- Antigua and Barbuda, Belize, Brazil, Dominica, the Dominican Republic, Haiti, Mexico, and Suriname are not members of ICSID.

The World Bank in Latin America and the Caribbean

Latin America and the Caribbean is a region of broad diversity, with people who speak Spanish, Portuguese, English, French, and some 400 indigenous languages. Its topography and ecosystems range from tropical islands to high sierras and altiplanos, rainforests, deserts, and sprawling plains. It is the most urbanized region in the developing world, with three-quarters of its people living in and around cities, but natural resources and agriculture are also important to many of its economies, which include some of the developing world's largest, such as Brazil and Mexico, and some of the smallest. Despite immense resources and dynamic societies, deep inequalities of wealth persist in most countries. About a quarter of the region's population lives in poverty (defined as living on less than $2 a day), roughly the same as in the late 1980s. Approximately 50 million of these people (9.5 percent) are extremely poor (living on less than $1 a day). Box 3.7 presents key regional facts.

Despite ongoing recovery and improved economic prospects in recent years, the region still faces the significant challenge of persistent poverty because of both entrenched high inequality, which is exacerbated by the exclusion of marginal groups, and modest and volatile growth in recent decades. World Bank support to the region aims to reduce poverty through sustained, equitable growth and a focus on the poorest and most vulnerable people. Priorities include

- improving the investment climate and competitiveness to foster job creation;
- strengthening education and creating innovative systems for enhancing human capital and increasing productivity;
- improving public sector governance and institutions;

Box 3.7 Latin America and the Caribbean Fast Facts

0.6 billion	Total population
1.4 percent	Population growth
72 years	Life expectancy at birth
27	Infant mortality per 1,000 births
97 percent	Female youth literacy
$3,990	2005 gross national income per capita
1.9 million	Number of people living with HIV/AIDS

Source: World Bank 2006.

▓ fostering social equity and inclusion and achieving an inclusive, but affordable, welfare system;

▓ strengthening environmental institutions and promoting effective use of natural resources; and

▓ consolidating macroeconomic and financial stability and using fiscal resources for infrastructure investments.

The Bank is tailoring assistance to meet the needs of citizens in Latin America and the Caribbean, particularly in middle-income countries with high poverty. In Chile, for instance, the Bank has moved from financing a broad range of projects to supporting selected areas of focus (education, social protection, and innovation) that are part of the country's overall strategy to ensure high growth with equity.

Figures 3.12 and 3.13 provide thematic and sectoral breakdowns of lending for fiscal 2006. The region's Web site is at http://www.worldbank.org/lac.

IFC in Latin America and the Caribbean

IFC has had one of the largest regional programs in its 50-year history in Latin America and the Caribbean, which continues to present challenges in relation to its investment climate, financial sector development, and infrastructure. IFC is working to help develop a broadly based private sector whose benefits can reach poorer segments of the population. IFC provided countercyclical support during the region's recent crisis—supporting export-earning projects in Argentina, for example, and helping reactivate trade financing in Brazil—and is now focusing on providing longer-term funding for private enterprises and for select projects with a broad impact on social and economic inclusion. IFC's investments emphasize enhancing competitiveness, providing support to high-growth industries, and helping the region's firms become global players. The region is also a focus for IFC's work in structured finance, risk management, and local currency transactions.

Advisory services for the region are being delivered through a multidonor facility set up by IFC to provide consulting and business services in support of private sector development. The facility is working with governments and key stakeholders to improve conditions for private sector development, with IFC clients to enhance the development impact of investments, and with financial institutions to help small businesses gain better access to finance.

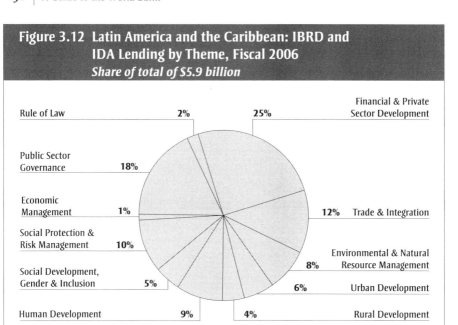

Figure 3.12 Latin America and the Caribbean: IBRD and IDA Lending by Theme, Fiscal 2006
Share of total of $5.9 billion

Rule of Law 2%

Financial & Private Sector Development 25%

Public Sector Governance 18%

Economic Management 1%

Trade & Integration 12%

Social Protection & Risk Management 10%

Environmental & Natural Resource Management 8%

Social Development, Gender & Inclusion 5%

Urban Development 6%

Human Development 9%

Rural Development 4%

Source: World Bank 2006.

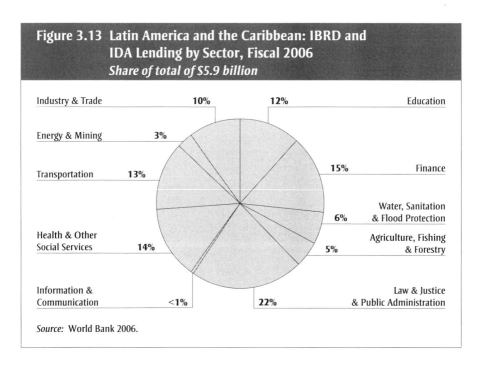

Figure 3.13 Latin America and the Caribbean: IBRD and IDA Lending by Sector, Fiscal 2006
Share of total of $5.9 billion

Industry & Trade 10%

Education 12%

Energy & Mining 3%

Transportation 13%

Finance 15%

Water, Sanitation & Flood Protection 6%

Health & Other Social Services 14%

Agriculture, Fishing & Forestry 5%

Information & Communication <1%

Law & Justice & Public Administration 22%

Source: World Bank 2006.

The Latin America and the Caribbean Department is managed from IFC's regional hub in Rio de Janeiro. Its Web site is at http://www.ifc.org/lac.

MIGA in Latin America and the Caribbean

MIGA supports projects in Latin America and the Caribbean through its guarantee program. MIGA also undertakes technical assistance activities in the region, focusing on investment promotion in countries that have not been recipients of substantial foreign direct investment in the past.

Regional Initiatives

The following initiatives are among those in place in Latin America and the Caribbean:

- *Clean Air Initiative in Latin American Cities.* This initiative focuses on reversing the deterioration of urban air quality caused by rapid urbanization, increased vehicular transport, and industrial production. It is a partnership of city governments, private sector companies, international development agencies and foundations, NGOs, and academic institutions, with a technical secretariat at the World Bank. See http://www.cleanairnet.org/lac.
- *Global Telemedicine and Teaching Network.* Through an expanded network and partnerships, the Global Telemedicine and Teaching Network—a satellite-based and Internet-based communications platform, the Global Development Learning Network, and Medical Missions for Children improve treatment of critically ill children in remote areas in real time. See "Regional Initiatives" at http://www.worldbank.org/lac.
- *Landfill Gas-to-Energy Initiative for Latin American Cities.* The objectives of this program are to develop outreach activities to promote this environmentally sound, nonconventional energy source; document experiences in the region and in selected cities elsewhere; and help implement a regional approach aimed at maximum reduction of methane emissions and the development of carbon trading opportunities. See "Regional Initiatives" at http://www.worldbank.org/lac.
- *Mesoamerican Biological Corridor.* Home to rare and endangered species, as well as human inhabitants, the goal of the Mesoamerican Biological Corridor is to integrate conservation, protection, and ecological balance within the framework of sustainable economic development. See http://www.biomeso.net.

- *The Multi-Country HIV/AIDS Prevention and Control Lending Program for the Caribbean.* This program provides loans or credits to help individual countries finance their national HIV/AIDS prevention and control projects. See "Regional Initiatives" at http://www.worldbank.org/lac.
- *Pilot Program to Protect the Brazilian Rain Forest.* This multilateral initiative of the Brazilian government, civil society, and the international community is aimed at developing innovative tools and methodologies for conserving Brazil's rain forests. See "Regional Initiatives" at http://www.worldbank.org/lac.

Key Publications

Publications about Latin America and the Caribbean include the following:

- *Beyond the City: The Rural Contribution to Development*
- *Beyond Survival: Protecting Households from Health Shocks in Latin America*
- *Challenges of CAFTA: Maximizing the Benefits for Central America*
- *Close to Home: The Development Impact of Remittances*
- *Citizens, Politicians, and Providers: The Latin American Experience with Service Delivery Reform*
- *Emerging Capital Markets and Globalization: The Latin American Experience*
- *Inequality in Latin America and the Caribbean: Breaking with History?*
- *Infrastructure in Latin America and the Caribbean: Recent Developments and Key Challenges*
- *Keeping the Promise of Social Security In Latin America*
- *Lessons from NAFTA for Latin America and the Caribbean*
- *Natural Resources: Neither Curse Nor Destiny*
- *Poverty Reduction and Growth: Virtuous and Vicious Circles*
- *A Time to Choose: Caribbean Development in the 21st Century*
- *The Urban Poor in Latin America*

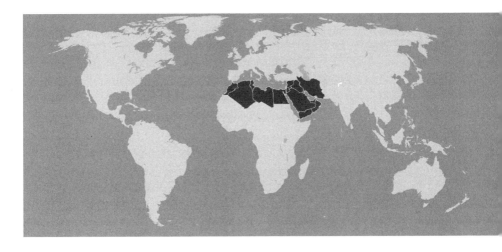

Middle East and North Africa

This World Bank region includes the following countries that are eligible for borrowing:

Algeria	Iraq	Syrian Arab Republic
Djibouti	Jordan	Tunisia
Arab Republic of Egypt	Lebanon	Republic of Yemen
Islamic Republic of Iran	Morocco	

All these countries are members of IBRD. There are also World Bank activities in the West Bank and Gaza. As for the other institutions,

- Afghanistan, Kuwait, Oman, Pakistan, Saudi Arabia, and the United Arab Emirates are also included in IFC's Middle East and North Africa region, which also covers the West Bank and Gaza; Djibouti is included in IFC's Africa region;
- Iraq is not a member of MIGA; and
- Djibouti, the Islamic Republic of Iran, and Iraq are not members of ICSID.

The World Bank in the Middle East and North Africa

The Middle East and North Africa is an economically diverse region that includes the oil-rich economies in the Gulf and countries that are resource-scarce in relation to population, such as Egypt, Morocco, and the Republic

---

Box 3.8 Middle East and North Africa Fast Facts

0.3 billion	Total population
1.8 percent	Population growth
69 years	Life expectancy at birth
44	Infant mortality per 1,000 births
81 percent	Female youth literacy
$2,240	2005 gross national income per capita
0.4 million	Number of people living with HIV/AIDS

Source: World Bank 2006.

---

of Yemen. The region's economic fortunes over much of the past quarter century have been heavily influenced by two factors: the price of oil and the legacy of economic policies and structures that emphasized a leading role for the state. Box 3.8 presents key regional facts.

Beginning in the late 1980s, many of the region's economies were committed to far-reaching economic reforms to restore macroeconomic balances and promote private sector–led development. As a result, the late 1990s saw improvements: average gross national income per capita for the region increased from $1,800 in 1985 to $2,080 in 2000. Annual gross domestic product growth in the region has remained steady at 3.1 percent for the past decade.

Despite its improved performance, the region continues to face important economic and social challenges. A key issue is unemployment, which is around 15 percent, although more than 20 percent of the workforce is unemployed in Algeria, Libya, Morocco, and the West Bank and Gaza. Unemployment is only slightly less pressing in the Islamic Republic of Iran, Jordan, Lebanon, and Tunisia. Jobless rates among youth are twice the regional average in some countries, requiring the region to create about 4 million jobs a year in the next few years to accommodate new entrants into the labor market.

The Bank has identified five areas that represent a common challenge across the region—public sector efficiency and governance, private sector development and employment creation, education, sustainable water resource management, and the gender gap—and takes their impact into account for each intervention it undertakes in a country.

Figures 3.14 and 3.15 provide a thematic and sectoral breakdown of lending for fiscal 2006. The region's Web site is at http://www.worldbank.org/mena.

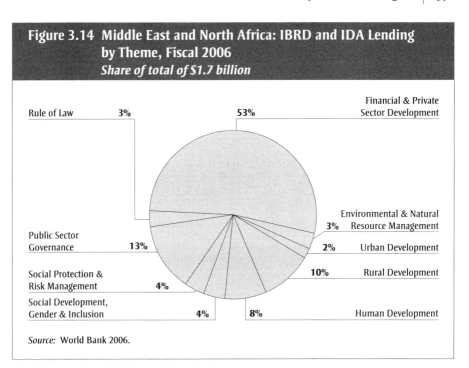

Figure 3.14 Middle East and North Africa: IBRD and IDA Lending by Theme, Fiscal 2006
Share of total of $1.7 billion

Rule of Law 3%

53% Financial & Private Sector Development

Public Sector Governance 13%

Social Protection & Risk Management 4%

Social Development, Gender & Inclusion 4%

Environmental & Natural Resource Management 3%

Urban Development 2%

Rural Development 10%

Human Development 8%

Source: World Bank 2006.

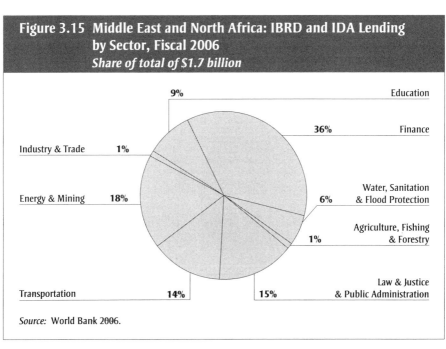

Figure 3.15 Middle East and North Africa: IBRD and IDA Lending by Sector, Fiscal 2006
Share of total of $1.7 billion

9% Education

36% Finance

Industry & Trade 1%

Energy & Mining 18%

Water, Sanitation & Flood Protection 6%

Agriculture, Fishing & Forestry 1%

Transportation 14%

Law & Justice & Public Administration 15%

Source: World Bank 2006.

IFC in the Middle East and North Africa

IFC aims to increase private investment and job creation to accelerate growth and promote economies that are more open. In support of this strategy, IFC's field presence has expanded rapidly. Recent investments cover many sectors, including the financial sector, manufacturing, oil and gas, education, agribusiness, and infrastructure.

IFC is using advisory services, separately or in combination with long-term capital, to strengthen the region's private sector and promote best practices. Through its Private Enterprise Partnership for the Middle East and North Africa, IFC provides a wide range of advisory services. Because small and medium enterprises are crucial to many economies in the region, the partnership is helping facilitate their development and their access to finance. It also provides advice on privatization and on business-enabling environments, including for women entrepreneurs, and it provides support for public-private partnerships.

The Middle East and North Africa Department is managed from IFC's regional hub in Cairo. Its Web site is at http://www.ifc.org/mena.

MIGA in the Middle East and North Africa

MIGA offers guarantee services in the region and provides support to regional investors making investments outside the region. It undertakes technical assistance initiatives and participates in a broader World Bank Group outreach effort aimed at promoting the use of a wider array of World Bank Group tools for developing the private sector.

Regional Initiatives

Regional initiatives in the Middle East and North Africa include the following:

- *Governance in the Middle East and North Africa Initiative.* This initiative seeks to improve governance institutions and processes, the weaknesses of which may lead to disappointing economic performance. It is a partnership of individual researchers from the region, local think tanks, and donor agencies. The Web site is at http://www.worldbank.org/mena/governance.
- *The Middle East and North Africa Development Forum.* This is a partnership, with participation by the World Bank Institute, the Bank's Middle East and North Africa Regional Vice Presidency, the UN Development Programme, and think tanks. Its goals include empowering civil society to participate in shaping public policy, contributing to the policy debate

in key areas of regional interest, improving the extent and quality of research on economic and social policy issues, and improving networks to promote development in the region. The Web site is at http://www.worldbank.org/wbi/mdf.

- *Trade and Investment Climate.* The main objective of this program is to use global integration as a way to enhance growth, expand jobs, and increase productivity. To achieve greater global integration, the program calls for joint liberalization of trade in goods and services, involving, among other things, much freer flows of labor and capital than has thus far been the case.

Key Publications

The following publications deal with the Middle East and North Africa:

- *Better Governance for Development in the Middle East and North Africa: Enhancing Inclusiveness and Accountability*
- *HIV/AIDS in the Middle East and North Africa: The Costs of Inaction*
- *Making the Most of Scarcity: Accountability for Better Water Management in the Middle East and North Africa*
- *Pensions in the Middle East and North Africa: Time for Change*
- *Sustaining Gains in Poverty Reduction and Human Development in the Middle East and North Africa*
- *Trade, Investment, and Development in the Middle East and North Africa: Engaging with the World*
- *Unlocking the Employment Potential in the Middle East and North Africa: Toward a New Social Contract*

Aircraft workers lay down flooring in Brazil as part of an IFC-financed project. IFC invests in private enterprises throughout most of the developing world. Its investments help to create jobs, build economies, and generate tax revenue.

4 Topics in Development

This chapter provides an overview of major aspects of development in which the World Bank Group is involved. These topics are listed alphabetically with a focus on key initiatives, Web sites, and publications. Because of space constraints, the listing of topics is not intended to be comprehensive.

The broad themes in Bank Group work are covered under "Strategies" in chapter 2. As discussed in that section, the Bank Group is increasingly emphasizing the social aspects of development. A key organizing principle of its work is the Millennium Development Goals (MDGs) as defined by the United Nations.

Another key aspect of Bank Group activities, as explained in chapter 1, is the matrix in which units focused on development sectors (called "networks") intersect with units focused on world regions. The networks correspond to many of the topics covered in this chapter. These topics are as follows:

- Agriculture and rural development
- Aid effectiveness
- Combating corruption
- Conflict prevention and fragile states
- Debt relief
- Economic research and data
- Education
- Empowerment and participation
- Energy and mining
- Environment
- Financial sector
- Gender
- Globalization
- Governance
- Health, nutrition, and population
- Indigenous peoples
- Information and communication technologies
- Infrastructure
- Labor and social protection
- Law, regulation, and the judiciary
- Manufacturing and services
- Poverty
- Private sector development
- Social development
- Sustainable development
- Trade
- Transport
- Urban development
- Water

Agriculture and Rural Development

Seventy percent of the world's poor live in rural areas, and this rural population relies on agriculture as its main source of income. The Bank Group pursues its work in agriculture and rural development through the units and programs discussed in this section.

Agriculture and Rural Development Department (World Bank)

The Agriculture and Rural Development Department, one of the departments that make up the Sustainable Development Network, works to reduce poverty through sustainable rural development. To this end, the department provides analytic and advisory services to the Bank's regions on a wide range of agriculture and rural development topics. These services include preparing and implementing the World Bank's corporate strategy on rural development, monitoring the Bank's portfolio of agriculture and rural projects, and promoting knowledge sharing among agriculture and rural development practitioners inside and outside the Bank to continually improve the Bank's activities in rural areas. The department's focus includes gender and rural development, rural producer organizations, sustainable agriculture, water resources management, and forests and forestry. The department's Web site is at http://www.worldbank.org/rural. Additional information appears on the Sustainable Development Web site at http://www.worldbank.org/sustainabledevelopment.

Agribusiness Department (IFC)

The technical, financial, and market expertise necessary to evaluate agribusiness projects is centralized in IFC's Agribusiness Department. Its staff comprises investment officers, engineers, and economists, all with specialized international experience. IFC supports projects involving primary agricultural production, aquaculture, and fishing, as well as marketing (for example, silos, cold and controlled-atmosphere storage facilities, and wholesale markets), food processing, and distribution. As a rule, preference is given to investment projects that have the largest demonstrated benefits for the efficiency and competitiveness of the supply chain and that have the highest overall contribution to economic development. For more on IFC and agribusiness, see http://www.ifc.org/agribusiness.

Other Resources

Other resources include the following:

- The *Consultative Group on International Agricultural Research,* a Bank Group affiliate whose secretariat is at Bank headquarters, is a strategic alliance of members, partners, and international agricultural centers that mobilizes science to benefit the poor. Its Web site is at http://www.cgiar.org.
- *World Bank research* focused on agriculture and rural development can be found at http://go.worldbank.org/8PZ5ZCHZK0.

Key Publications

Following are some key publications that address agriculture and rural development:

- *Agricultural Growth and the Poor*
- *Agricultural Investment Sourcebook*
- *Agricultural Trade Reform and the Doha Development Agenda*
- *Enhancing Agricultural Innovation: How to Go Beyond the Strengthening of Research Systems*
- *Reaching the Rural Poor*
- *Reengaging in Agricultural Water Management*
- *Shaping the Future of Water for Agriculture*
- *Sustainable Land Management: Challenges, Opportunities, and Trade-Offs*
- *Sustaining Forests*
- *World Development Report 2008: Agriculture for Development*

Aid Effectiveness

The effectiveness of aid in reducing poverty, improving lives, and stimulating economic growth has always been a central concern of the Bank Group. The international community's broad acceptance of the MDGs brought aid effectiveness into even sharper relief as the Bank Group (among others) began focusing on measuring progress toward achieving the MDGs.

Independent Evaluation

The World Bank's Independent Evaluation Group and equivalent units within IFC and MIGA assess the effectiveness of specific programs and projects for the people and countries participating in them. These units provide advice to the Boards of Directors based on evaluations at the project, country, and sector levels. Each year, evidence from those evaluations is marshaled to produce a summary report on the Bank's development effectiveness. As covered in chapter 2, evaluation is an integral part of the life cycle of every project, as is monitoring for quality while a project is under way. The Web site for the Independent Evaluation Group is at http://www.worldbank.org/ieg.

Quality Assurance Group

As part of the Bank's goal of fighting poverty with passion and professionalism while decreasing defects in implementation, the Quality Assurance Group conducts real-time assessments of the Bank's performance in relation to its major product lines. The Quality Assurance Group systematically assesses quality in each of the Bank's three areas of operation: new lending, portfolio management, and advisory services. These examinations cover economic, financial, technical, environmental, social, and institutional aspects of operations and assess the degree to which operations align with Country Assistance Strategies and the extent of client participation.

Other Resources

The following Web sites are also useful:

- The *Independent Evaluation Group Help Desk* has a Web site at http://www. worldbank.org/ieg/contact.html. Its e-mail address is eline@worldbank.org.
- *World Bank research* focused on aid effectiveness can be found at http:// www.worldbank.org/research/aid.

Key Publications

Publications on aid effectiveness include the following:

- *Aid That Works: Successful Development in Fragile States*
- *Annual Review of Development Effectiveness*
- *Assessing Aid: What Works, What Doesn't, and Why*
- *A Case for Aid: Building a Consensus for Development Assistance*
- *Global Monitoring Report 2006: Strengthening Mutual Accountability— Aid, Trade, and Governance*
- *The Market for Aid*

Combating Corruption

The Bank Group has identified corruption as one of the single greatest obstacles to economic and social development. Through bribery, fraud, and the misappropriation of economic privileges, corruption diverts resources away from those who need them most. Since the mid-1990s, the Bank Group has supported more than 600 anticorruption programs and governance initiatives developed by its member countries. The goals include increasing political accountability, strengthening civil society participation, creating a competitive private sector, establishing institutional restraints on power, and improving public sector management.

Initiatives include encouraging disclosure of assets by public officials, training judges, teaching investigative reporting to journalists, and supporting strong corporate governance through IFC's outreach and advisory services. Nearly one-quarter of new projects now include public expenditure and financial reform components. The Bank Group is working to integrate governance and anticorruption measures into all of its planning and operational work.

In March 2007, the World Bank's Board of Executive Directors unanimously approved a new Governance and Anticorruption Strategy for the World Bank Group. The strategy paper—originally presented to the Development Committee at the Bank's 2006 Annual Meetings in Singapore—was revised to take into account main messages resulting from multistakeholder consultations that the Bank held with over 3,200 representatives from government, civil society, donor agencies, business, parliaments, and other interested parties through 47 country consultations, 4 meetings with global audiences, and Web-based feedback. An implementation plan was scheduled to be finalized by June 2007. The Bank Group is also committed to ensuring that the projects it finances are free from corruption. The Bank Group has stringent procurement and anticorruption guidelines and an anonymous hotline for corruption complaints. It maintains a list of firms and individuals ineligible to be awarded Bank Group–financed contracts. The Web site for governance and anticorruption issues is at http://www.worldbank.org/governance.

The World Bank Institute (WBI) supports countries in improving governance and controlling corruption by linking empirical diagnostic surveys, their practical application, collective action, and prevention. WBI's thematic learning programs include courses, seminars, and policy advice on topics that are important to the international development process. Aligned with the Millennium Development Goals and the Bank Group's corporate operational goals, these programs are normally tailored to specific country needs, but may also address global issues such as governance or knowledge for development. Programs also include parliamentary oversight, legal and judicial reform, and information and the media. For more information, visit http://www.worldbank. org/wbi/governance.

Other Resources

The Bank's Department of Institutional Integrity investigates allegations of fraud or corruption in World Bank Group–financed operations, as well as allegations of misconduct by Bank Group staff, by means of the fraud and corruption hotline. For more information, click on "Reporting Fraud and Corruption" at http://www.worldbank.org/investigations.

Key Publications

The following publications address corruption issues:

- *Anticorruption in Transition: A Contribution to the Policy Debate*
- *Anticorruption in Transition 2: Corruption in Enterprise—State Interactions in Europe and Central Asia*
- *Anticorruption in Transition 3: Who Is Succeeding . . . and Why?*
- *Fighting Corruption in East Asia: Solutions from the Private Sector*
- *Governance Matters V: Governance Indicators for 1996–2005*
- *Governance Reform: Bridging, Monitoring, and Action*
- *The Many Faces of Corruption: Tracking Vulnerabilities at the Sector Level*
- *Reference Guide to Anti-Money Laundering and Combating the Financing of Terrorism,* second edition
- *The Role of Parliaments in Curbing Corruption*
- *1 World Manga: Investigating Corruption—Broken Trust* (comic book)

Conflict Prevention and Fragile States

The Bank Group works in countries afflicted by conflict, supporting international efforts to assist war-torn populations in resuming peaceful development. It also seeks to understand the causes of conflict and to determine ways that conflict can be prevented. The Fragile and Conflict-Affected Countries Group of the World Bank takes the lead in this area: it conducts research and provides analysis on conflict and development to support country units working in conflict-affected countries. The Bank also supports the disarmament, demobilization, and reintegration of former combatants, as well as mine survey and awareness initiatives. It has established the Post-Conflict Fund, which provides financing for physical and social reconstruction initiatives in postwar societies. The Web site is at http://www.worldbank.org/conflict.

Other Resources

World Bank research focused on the economics of civil war, crime, and violence, for which information can be found under "Conflict" at http://econ.worldbank.org/programs.

Key Publications

Publications dealing with conflict prevention and fragile states include the following:

- *Breaking the Conflict Trap: Civil War and Development Policy*
- *Gender, Conflict, and Development: Toward Gender Equality in Conflict-Affected Countries*
- *The Other Half of Gender: Men's Issues in Development*
- *Reshaping the Future: Education and Post-Conflict Reconstruction*
- *Risks and Reconstruction: Experiences of Resettlers and Refugees*
- *Understanding Civil War,* volume 1: *Africa*
- *Understanding Civil War,* volume 2: *Europe, Central Asia, and Other Regions*
- *The World Bank's Experience with Post-Conflict Reconstruction*
- *1 World Manga: Child Soldiers—Of Boys and Men* (comic book)

Debt Relief

Much of the debt burden in low-income countries dates back to the 1970s and 1980s. Many poor countries had borrowed to fund domestic projects on the back of the commodity price boom, believing that high prices and export earnings would be sustained. Oil price shocks during that time, which caused recessions throughout the world, combined with high interest rates and low commodity prices to hit borrowing countries especially hard. Although a number of countries recovered, many others did not. Despite several rounds of debt restructuring to alleviate the debt burdens these countries faced, the Bank Group soon realized that a multilateral debt reduction effort would be needed to address the severe debt burdens of these countries effectively. The outcome was the Heavily Indebted Poor Country (HIPC) Initiative.

The new Debt Department builds on the work of the HIPC Initiative. The department serves several purposes, including implementation of the proposed new debt sustainability framework for low-income countries and continued implementation of the HIPC Initiative. The department is also responsible for shaping the World Bank's position—when possible, in coordination with the debt policy community in general—on global debt issues facing developing countries. The e-mail address for comments on the HIPC Initiative is hipc@worldbank.org.

In March 2006, the World Bank's Board of Executive Directors approved financing and implementation details for the Bank's contribution to the Multilateral Debt Relief Initiative, which provides for 100 percent relief of eligible debt from three multilateral institutions (the IMF, IDA, and the African Development Fund) to a group of low-income countries. This initiative is intended to help some of the world's poorest countries make progress toward achieving the MDGs by freeing up additional resources.

For more information on the HIPC Initiative and the Multilateral Debt Relief Initiative, visit http://www.worldbank.org/debt.

Other Resources

Many Bank Group countries also participate in the Paris Club, an informal group of official creditors—industrial countries in most cases—that seek solutions for debtor nations facing payment difficulties. Paris Club creditors agree to reschedule debts due to them. Although the Paris Club has no legal basis, its members agree to a set of rules and principles designed to reach a coordinated agreement on debt rescheduling quickly and efficiently. This voluntary gathering dates back to 1956, when Argentina agreed to meet its public creditors in Paris. Since then, the Paris Club and related ad hoc groups have reached more than 300 agreements covering 76 debtor countries. Because the Paris Club normally requires countries to have an active IMF-supported program in order to qualify for a rescheduling agreement, it has extensive contact with the IMF and the Bank Group. The Web site is at http://www.clubdeparis.org.

The Paris Club is paralleled by the London Club, an informal organization of commercial creditors. Officials of the Bank Group have been invited to meetings of the London Club in an effort to coordinate debt relief and repayment efforts with economic policy advice.

Key Publications

Publications dealing with debt relief and the HIPC Initiative include the following:

- *Debt Relief for the Poorest: An Evaluation Update of the HIPC Initiative*
- *Little Book on External Debt*

Economic Research and Data

The Bank Group conducts extensive economic research and, with the help of country governments and other partners, assembles a wide range of economic data.

Data and Statistics

The Bank Group is a leading publisher of economic data and statistics on all aspects of development, both in print and online (see box 4.1 for Web links). Some information is free and some is available with a subscription. Major titles appear under "Key Publications" at the end of this section. The Development Data Group is the lead unit in this area; the Web site is at http://www.worldbank.org/data. The Development Data Group can also be reached by phone at 1-202-473-7824 or 1-800-590-1906, by fax at 1-202-522-1498, or by e-mail at data@worldbank.org.

The Office of the Publisher handles commercial sales of print and electronic publications. This unit can be contacted through its Web site

---

Box 4.1 Web Links for Data and Statistics

World Bank Group data and statistics: http://www.worldbank.org/data
Online databases: http://www.worldbank.org/data/onlinedatabases
Financial sector databases: http://www.worldbank.org/finance
Financial sector statistics: http://www.worldbank.org/finance
Living standards measurement study: http://www.worldbank.org/lsms
PovertyNet (data on poverty): http://www.worldbank.org/poverty/data
Doing Business indicators: http://www.doingbusiness.org/
Statistical capacity building: http://www.worldbank.org/data
World Bank—Global Environment Facility projects database: http://www.worldbank.org/gef
World Bank research datasets: http://econ.worldbank.org/resource.php?type=18

at http://publications.worldbank.org/ecommerce, by phone at 1-703-661-1580 or 1-800-645-7247, by fax at 1-703-661-1501, or by e-mail at books@worldbank.org.

Research

The Bank Group's economic analysis identifies specific development indicators that provide a big picture of economic trends, the cumulative effectiveness of development programs, and other factors that affect economic progress. The Web site for World Bank research is at http://econ.worldbank.org; the e-mail for general queries is research@worldbank.org.

The World Bank and IFC also conduct economic research through the joint Financial and Private Sector Development Vice Presidency. One major activity is the Doing Business Project, which studies the effects of regulation on the business climate. The Web site for this vice presidential unit is http://www.ifc.org/economics.

Other Resources

Various resources are available on the Internet:

- The *Poverty Reduction and Economic Management (PREM) Advisory Service* focuses on economic policy, gender, governance and public sector reform, and poverty, among other issues. It publishes *PREM Notes,* which summarizes good practice and key policy findings on those topics. Its Web site is at http://www.worldbank.org/prem. The e-mail address is premadvisory@worldbank.org.
- The *World Bank Research Observer* and the *World Bank Economic Review* are journals published by the World Bank and Oxford University Press. Current issues are available by subscription. The archive database is searchable on the home page, but back issues must be ordered from Oxford Journals. The Web site is at http://www.worldbank.org/research/journals.

Key Publications

The following are some of the Bank's key research publications:

- *Annual World Bank Conference on Development Economics*
- *Doing Business*
- *Frontiers of Development Economics*

- *Global Development Finance* (available in print and online)
- *Global Economic Prospects*
- *Global Monitoring Report*
- *Little Data Book*
- *Little Green Data Book*
- *Policy Research Reports*
- *Policy Research Working Papers*
- *Atlas of Global Development: A Visual Guide to the World's Greatest Challenges*
- *World Development Indicators* (available in print and online)
- *World Development Report*

Education

The Bank Group recognizes that universal, high-quality education reduces poverty and inequality and sustains economic growth. Such education is also fundamental for the construction of democratic societies and globally competitive economies. It improves people's skills, which, in turn, improve their incomes. Consequently, achieving universal primary education for all is one of the eight MDGs. The Web site for education issues is at http://www.worldbank.org/education.

The Bank Group pursues its work in education and training through the following units and programs.

Education Department (World Bank)

The Education Department is part of the Human Development Network. Education activities, programs, and projects at the region or country level can be accessed through the Web sites of the Bank's regions. Major education initiatives include the following:

- *Education for All* is a commitment by the international community to achieving education for every citizen in every society. The Education for All partnership believes that education is key to sustainable development, to peace and stability within and among countries, and to people's full participation in the societies and economies of the 21st century. The partnership is committed to ensuring that, by 2015, *all children* are enrolled in and able to complete a primary education. Achieving this goal necessitates giving special attention to girls and disadvantaged children, who are at greatest risk of failing to complete their schooling.

▪ *Education for the Knowledge Economy* is an analytical program for understanding how education and training systems need to change to meet the challenges of the knowledge economy. The program offers practical and sustainable policy options for developing countries.

▪ *Early Child Development* is a knowledge source that assists policy makers, program managers, and practitioners in their efforts to promote the healthy growth and development of young children. Visit Early Child Development at http://www.worldbank.org/children.

World Bank Institute

Capacity for development is the ability of individuals, institutions, and entire societies to solve problems, make informed choices, order their priorities, and plan their futures, as well as implement programs and projects and sustain them over time. Building capacity is at the heart of development and development effectiveness and depends heavily on society's ability to acquire and use knowledge.

WBI is the capacity development arm of the World Bank that helps countries share and apply global and local knowledge to meet development challenges. WBI's capacity development programs are designed not only to build skills among groups of individuals, but also to strengthen the organizations in which they work and the sociopolitical environment in which they operate.

WBI conducts training sessions and policy consultations and creates and supports knowledge networks related to international economic and social development. The focus includes distance learning and other emerging technologies for education and training. WBI serves member countries, Bank Group staff members and clients, and other people working in the areas of poverty reduction and sustainable development. WBI has programs focused on education, environment and natural resources management, the financial sector, health and HIV/AIDS, knowledge for development, poverty and growth, private sector development, public-private partnerships in infrastructure, public sector governance, social protection and risk management, trade, urban and local government, and water and rural development. Visit http://www.worldbank.org/wbi.

IFC Investments in Private Education

IFC supports the development of private educational activities in its client countries and believes that such support can help improve access to and the quality of the education sector. To further this commitment, IFC's Health and Education Department invests in or advises on the start-up or expansion of initiatives in many subsectors of education. These subsectors include primary, secondary, and postsecondary schooling, with a particular interest in school networks, e-learning initiatives, and student financing programs and other ancillary services. IFC has also been instrumental in establishing the Global Business School Network, which links institutions in developing and industrial countries, with an emphasis on Sub-Saharan Africa.

Other Resources

The following resources are also useful:

- *Education Advisory Service.* The Web site is at http://www.worldbank. org/education. The service may be contacted by e-mail at eservice@ worldbank.org.
- *World Bank research.* To visit the Web site, click "Topic" at http://econ. worldbank.org and select "Education."
- *WBI* has an education learning program. The Web site is at http://www. worldbank.org/wbi/education.

Key Publications

Publications addressing education issues include the following:

- *Achieving Universal Primary Education by 2015: A Chance for Every Child*
- *A Chance to Learn: Knowledge and Finance for Education in Sub-Saharan Africa*
- *Closing the Gap in Education and Technology*
- *Higher Education in Latin America: The International Dimension*
- *How Universities Can Promote Economic Growth*
- *Meeting the Challenges of Secondary Education in Latin America and East Asia*
- *A New Social Contract for Peru: An Agenda for Improving Education, Health Care, and the Social Safety Net*

The following are some key WBI publications:

- *Cities in a Globalizing World*
- *Development Outreach Magazine*
- *Diaspora Networks and the International Migration of Skills*
- *Japan: Moving Toward a More Advanced Knowledge Economy*

- *Managing the Implementation of Development Projects: A Resource Kit on CD-ROM*
- *Promoting Social Cohesion through Education*
- *The Role of Parliaments in Curbing Corruption*

Empowerment and Participation

Empowerment is the process of enhancing the capacity of individuals or groups to make choices and to transform those choices into desired actions and outcomes. Central to this process are actions that both build individual and collective assets and improve the efficiency and fairness of the organizational and institutional contexts that govern the use of these assets.

The World Bank's *Empowerment Sourcebook,* published in 2002, set out to bring together the thinking and practice of empowerment as a first step toward developing a better understanding of this component of the Bank's work. Since then, staff members and teams around the World Bank have been engaged in a broad range of activities that seek to operationalize the concept of empowerment. Some practical illustrations from Bank operations and non-Bank activities include

- providing basic services,
- improving local governance,
- improving national governance,
- developing pro-poor markets, and
- providing access to justice and legal aid.

In the past, the strategies of the World Bank and its clients for improved development and poverty reduction have focused on formal systems, with little connection to citizens and those working at the community level. An empowering approach creates a link between the supply and demand sides of development. A demand-side approach to improving governance focuses on educating, informing, and enabling citizens and poor people's organizations so that they can interact effectively with their governments. A supply-side approach focuses on macro-level institutions and the legal framework, which determine how poor people can access development opportunities. The empowerment process ensures that the two approaches act in synergy.

IFC supports public participation and community empowerment through extensive civil society outreach efforts with local nongovernmental organizations (NGOs), community leaders, media representatives, and all other stakeholders. IFC believes that early engagement with the community, along with maximum public disclosure, is the best business model in the developing world and emerging markets.

For more information, see http://www.worldbank.org/empowerment.

Other Resources

Further resources include the following:

- *WBI* has a socially sustainable development Web site at http://www. worldbank.org/wbi/empowerment.
- *World Bank research* focused on inequity around the world can be found at http://www.worldbank.org/research/inequality.

Key Publications

These publications also address empowerment and participation issues:

- *Empowerment and Poverty Reduction: A Sourcebook*
- *Empowerment in Practice: From Analysis to Implementation*
- *Measuring Empowerment: Cross-Disciplinary Perspectives*
- *Voices of the Poor*
- *World Development Report 2000/2001: Attacking Poverty*

Energy and Mining

The Bank Group views energy as a fundamental driver of economic development and believes that countries must develop their own energy programs in careful and sustainable ways. The Bank Group's objectives in the energy sector include helping the poor directly, improving macroeconomic and fiscal balances, promoting good governance and private sector development, and protecting the environment. The Bank Group's energy program includes some joint units of the World Bank and IFC. The Web site for energy issues is at http://www.worldbank.org/energy.

The Bank Group also works to help countries ensure environmentally and socially responsible development of their mineral resources. The Bank Group pursues its work in this area through the Oil, Gas, Mining, and Chemicals Department, a joint unit of the World Bank and IFC that aims to improve coordination between work on public sector policy and private sector investment activities. The department is the lead unit in implementing the

Bank Group's response to the Extractive Industries Review, an independent stakeholder consultation process that concluded in 2004. The department focuses on such issues as gas flaring, carbon emissions trading, and revenue management and transparency, and it works with an advisory group to identify best practices in the oil, gas, and mining industries.

IFC is developing new business models for investments involving renewable energy, energy efficiency, recovery and use of methane, and use of cleaner fuels. IFC helps companies in emerging markets increase their incomes while reducing environmental impacts by arranging for the purchase of carbon credits under the terms of the Kyoto Protocol. IFC also works with the Global Environment Facility and other donors to help commercialize climate-friendly investments.

Other Resources

These resources are also useful:

- The *Energy Help Desk* can be contacted at energyhelpdesk@worldbank.org.
- The *Extractive Industries Review* is an independent evaluation of Bank Group involvement in the sector. To access the report, visit http://www.ifc.org and search for "Extractive Industries Review."
- Information on *IFC's power projects* can be found at http://www.ifc.org/ifcext/infrastructure.nsf/Content/Power.
- The *Mining Help Desk* can be contacted at omgc@worldbank.org.
- The *Oil, Gas, Mining, and Chemicals Department* Web site is at http://www.worldbank.org/mining.

Key Publications

These publications deal with energy and mining issues:

- *Breathing Clean: Considering the Switch to Natural Gas Buses*
- *From Crisis to Stability in the Armenian Power Sector: Lessons Learned from Armenia's Energy Reform Experience*
- *The Little Green Data Book 2006*
- *Mining Royalties: A Global Study of Their Impact on Investors, Government, and Civil Society*
- *People and Power: Electricity Sector Reforms and the Poor in Europe and Central Asia*

- *Power for Development: A Review of the World Bank Group's Experience with Private Participation in the Electricity Sector*
- *Rural Energy and Development: Improving Energy Supplies for Two Billion People*

Environment

Many view concern for the environment as a rich-country luxury. It is not. Natural and man-made environmental resources—fresh water, clean air, forests, grasslands, marine resources, and agro-ecosystems—provide sustenance and a foundation for social and economic development. The World Bank is one of the key promoters and financiers of environmental upgrading in the developing world, supporting environmental protection and improvement. It conducts research and advocacy on environmental issues and ensures environmental protection in its own work through careful adherence to safeguards it has established.

Environment Department (World Bank)

Part of the Sustainable Development Network, the Environment Department is responsible for the World Bank's environment strategy for developing countries. This strategy has the following priorities: improving aspects of the quality of life (people's health, livelihoods, and vulnerability) that are affected by environmental conditions; improving the quality of growth by supporting policy, regulatory, and institutional frameworks for sustainable environmental management and by promoting sustainable private development; and protecting the quality of the regional and global commons, such as the climate, forests, water resources, and biodiversity. The unit also maintains the Bank Group's Web site for environmental issues at http://www.worldbank.org/environment.

Environment and Social Development Department (IFC)

The Environment and Social Development Department works to meld the concerns of the environment with the needs of the private sector. The key Web site is at http://www.ifc.org/enviro. In early 2006, IFC announced its strengthened environmental and social standards, which set forth its requirements for its client companies. Also known as the performance standards, these are the basis of the Equator Principles—a benchmark for the financial industry to manage social and environmental issues in project financing—that some 40 of the world's leading commercial banks have adopted for their project finance lending.

IFC's team of environmental specialists provides risk management and insurance services to reduce and manage environmental, social, and business risks, and it provides support for innovative products and business lines that contribute to the sustainability of private sector enterprises.

Other Resources

For information on the Bank Group's environmental safeguards, see chapter 2, as well as the following resources:

- IFC's *environmental and social standards* Web site provides information on the corporation's sustainability policy; environmental and social review procedure; performance standards; and environmental, health, and safety guidelines. It also lists those sectors in which IFC does not invest. Click "Environmental and Social Standards" at http://www.ifc.org/enviro.
- MIGA's *environmental and disclosure policies* are available at "NGOs and Civil Society" at http://www.miga.org.
- The *Operational Manual* includes safeguard policies. The Web site is at http://www.worldbank.org/opmanual.
- The *Global Environment Facility* is a Bank Group affiliate whose secretariat is located at Bank headquarters. For more information, see "Programmatic Partnerships" under "Partnerships" in chapter 2 or http://www.worldbank.org/gef.
- The *Prototype Carbon Fund* seeks to mitigate climate change through reductions in greenhouse gases and encourages public-private partnerships. An initiative of the Bank Group, donor governments, and private industry, the fund has a help desk at "About Us" on its Web site: http://www.prototypecarbonfund.org.
- *World Bank research.* For environmental resources, click "Topic" at http://econ.worldbank.org and select "Environment." For the Infrastructure and the Environment Program, see http://econ.worldbank.org/programs/2328.

Key Publications

Many publications address environmental issues, for example:

- *At Loggerheads: Agricultural Expansion, Poverty Reduction, and the Environment in the Tropical Forests*
- *Environment Matters*

- *Environmental Health: Bridging the Gaps*
- *Faith in Conservation: New Approaches to Religions and the Environment*
- *Green miniAtlas*
- *How Much Is an Ecosystem Worth? Assessing the Economic Value of Conservation*
- *Little Green Data Book*
- *Natural Disaster Hotspots: A Global Risk Analysis*
- *Natural Resources: Neither Curse nor Destiny*
- *Overcoming Drought: Adaptation Strategies for Andhra Pradesh*
- *Strategic Environmental Assessment for Policies: An Instrument for Good*
- *Where Is the Wealth of Nations? Measuring Capital for the 21st Century*
- *World Development Report 1992: Development and the Environment*
- *World Development Report 2002: Sustainable Development in a Dynamic World*
- *1 World Manga Passage 3: Global Warming—The Lagoon of the Vanishing Fish* (comic book)

Financial Sector

A healthy, trustworthy financial system is fundamental to economic development. The Bank Group helps countries strengthen their financial systems, grow their economies, restructure and modernize institutions, and respond to the savings and financing needs of all people. Major initiatives are as follows.

Financial and Private Sector Development Vice Presidency (World Bank Group)

The Financial and Private Sector Development Vice Presidency works to provide opportunities for the poor through market-friendly, enterprise-led growth and to provide better services through efficient delivery systems and well-targeted subsidies. This joint World Bank–IFC vice presidency focuses on the following three core areas:

- Creating the institutional foundations for effective markets, such as property rights, collateral systems, corporate governance, and financial market infrastructure
- Promoting open and competitive markets, for example, by opening up entry and providing access to finance for promising firms, by helping these firms to access deeper and more liquid financial markets, and exit for failing firms

- Supporting social safety nets using market-based instruments, such as financial market-based instruments and risk management for pensions and insurance systems as well as low-income housing

The Web site is at http://www.worldbank.org/finance.

IFC Investments and Advisory Services

IFC considers support for financial markets a cornerstone of its investment policies and a critical tool for private sector development. IFC's Global Financial Markets Department is the lead unit for investments in and technical support for banks and other financial institutions. More information is available at http://www.ifc.org/gfm. IFC also seeks innovative ways to finance microentrepreneurs, who play a key role in the private sectors of many economies in the developing world. See also the "Small and Medium Enterprise Department (World Bank Group)" in the section on "Private Sector Development" in this chapter.

In addition to providing funding and asset management for the corporation, IFC's Finance Vice Presidency offers products and services to clients, including many in the financial sector. These products and services include structured finance transactions, derivative-based products, loan participations with commercial banks, and local currency financing. In some instances, the vice presidency has funded IFC's own operations through local currency bond issues that have helped develop domestic capital markets in developing countries. See http://www.ifc.org/finance.

Through its Private Equity and Investment Funds Department, IFC also invests in emerging market investment funds and fund management companies. IFC has become a center of expertise for this sector and works through conferences and industry organizations to make emerging market private equity more visible to investors. See http://www.ifc.org/funds.

Other Resources

Additional resources include the following:

- The *Consultative Group to Assist the Poor* is a Bank Group affiliate that focuses on microfinance. Its secretariat is located at Bank headquarters. For more information, see "Programmatic Partnerships" under "Partnerships" in chapter 2 or http://www.cgap.org.
- The *Financial Sector Advisory Service* answers questions about the financial sector. The e-mail address is askfinancialsector@worldbank.org.

- The *Interest Bearing Notes Newsletter* is a periodical publication of the World Bank's Financial Sector. See http://www.worldbank.org/subscriptions.
- *WBI* has a financial sector learning program. The Web site is at http://www.financelearning.org.
- *World Bank research.* For financial sector resources, click "Topic" at http://econ.worldbank.org and select "Financial Sector." The Bank also has research programs focused on credit reporting systems, finance, and policies and institutions that promote savings.

Key Publications

Publications about financial matters include the following:

- *Access for All: Building Inclusive Financial Systems*
- *Access to Financial Services in Brazil*
- *Development of Non-Bank Financial Institutions and Capital Markets in European Union Accession Countries*
- *Electronic Finance: A New Approach to Financial Sector Development?*
- *Finance for Growth: Policy Choices in a Volatile World*
- *Financial Sector Assessment: A Handbook*
- *Financial Sector Development and the Millennium Development Goals*
- *International Financial Reporting Standards: A Practical Guide,* fourth edition
- *Microfinance Handbook: An Institutional and Financial Perspective*
- *The Microfinance Revolution*
- *A Reader in International Corporate Finance,* volumes I and II
- *Remittances: Development Impact and Future Prospects*
- *Transforming Microfinance Institutions: Providing Full Financial Services to the Poor*

Gender

Through its programs and projects, the Bank Group seeks to reduce gender disparities and to enhance women's participation in economic development. It summarizes knowledge and experience, provides gender statistics, and promotes discussion on issues of gender and development. The Gender and Development Group within the Poverty Reduction and Economic Management Network is the lead unit in this area. The key gender-related goal is the MDG to eliminate gender-related disparities at all levels of education by 2015; see the Web site at http://www.worldbank.org/gender. IFC assists women entrepreneurs through the Gender Entrepreneurship Markets Program; visit http://www.ifc.org/GEM.

Other Resources

Other resources include the *PREM Advisory Service,* which deals with many issues, including gender. The service publishes *PREM Notes,* which summarizes good practice and key policy findings. The Web site is at http://www. worldbank.org/prem. The e-mail address is premadvisory@worldbank.org.

Key Publications

Many publications address gender issues, including the following:

- *Engendering Development Through Gender Equality in Rights, Resources, and Voice*
- *Gender, Conflict, and Development*
- *Gender and Development in the Middle East and North Africa: Women in the Public Sphere*
- *Gender and Economic Growth in Uganda: Unleashing the Power of Women*
- *Gender, Time Use, and Poverty in Sub-Saharan Africa*
- *The Other Half of Gender: Men's Issues in Development*
- *1 World Manga: Girls' Education—Life Lessons* (comic book)

Globalization

Globalization—the growing integration of economies and societies around the world—has been one of the most hotly debated topics in international economics over the past few years. Rapid growth and poverty reduction in China, India, and other countries that were poor 20 years ago has been a positive aspect of globalization, but globalization has also generated significant international opposition over concerns that it has increased inequality and environmental degradation. The Bank Group's Web site on globalization issues is at http://www.worldbank.org/globalization.

Key Publications

Globalization is also the subject of these publications:

- *Addressing the Challenges of Globalization: An Independent Evaluation of the World Bank's Approach to Global Programs*
- *Atlas of Global Development: A Visual Guide to the World's Greatest Challenges*
- *Cities in a Globalizing World: Governance, Performance, and Sustainability*

- *Development Challenges in the 1990s: Leading Policymakers Speak from Experience*
- *Diaspora Networks and the International Migration of Skills: How Countries Can Draw on Their Talent Abroad*
- *Global Issues for Global Citizens: An Introduction to Key Development Challenges*
- *Globalization and Development: A Latin American and Caribbean Perspective*
- *Globalization for Development,* revised edition: *Trade, Finance, Aid, Migration, and Policy*
- *Globalization, Growth, and Poverty: Building an Inclusive World Economy*
- *miniAtlas of Global Development*
- *World Development Report 1999/2000: Entering the 21st Century*

Governance

The Bank Group works to promote effective governance in the public sector and high standards of corporate governance in the private sector.

Public Sector Governance

A fundamental role of the Bank Group is to help the governments of client countries function better. Although this goal is simple to define, it is both complex and difficult to accomplish. The Bank Group has a number of initiatives dealing with governance issues, including Public Sector Group activities, public services research, and WBI governance and knowledge-sharing programs.

The Public Sector Group is the lead unit in this area and is responsible for the World Bank's governance and public sector strategy. The unit focuses on building efficient and accountable public sector institutions rather than simply providing policy advice, and it also maintains the Web site on governance and public sector reform at http://www.worldbank.org/publicsector.

Several units of IFC work with governments to strengthen institutions, laws, and regulations related to the private sector. The Foreign Investment Advisory Service, a joint unit of IFC and the World Bank, focuses specifically on helping developing country governments attract and retain foreign direct investment; see http://www.fias.net.

Corporate Governance

The joint IFC–World Bank Corporate Governance Group helps companies and countries improve standards of governance for corporations, focusing on shareholders' and stakeholders' rights, board members' duties, disclosure, and effective enforcement. The Bank Group provides technical assistance on such governance issues to a wide range of government and financial institutions. IFC has developed a methodology for assessing corporate governance, which it uses in its own risk analysis and investment decisions as well as to help client companies improve their practices. For more information, click "Corporate Governance and Capital Markets" at http://www.ifc.org/economics.

Other Resources

Various resources are available on the Internet:

- The *PREM Advisory Service* deals with many issues, including governance and public sector reform. The service publishes *PREM Notes,* which summarizes good practice and key policy findings. The Web site is at http://www.worldbank.org/prem. The e-mail address is premadvisory@ worldbank.org.
- *WBI* has a public sector governance learning program. The Web site is at http://www.worldbank.org/wbi/governancelp.

Key Publications

Publications in this area include the following:

- *Public Sector Governance and Accountability series.* This WBI book series provides conceptual guidance and practical lessons on how to establish a well-functioning public sector that focuses on poverty reduction; delivers quality public services; fosters private, market-led growth; and is accountable to its citizens for all actions. All the books in the series present ideas and practices that promote responsive, responsible, and accountable public governance in developing countries. Titles include
  - *Budgeting and Budgetary Institutions*
  - *Intergovernmental Fiscal Transfers*
  - *Local Budgeting*
  - *Local Governance in Developing Countries*
  - *Local Governance in Industrial Countries*
  - *Local Public Financial Management*
  - *Performance Accountability and Combating Corruption*

■ *Public Expenditure Analysis*
■ *Public Services Delivery*
■ *World Development Report 1997: The State in a Changing World*
■ *World Development Report 2002: Building Institutions for Markets*

Health, Nutrition, and Population

Ensuring adequate levels of basic health and nutrition lies at the heart of poverty reduction and economic development. In recent decades, improvements in income, education, hygiene, housing, water supply and sanitation, nutrition, and access to contraception have brought about notable health gains for much of the world, yet the health, nutrition, and population challenges remain great for most developing countries.

The World Bank and Health

The World Bank commits an average of $1 billion in new lending each year for health, nutrition, and population projects in the developing world. It seeks to focus its assistance where the impact will be greatest—directly on people. The lead unit is Health, Nutrition, and Population, a sector unit of the Human Development Network. The unit organizes its work into the broad categories of health systems development; health, nutrition, and population MDGs; population and reproductive health; HIV/AIDS; nutrition; poverty and health; and public health. Public health is further broken down into categories that include avian flu, child heath, malaria, mental health, onchocerciasis, road safety, school health, tobacco, and tuberculosis.

The unit's Web site is at http://www.worldbank.org/hnp.

IFC and Health

IFC's Health and Education Department seeks to boost the private health care infrastructure in developing countries and emerging markets through investments in medical facilities, ancillary services, pharmaceutical devices, education and training, e-health (a relatively recent term for health care practice supported by electronic processes and communication), and insurance. For more information, see http://www.ifc.org/ifcext/che.nsf.

With respect to HIV/AIDS, IFC has prepared *Good Practice Note: HIV/AIDS in the Workplace* as part of the IFC Against AIDS Program. Its purpose is to help clients and others in the private sector understand and manage the risks HIV/AIDS poses to their workforces and communities. The publication can be found at http://www.ifc.org/ifcext/aids.nsf/Content/Publications.

Other Resources

Other health resources include the following:

- The *Global Partnership for Eliminating River Blindness* is discussed in the subsection on "Regional Initiatives" under "Africa (Sub-Saharan)" in chapter 3 and at http://www.worldbank.org/gper.
- The *Health and Population Advisory Service* handles queries to the Health, Nutrition, and Population unit in all areas except nutrition, which has its own advisory service (see below). The service may be contacted by phone at 1-202-473-2256, by fax at 1-202-522-3234, or by e-mail at healthpop@worldbank.org.
- The *health systems development* Web site examines all aspects of health systems, including market demand, financing, human resources, and service delivery. Go to "Topics" at http://www.worldbank.org/hnp.
- The *HIV/AIDS* Web site emphasizes that HIV/AIDS is not only a health problem, but is also a development problem that threatens human welfare, socioeconomic advances, productivity, social cohesion, and even national security. The World Bank is a key source of funding to combat HIV/AIDS. For information and resources, visit "Topics" at http://www.worldbank.org/hnp.
- The *Joint UN Programme on HIV/AIDS* has information on its Web site at http://www.unaids.org.
- The *malaria* Web site at http://www.worldbank.org/malaria addresses this devastating illness. Malaria is one of the world's most important public health concerns, causing more than a million deaths and up to 500 million clinical cases each year. Most of the 3,000 deaths each day—10 new cases every second—are in Africa, and more than a third of the world's population now lives in malaria-endemic areas. The Bank has intensified its support for malaria control through the new *Global Strategy and Malaria Booster Program,* begun in 2005. This program combines an emphasis on monitoring results and outcomes with flexibility in approaches and lending instruments.
- The *mental health* Web site at http://www.worldbank.org/mentalhealth provides information about this issue.

- The *Multi-Country HIV-AIDS Program* is described in the subsection on "Regional Initiatives" under "Africa (Sub-Saharan)" in chapter 3 and at http://www.worldbank.org/afr/aids/map.htm.

- The *Nutrition Advisory Service* provides information about nutrition. Nearly half of child mortality in low-income countries can be linked to malnutrition. The World Bank's approach to nutrition targets poor people, especially young children and their mothers, with an emphasis on community- and school-based nutrition programs, food fortification programs, and food policy reforms. To date, the World Bank has committed nearly $2 billion to support nutrition programs. The Web site is at http://www.worldbank.org/nutrition. Contact the Nutrition Advisory Service by phone at 1-202-473-2255, by fax at 1-202-522-3234, or by e-mail at nutrition@worldbank.org.

- The *population and reproductive health* Web site describes Bank activities and resources in this area. Problems such as early and unwanted childbearing, sexually transmitted infections, and pregnancy-related illness and death account for much of the burden of disease in developing countries, especially among the poor, who often lack access to minimal health care. The Web site is at http://www.worldbank.org/population.

- The *poverty and health* Web site focuses on how developments in health affect efforts to reduce poverty in developing countries. Visit "Topics" at http://www.worldbank.org/hnp.

- The *tobacco* Web site provides information on tobacco policies and control measures. The World Bank has a formal policy of not lending for tobacco production or processing, directly or indirectly, and of encouraging tobacco control in developing countries. Visit http://www.worldbank.org/tobacco.

- The *tuberculosis* Web site details the World Bank's efforts to fight tuberculosis. The World Bank combats tuberculosis by providing policy dialogue and advice, by lending to countries to strengthen health systems and control the disease, by undertaking analysis, and by becoming involved in global partnerships. The Web site is at http://www.worldbank.org/tuberculosis.

- The *vaccines and immunization* Web site provides a summary of key facts, priority interventions, indicators, useful implementation lessons, and links to additional resources and information. The Bank Group supports immunization worldwide because it saves lives and is one of the most cost-effective, equitable health interventions available. Vaccine-preventable diseases disproportionately affect the poorest people in developing countries. Visit "Public Health at a Glance" at http://www.worldbank.org/hnp, then click on "Immunization."

- *WBI* has a program on health and AIDS. See http://www.worldbank.org/wbi/healthandaids.
- *World Bank research.* Click "Topic" at http://econ.worldbank.org, and select "Health, Nutrition, and Population."

Key Publications

Numerous publications address health and population issues, including the following:

- *Battling HIV/AIDS: A Decision Maker's Guide to the Procurement of Medicines and Related Supplies*
- *Combating Malnutrition: Time to Act*
- *The Disease Control Priorities Project,* available at http://www.dcp2.org
  - *Disease Control Priorities in Developing Countries,* second edition
  - *Global Burden of Disease and Risk Factors*
  - *Priorities in Health*
- *Health Economics in Development*
- *Health Financing Revisited: A Practitioner's Guide*
- *International Trade in Health Services and the GATS: Current Issues and Debates*
- *The Millennium Development Goals for Health: Rising to the Challenges*
- *Reproductive Health: The Missing Millennium Development Goal*
- *A Sourcebook of HIV/AIDS Prevention Programs*
- *World Development Report 1993: Investing in Health*
- *1 World Manga: Passage 2: HIV/AIDS—First Love* (comic book)

Indigenous Peoples

The Bank Group seeks to promote indigenous peoples' development while ensuring that the development process fosters respect for their dignity, human rights, and unique qualities. The lead unit in this area is the Bank's Indigenous Peoples Group, which is responsible for policies and guidelines to promote greater understanding within the Bank Group and its member countries of the value of cultural diversity in poverty reduction, sustainable development, and effective nation building. The Bank Group also works in this area through partnerships with indigenous organizations, other donor agencies, and governments. The Web site is at http://www.worldbank.org/indigenous.

IFC and Indigenous Peoples

IFC takes seriously the potentially disruptive nature of some private investments that involve the resettling of indigenous peoples. At the same time, private sector projects may create opportunities for indigenous peoples to participate in and benefit from project-related activities that may help them fulfill their aspirations for economic and social development. IFC's performance standards recognize that indigenous peoples may play a role in sustainable development by promoting and managing activities and enterprises as partners in development. To learn more about IFC's policy on indigenous peoples, see http://www.ifc.org/ifcext/enviro.nsf/Content/PerformanceStandards.

Other Resources

The *Indigenous Knowledge Program* documents local or traditional knowledge in developing countries and applies this knowledge to development issues. This program is a partnership of the World Bank's Africa Region with various UN agencies, bilateral development agencies, and NGOs. The Web site is at http://www.worldbank.org/afr/ik.

Key Publications

The following publications deal with the involuntary resettlement of indigenous peoples:

- *The Economics of Involuntary Resettlement: Questions and Challenges*
- *Handbook for Preparing a Resettlement Action Plan*
- *Involuntary Resettlement Sourcebook: Planning and Implementation in Development Projects*

Information and Communication Technologies

Information and communication technologies have the potential to speed development and improve a variety of social services. The Bank Group's Global Information and Communication Technologies Department—a joint department of the World Bank and IFC—focuses on the best ways to support technology implementation by helping to develop and promote access to information and communication technologies in developing countries. It provides governments, private companies, and community organizations with the capital and expertise needed to develop and exploit these technologies to reduce poverty and foster development. The Web site is at http://www.worldbank.org/gict.

Other Resources

Other resources include the following:

- The *Development Gateway* is an interactive portal for information and knowledge sharing on sustainable development and poverty reduction that offers, for example, a comprehensive database of development projects, an international procurement marketplace, and knowledge sharing on key development topics. It is operated by the Development Gateway Foundation, a not-for-profit organization based in Washington, DC. The foundation is governed by a board of directors representing major donors and partners from international organizations, the public and private sectors, and civil society. The Development Gateway connects to Country Gateways, a network of 44 locally owned and managed public-private partnerships with the mission of facilitating country-level innovative and effective use of the Internet and other information and communication technologies. The Web site is at http://www.developmentgateway.org.
- The *Global Development Learning Network* is discussed in the subsection "Capacity Development" under "Knowledge Sharing" in chapter 2. The Web site is at http://www.gdln.org.

Key Publications

Publications addressing information and communication technologies include the following:

- *China's Information Revolution: Managing the Economic and Social Transformation*
- *Connecting Sub-Saharan Africa: A World Bank Group Strategy for Information and Communication Technology Sector Development*
- *E-Development: From Excitement to Effectiveness*
- *Financing Information and Communication Infrastructure Needs in the Developing World: Public and Private Roles*
- *Global Integration and Technology Transfer*
- *Information and Communications for Development 2006: Global Trends and Policies*

Infrastructure

Infrastructure development remains a fundamental focus of the Bank Group, and poor people are acutely aware that infrastructure could significantly improve the quality of their lives. The Bank Group's infrastructure work is organized by departments that focus on energy; information and communication technologies; mining; oil, gas, and chemicals; transport; urban development; and water supply and sanitation. Some of these departments are joint World Bank–IFC units. The Web site for infrastructure issues is at http://www.worldbank.org/infrastructure.

IFC and Infrastructure

Infrastructure is a significant part of IFC's work of assisting the development of private sector business opportunities in emerging economies. IFC's Infrastructure Department offers expertise in helping private sector sponsors finance infrastructure projects in client countries. It focuses on investments in power, transport, and utilities; its Web site is http://www.ifc.org/infrastructure. Other departments handle some related sectors, including telecommunications and oil and gas.

In close partnership with the World Bank, IFC has also established the Subnational Finance Department to make direct investments in subsovereign governments and entities they control that bear much of the responsibility for infrastructure; see http://www.ifc.org/municipalfund. In addition, IFC's Advisory Services Department assists client countries with privatizations and public-private partnerships in infrastructure and other essential services; see http://www.ifc.org/advisory.

Other Resources

The following resources are also useful:

- The *energy Web site* can be found at http://www.worldbank.org/energy.
- The *Global Information and Communication Technologies Department* can be contacted by e-mail at gict@worldbank.org, and its Web site is at http://www.worldbank.org/gict.
- The *Oil, Gas, Mining and Chemicals Group* can be contacted by e-mail at ogmc@worldbank.org. Visit its Web site by selecting "Oil, Gas, Mining & Chemicals" at http://www.worldbank.org/infrastructure.
- The *Public-Private Infrastructure Advisory Facility* is a multidonor technical assistance facility aimed at helping developing countries improve the quality of their infrastructure through private sector involvement. Launched in July 1999, the facility was developed as a joint initiative of the governments of Japan and the United Kingdom working closely with the World Bank. The Web site is at http://www.ppiaf.org.

- The *Transport Group* can be contacted by e-mail at transport@worldbank. org. Visit its Web site by selecting "Transport" at http://www.worldbank. org/infrastructure.
- The *Urban Development Group* can be contacted by e-mail at urbanhelp@ worldbank.org. Visit its Web site by selecting "Urban Development" at http://www.worldbank.org/infrastructure.
- The *Water Supply and Sanitation Group* Web site can be found at http:// www.worldbank.org/watsan.
- *WBI* has a learning program on public-private partnerships in infrastructure. The Web site is at http://www.worldbank.org/wbi/infrastructure. *WBI's* urban and local government learning program Web site is at http://www.worldbank.org/wbi/urban, and its water-related Web site is at http://www.worldbank.org/wbi/water.

Key Publications

Much has been published about infrastructure, including the following:

- *Building Safer Cities: The Future of Disaster Risk*
- *Handbook for Evaluating Infrastructure Regulatory Systems*
- *Infrastructure at the Crossroads: Lessons from Twenty Years of World Bank Experience*
- *Infrastructure for Poor People: Public Policy for Private Provision*
- *Labor Issues in Infrastructure Reform: A Toolkit*
- *Port Reform Toolkit,* second edition: *Effective Support for Policymakers and Practitioners*
- *Reforming Infrastructure: Privatization, Regulation, and Competition*
- *Street Addressing and the Management of Cities*
- *World Development Report 1994: Infrastructure for Development*
- *World Development Report 2004: Making Services Work for Poor People*

Labor and Social Protection

The Bank Group studies and generally supports measures that seek to improve or protect human capital, such as labor market interventions, publicly mandated unemployment or old-age insurance, and targeted income support. Such measures help individuals, households, and communities better manage the income risks that leave people vulnerable, and they contribute to a country's solidarity, social cohesion, and social stability. Topics on which the Bank Group provides information and resources through its Human Development Network include child labor, disability, labor markets, pensions, safety nets and transfers, social funds, and social risk management. The Web site for social protection issues is at http://www.worldbank.org/sp. The World Bank also maintains the Social Protection Advisory Service: fax queries to 1-202-614-0471 or e-mail socialprotection@worldbank.org.

IFC and Social Protection

IFC will not support projects that use forced or harmful child labor. Projects should comply with the national laws of host countries, including laws that protect core labor standards, and with related treaties ratified by host countries.

Forced labor consists of all work or service not voluntarily performed that is exacted from an individual under threat of force or penalty. Harmful child labor consists of the employment of children that is economically exploitative; likely to be hazardous to the child or to interfere with the child's education; or likely to be harmful to the child's health or physical, mental, spiritual, moral, or social development. IFC's performance standards address labor and working conditions. Learn more from http://www.ifc.org/ifcext/enviro.nsf/Content/PerformanceStandards.

Other Resources

Other resources include the following:

- The *Social Protection Help Desk* can provide useful information. Contact the help desk by e-mail at socialprotection@worldbank.org.
- *WBI* has a social protection and risk management learning program. The Web site is at http://www.worldbank.org/wbi/socialprotection.
- *World Bank research.* Click "Topic" at http://econ.worldbank.org and select "Social Protections and Labor."

Key Publications

Some publications about social protection follow:

- *Chains of Production, Ladders of Protection: Social Protection for Workers in the Informal Economy*
- *Household Risk Management and Social Protection in Chile*
- *Income Support for the Unemployed: Issues and Options*
- *Labor Issues in Infrastructure Reform: A Toolkit*
- *Labor Markets and Social Policy in Central and Eastern Europe: The Accession and Beyond*

- *Old-Age Income Support in the 21st Century: An International Perspective on Pension Systems and Reform*
- *Pensions in the Middle East and North Africa: Time for Change*
- *Pensions Panorama: Retirement-Income Systems in 53 Countries*
- *Reducing Vulnerability and Increasing Opportunity: Social Protection in the Middle East and North Africa*
- *Trade and Migration: Building Bridges for Global Labor Mobility*
- *World Development Report 1995: Workers in an Integrating World*

Law, Regulation, and the Judiciary

The Bank Group is an active supporter of legal and judicial reforms that address the needs of the poor and the most vulnerable in developing countries. The lead unit in this area, the Legal and Judicial Reform Practice Group of the World Bank, works with governments, judges, lawyers, scholars, civil society representatives, and other organizations to build better legal institutions and judicial systems. Other areas of activity for the Bank include environmental and international law and the role of legal systems in private sector development, finance, and infrastructure. The Bank's law and justice Web site at http://www4.worldbank.org/legal provides information on all these activities and links to several legal databases.

The Bank Group is working with governments to make laws and regulations more conducive to private sector development. Efforts include the Doing Business Project, a joint World Bank–IFC effort that compares administrative barriers facing private sector enterprises in more than 150 countries. The project is now being extended to the subnational level in selected countries and regions. Many of IFC's regional advisory services facilities and the joint World Bank–IFC Foreign Investment Advisory Service work with governments to assess administrative barriers and help develop legislative or judicial solutions. IFC has helped establish alternative dispute resolution in several countries in an effort to ensure that conflicts among private enterprises are addressed more quickly and at lower cost than through court proceedings.

Other Resources

Other legal resources are as follows:

- The *Bank documents* Web resource has links to key Bank Group documents, including articles of agreement, manuals and guidelines, and other materials. See http://www.worldbank.org/lawlibrary.

▦ The *Legal Help Desk* has a Web site at "Legal Help Desk" at http://www.worldbank.org/legal. The e-mail address is legalhelpdesk@ worldbank.org.

Key Publications

These publications deal with law and justice:

▦ *Competition Law and Regional Economic Integration: An Analysis of the Southern Mediterranean Countries*
▦ *A Framework for the Design and Implementation of Competition Law and Policy*
▦ *Intellectual Property and Development: Lessons from Recent Economic Research*
▦ *Judicial Systems in Transition Economies: Assessing the Past, Looking to the Future*
▦ *Land Law Reform: Achieving Development Policy Objectives*
▦ *Reforming Collateral Laws to Expand Access to Finance*
▦ *The Transit Regime for Landlocked States: International Law and Development Perspectives*
▦ *The World Bank Legal Review: Law and Justice for Development*, volume 1

Manufacturing and Services

Manufacturing accounts for some 40 percent of the gross domestic product of developing countries. By engaging in the manufacturing and services industries, primarily through IFC investments and advisory services and MIGA guarantees, the Bank Group is helping countries improve their economic competitiveness and the environmental and social sustainability of their industrial operations.

Global Manufacturing and Services Department (IFC)

This department coordinates IFC's investments and advisory services in a wide range of enterprises, including heavy industries, such as building materials, metals, forest products, automotives, glass, and other industrial and consumer products; light industries, such as electronics, appliances, pharmaceuticals, and textiles; and services, such as retail and tourism. The goal is to help clients achieve international competitiveness through financing, industry-specific expertise, and assistance in meeting international standards, including on corporate governance and environmental and social performance. In some instances, IFC also helps link small local suppliers of goods and services to larger clients in which it has invested. For more information, see http://www.ifc.org/ifcext/gms.nsf/Content/home.

Key Publications

Some publications that address manufacturing and services follow:

- *Forest Management in Nepal: Economics and Ecology*
- *Nature Tourism, Conservation, and Development in KwaZulu Natal, South Africa*
- *Radical Reform in the Automotive Industry: Policies in Emerging Markets*
- *Structural Aspects of Manufacturing in Sub-Saharan Africa: Findings from a Seven Country Enterprise*
- *Technology Institutions and Policies: Their Role in Developing Technological Capability in Industry*
- *Toward the Rural-Based Development of Commerce and Industry: Selected Experiences from East Asia*
- *Trade and Transport Facilitation: An Audit Methodology*
- *The World Bank Forest Strategy: Striking the Right Balance*

Poverty

Fighting poverty is central to the Bank Group's mission. The Bank Group considers a comprehensive understanding of poverty and its possible solutions to be fundamental for everyone involved in development. This understanding involves defining poverty, studying trends over time, setting goals to reduce poverty, and measuring results. The Bank Group's Web site on this topic is PovertyNet at http://www.worldbank.org/poverty, which introduces key issues and provides in-depth information on poverty measurement, monitoring, and analysis and on poverty reduction strategies for researchers and practitioners.

IFC and Poverty

IFC assists in the fight against poverty by focusing many of its investments on sectors that have the most direct effect on living standards. Such sectors include the financial sector, infrastructure, information and communication technologies, small and medium enterprises, microfinance, health, and education.

Other Resources

Other resources include the following:

- The *PREM Advisory Service,* whose focus includes poverty, publishes *PREM Notes,* which summarizes good practice and key policy findings. The Web site is at http://www.worldbank.org/prem. The e-mail address is premadvisory@worldbank.org.
- *WBI* has a program on poverty and growth. The Web site is at http://www.worldbank.org/wbi/povertyandgrowth.
- *World Bank research.* Click "Topic" at http://econ.worldbank.org and select "Poverty Reduction."

Key Publications

These publications address poverty:

- *Attacking Africa's Poverty: Experience from the Ground*
- *Can the Poor Influence Policy? Participatory Poverty Assessments in the Developing World*
- *Delivering on the Promise of Pro-Poor Growth: Insights and Lessons from Country Experiences*
- *The Impact of Microeconomic Policies on Poverty and Income Distribution*
- *Improving the Lives of the Poor through Investment in Cities*
- *Participatory Approaches to Attacking Extreme Poverty*
- *Poverty and Social Impact Analysis*
- *Power, Rights, and Poverty: Concepts and Connections*
- *Reaching the Rural Poor: A Renewed Strategy for Rural Development*
- *Reducing Poverty on a Global Scale: Learning and Innovating for Development*
- *A Sourcebook for Poverty Reduction Strategies,* two volumes
- *Targeting of Transfers in Developing Countries: Review of Lessons and Experience*
- *Voices of the Poor* (series)
- *World Development Report 2000/2001: Attacking Poverty*
- *1 World Manga: Passage 1: Poverty—A Ray of Light* (comic book)
- *2004 Annual Review of Development Effectiveness: The World Bank's Contributions to Poverty Reduction*

Private Sector Development

The Bank Group places major emphasis on the role of the private sector in spurring economic growth and reducing poverty, with two of its institutions, IFC and MIGA, focusing specifically on private enterprises. In addition to IFC investments and MIGA guarantees, the Bank Group institutions provide research and advisory services in many areas of private sector development. The focus of Bank Group efforts includes private sector advisory services on corporate governance, corporate social responsibility, investment climate diagnostics and reform, private participation in infrastructure, privatization transactions, and micro and small business development.

Financial and Private Sector Development Vice Presidency (World Bank Group)

This joint World Bank–IFC vice presidency takes the lead on many aspects of private sector development. These include small and medium enterprises; corporate governance and capital markets; investment climate, including the Doing Business Project and the Foreign Investment Advisory Service; and the development effectiveness of IFC's investments and advisory services. See http://www.ifc.org/economics.

The activities of the Corporate Governance Department are aimed at helping companies and countries improve standards of governance for corporations, focusing on shareholders' and stakeholders' rights, board members' duties, disclosure, and effective enforcement. The department promotes the spirit of enterprise and accountability, encouraging fairness, transparency, and responsibility.

IFC Investments and Advisory Services

IFC's Industries Vice Presidency includes departments responsible for its investment portfolio across a wide range of industry sectors, including agribusiness, global financial markets, global manufacturing and services, health and education, infrastructure, and private equity and investment funds. Departments in this group also focus on grassroots business organizations, advisory services for privatization, and subnational finance. Departments dealing with global information and communication technologies and with oil, gas, mining, and chemicals report both to this group and to the World Bank's Infrastructure Vice Presidency. Increasingly, IFC is working to integrate its investments with related advisory services to improve the sustainability, competitiveness, governance, and development impact of private enterprises.

Private sector development is the focus of many Bank Group partnerships with other organizations. This includes IFC's donor-funded operations, which encompass trust funds and a network of facilities that serve developing regions or promote specific aspects of development. For information, including links to facilities, see "Advisory Services" at http://www.ifc.org/ifcext/about.nsf/Content/TAAS.

Small and Medium Enterprise Department (World Bank Group)

The Small and Medium Enterprise Department is a joint department of IFC and the World Bank that assists units across the World Bank Group in their efforts to develop small and medium enterprises (SMEs). This includes developing monitoring and evaluation tools for advisory services, supporting data collection and analysis on IFC's SME activities, promoting business links between companies in which IFC invests and local SMEs, and identifying best practices. The department also manages IFC's donor-supported trust funds.

The Doing Business Report and Database

In 2003, the World Bank and IFC launched the Doing Business Project, which measures the ease of doing business around the world. Now in its fifth edition, the project's reports are widely read and foster dialogue on business environment reforms at the local, regional, and global levels. *Doing Business* allows policy makers to compare their countries' regulatory performance with that of other countries, learn from best practices globally, and prioritize reforms.

A public database on the Doing Business Web site shares the data collected for the reports. These data provide objective measures of business regulations and their enforcement, with indicators comparable across 175 economies. They indicate the regulatory costs of business and can be used to analyze specific regulations that enhance or constrain investment, productivity, and growth. See http://www.doingbusiness.org.

Other Resources

Other resources include the following:

- The *Donor Committee for Enterprise Development* works to share information and coordinate the efforts of agencies in this field. The secretariat is housed in the joint World Bank–IFC Small and Medium Enterprise Department. Visit http://www.sedonors.org.

- The *Foreign Investment Advisory Service* advises governments of developing and transition countries on how to improve their investment climate for domestic and foreign investors. Visit http://www.fias.net/.
- The *Private Sector Development Blog* gathers news, resources, and ideas about the role of private enterprise in fighting poverty. The blog is informal and represents the quirks and opinions of the bloggers, not the World Bank Group. Visit http://psdblog.worldbank.org.
- *Public Policy for the Private Sector* is an online World Bank Group journal that covers public policy innovations for private sector–led and market-based solutions for development. Articles can be viewed and downloaded at http://rru.worldbank.org/PublicPolicyJournal/.
- The *Public-Private Infrastructure Advisory Facility* is a multidonor technical assistance facility aimed at helping developing countries improve the quality of their infrastructure through private sector involvement. The facility is a joint initiative of the governments of Japan and the United Kingdom working closely with the World Bank. The Web site is at http://www.ppiaf.org.
- The *Rapid Response Web Site* is an online knowledge resource specializing in policy for the private sector in developing countries. Areas of expertise are economywide interventions that shape the investment climate, including foreign investment and corporate governance; private participation in sectors with complex market design and regulatory issues (for example, energy, transport, telecommunications, health, and education); privatization transactions; and policy. The Web site provides links to expert analysis, powerful databases, quick solutions, and comprehensive how-to guides at http://rru.worldbank.org.
- *WBI* has a private sector development program that includes subprograms on business, competitiveness, and development and on the investment climate. The Web sites are at www.worldbank.org/wbi/bcd and www.worldbank.org/wbi/investmentclimate or www.investmentclimate.org. For microfinance and small and medium enterprises, see http://www.worldbank.org/wbi/banking/microfinance.
- *World Bank research.* Click on "Topic" at http://econ.worldbank.org and select "Private Sector Development."

Key Publications

Publications about private sector development include the following:

- *Doing Business in 2004: Understanding Regulation*
- *Doing Business in 2005: Removing Obstacles to Growth*

- *Doing Business in 2006: Creating Jobs*
- *Doing Business 2007: How to Reform*
- *The Private Sector in Development: Entrepreneurship, Regulation, and Competitive Disciplines*
- *World Development Report 2005: A Better Investment Climate for Everyone*

Social Development

The World Bank has consolidated its approach to social development in a single Bank-wide strategy and implementation plan titled "Empowering People by Transforming Institutions: Social Development in World Bank Operations," which was produced following a three-year effort that involved extensive stocktaking, research, and consultation. The plan focuses on efforts to empower the poor through enhanced Bank support for social inclusion, cohesive societies, and accountable institutions. Social development is defined as the transformation of institutions, and as such, promotes enhanced growth, improved projects, and better quality of life. The plan sets a vision, objectives, and a course of action for the long term and suggests specific actions, targets, and institutional measures for the next five years.

The Sustainable Development Network of the World Bank coordinates several thematic work programs. These include programs on community-driven development, conflict prevention and reconstruction, indigenous peoples, involuntary resettlement, participation and civic engagement, social analysis and policy, and social capital. The Web site is at http://www.worldbank.org/socialdevelopment. Additional information appears on the Sustainable Development Network Web site at http://www.worldbank.org/sustainabledevelopment. See also "Environment and Social Development Department (IFC)" under the "Environment" section in this chapter. Its Web site is at http://www.ifc.org/enviro.

Other Resources

More information about social development can be obtained from *World Bank research.* Click "Topic" at http://econ.worldbank.org and select "Social Development."

Key Publications

These publications deal with social development:

- *Evaluating Social Funds: A Cross-Country Analysis of Community Investments*
- *Measuring Social Capital: An Integrated Questionnaire*

- *Natural Resources and Violent Conflict: Options and Actions*
- *Putting Social Development to Work for the Poor: An OED Review of World Bank Activities*
- *Reshaping the Future: Education and Post-Conflict Reconstruction*
- *Social Cohesion and Conflict Prevention in Asia: Managing Diversity through Development*

Sustainable Development

The Sustainable Development Network was formed to advance sustainable development within the Bank Group by ensuring that actions taken today to promote development and reduce poverty do not result in environmental degradation or social exclusion tomorrow. That means dealing with the comprehensive nature of development in the implementation of projects and programs by the Bank Group and its partners. Specifically, participation, empowerment, strengthened institutions, environmental protection, conservation, and a focus on the rural poor are all foundations for sustained and inclusive economic growth. In 2006, the Bank merged the networks that deal with infrastructure and environment projects into a single unit to promote sustainable development. The purpose of consolidating the networks was to mainstream environmental issues, improve synergies, better integrate core operations, and ensure that the focus on sustainability is strengthened as the Bank increases its investment in infrastructure. The Web site for sustainable development issues is at http://www.worldbank.org/sustainabledevelopment.

IFC and Sustainability

Sustainability is at the heart of IFC's business model. The projects that it chooses to finance and the products and services it offers must fulfill development goals that go beyond financing. Therefore, when investing, IFC considers multiple dimensions of sustainability:

- Economic and financial growth through projects and client services to achieve development effectiveness
- Environmental protection by means of pollution prevention and abatement, biodiversity conservation, and sustainable natural resource management
- Social development through improved living standards, fair land acquisition, support of small businesses, health and safety of workers and communities, and respect for key human rights

- Corporate governance through transparent and professional systems of direction and control that lead to sustainable businesses
- Private sector development.

The Web site for IFC sustainability resources is at http://www.ifc.org/sustainability.

Other Resources

WBI has a sustainable development learning program. The Web site is at http://www.worldbank.org/wbi/sustainabledevelopment.

Key Publications

These publications address sustainable development:

- *At Loggerheads: Agricultural Expansion, Poverty Reduction, and Environment in the Tropical Forests*
- *Beyond the City: The Rural Contribution to Development*
- *Beyond Economic Growth,* second edition: *An Introduction to Sustainable Development*
- *Generating Public Sector Resources to Finance Sustainable Development: Revenue and Incentive Effects*
- *Green miniAtlas*
- *How Much Is an Ecosystem Worth? Assessing the Economic Value of Conservation*
- *The Little Green Data Book*
- *Strategic Environmental Assessment for Policies: An Instrument for Good*
- *Sustainable Amazon: Limitations and Opportunities for Rural Development*
- *Sustainable Land Management: Challenges, Opportunities, and Trade-Offs*
- *Water, Wealth, and Poverty*
- *World Development Report 2003: Sustainable Development in a Dynamic World*

Trade

The Bank Group's work on trade has two central objectives. At the global level, the Bank Group aims to promote changes in the world trading system to make it more supportive of development, especially of the poorest countries and of poor people across the developing world. That work entails continued collaboration with the World Trade Organization, other multilateral agencies, and donor countries, including work to maximize the development impact of regional trading agreements. At the country level, the Bank Group aims to promote integration through trade as a core aspect of development strategies. That effort involves providing strategic assistance to client countries to support trade-related reforms, with special efforts to target the low-income countries that are most in need of Bank support. The Bank Group's Web site on trade issues, maintained by WBI, is at http://www.worldbank.org/trade.

IFC and Trade

Through investments and advisory services, IFC supports banking institutions that provide trade enhancement facilities to local companies. In 2005, IFC launched the Global Trade Finance Program to help establish a worldwide network of bank partnerships to finance trade under risk coverage provided by IFC. The program aims to increase the developing countries' share of global trade and promote flows of goods and services between developing countries. Its Web site is at http://www.ifc.org/gtfp.

Other Resources

The following can provide more information on trade:

- *International Trade* has a Web site at http://www.worldbank.org/research/trade/index.htm.
- *World Bank research.* Click "Topic" at http://econ.worldbank.org, and select "International Economics and Trade."

Key Publications

Trade-related publications include the following:

- *Agricultural Trade Reform and the Doha Development Agenda*
- *Challenges of CAFTA: Maximizing the Benefits for Central America*
- *China and the WTO: Accession, Policy Reform, and Poverty Reduction Strategies*
- *Customs Modernization Handbook*
- *Development, Trade, and the WTO: A Handbook*
- *East Asia Integrates: A Trade Policy Agenda for Shared Growth*
- *Economic Development and Multilateral Trade Cooperation*

- *Global Economic Prospects 2005: Trade, Regionalism, and Development*
- *International Trade in Health Services and the GATS: Current Issues and Debates*
- *Poverty and the WTO: Impacts of the Doha Development Agenda*
- *Regional Integration and Development*

Transport

Transport is the key infrastructure asset for the movement of goods, people, and resources; it encompasses roads, rail, seaports, airports, and all manner of vehicles and management systems. This sector focuses on access, the role of the public and private sectors, and institutional and financial development. Areas of activity include economics and policy, ports and logistics, railways, roads and highways, and rural and urban transport. Special concerns include globalization of trade, congestion and pollution, operating deficits in public transport systems, and expenditure to maintain and modernize transport infrastructure. The Web site for transport issues is at http://www.worldbank.org/transport.

IFC and Transport

Sound transport infrastructure and services are crucial to private sector development. The private sector is playing a larger role in financing projects, as well as in providing managerial and technical expertise. Through its Infrastructure Department, IFC invests in ports, airlines and airports, roads, railroads, shipping, and trucking. Visit http://www.ifc.org/infrastructure. IFC's Advisory Services Department advises governments on private sector participation in transportation infrastructure and services; its Web site is at http://www.ifc.org/advisory.

Other Resources

The *Transport Help Desk* can be found at "Contact Us" at http://www.worldbank.org/transport.htm. The e-mail address is transport@worldbank.org.

Key Publications

The following publications concern transport issues:

- *Cities on the Move: A World Bank Urban Transport Strategy Review*
- *Customs Modernization Handbook*

- *Customs Modernization Initiatives: Case Studies*
- *Design and Appraisal of Rural Transport Infrastructure: Ensuring Basic Access for Rural Communities*
- *Improving Rural Mobility: Options for Developing Motorized and Non-motorized Transport in Rural Areas*
- *Port Reform Toolkit: Effective Decision Support for Policymakers*
- *A Primer on Efficiency Measurement for Utilities and Transport Regulators*
- *Trade and Transport Facilitation: A Toolkit for Audit, Analysis, and Remedial Action*

Urban Development

The Bank Group's work in the field of urban development focuses on improving the lives of poor people and promoting equity. That effort includes the creation of city development strategies; that is, an agenda for development modeled roughly on country strategies and created by local people with broad participation. Other areas of activity include disaster management, land and real estate, local economic development, municipal finance, urban community upgrades, urban poverty, and waste management. The main Web site for urban issues is at http://www.worldbank.org/urban.

A combined initiative of the World Bank and IFC, the Municipal Fund provides needed capital investment to municipalities and other local public entities in the developing world without central government guarantees. The Municipal Fund's offerings provide states, municipalities, and municipally controlled institutions with new financial products and access to capital markets. The objective is to strengthen their ability to deliver key infrastructure services such as water, wastewater management, transportation, electricity, and power and to improve efficiency and accountability. More information is available at http://www.ifc.org/municipalfund.

Other Resources

Other urban development resources include the following:

- *Cities Alliance* is a global alliance of cities and their development partners committed to improving the living conditions of the urban poor. The secretariat is housed at the World Bank. Visit http://www.citiesalliance.org.
- The *Urban Help Desk* offers e-mail advice at urbanhelp@worldbank.org.
- *WBI* has a program on urban and local government. Its Web site is at http://www.worldbank.org/wbi/urban.

■ *World Bank research.* Click "Topic" at http://econ.worldbank.org and select "Urban Development."

Key Publications

The following publications deal with urban development:

■ *Building Safer Cities: The Future of Disaster Risk*
■ *Cities in a Globalizing World: Governance, Performance, and Sustainability*
■ *Coping with the Cold: Heating Strategies for Eastern Europe and Central Asia's Urban Poor*
■ *Historic Cities and Sacred Sites: Cultural Roots for Urban Futures*
■ *Improving the Lives of the Poor through Investment in Cities: An Update on the Performance of the World Bank's Urban Portfolio*
■ *Street Addressing and the Management of Cities*
■ *Urban Environment and Infrastructure: Toward Livable Cities*
■ *Urban Planning in Africa: Addressing, Mapping, and Their Applications*
■ *The Urban Poor in Latin America*

Water

Water is the focus of Bank Group efforts in two broad areas: (1) water resources management, and (2) water supply and sanitation. Specific issues include coastal and marine management, dams and reservoirs, groundwater, irrigation and drainage, river basin and watershed management, water management across national boundaries, water and the environment, and water economics. Water is also the focus of one of the MDGs: the objective for 2015 is to reduce by half the proportion of people without sustainable access to safe drinking water. Web sites include water resources management at http://www.worldbank.org/water and water and water supply and sanitation at http://www.worldbank.org/watsan.

IFC and Water Resources

IFC is represented on the World Bank Group's Water and Urban Sector Board and contributes to the development of ideas and policies in this sector. IFC draws on its experience to provide inputs from an investor perspective. It often works in collaboration with the World Bank; however, IFC's main role is to support investors who undertake private sector water projects. IFC has invested in water projects in a wide range of countries; see http://www.ifc.org/infrastructure. IFC has also advised on the privatization of several water companies; learn more at http://www.ifc.org/advisory.

Other Resources

The *Water Help Desk* offers e-mail advice at whelpdesk@worldbank.org.

Key Publications

Publications on the water sector include the following:

- *The Human Right to Water: Legal and Policy Dimensions*
- *The Institutional Economics of Water: A Cross-Country Analysis of Institutions and Performance*
- *Making the Most of Scarcity: Accountability for Better Water Management in the Middle East and North Africa*
- *Shaping the Future of Water for Agriculture: A Sourcebook for Investment in Agricultural Water Management*
- *Water, Electricity, and the Poor*

Students take year-end exams in the Republic of Yemen. Since 1990, the World Bank's emphasis on girls' education has increased and gender equality has been integrated as an important component of the Bank's poverty reduction mission.

Appendixes

A. Contacting the World Bank Group

B. Timeline of World Bank Group History

C. Presidents of the World Bank Group

D. Country Membership in World Bank Group Institutions

E. Constituencies of the Executive Directors

F. Additional Country Resources

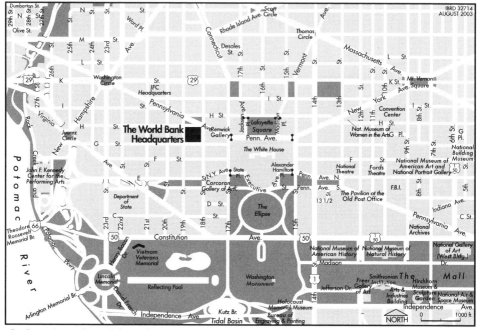

The location of World Bank Group headquarters.

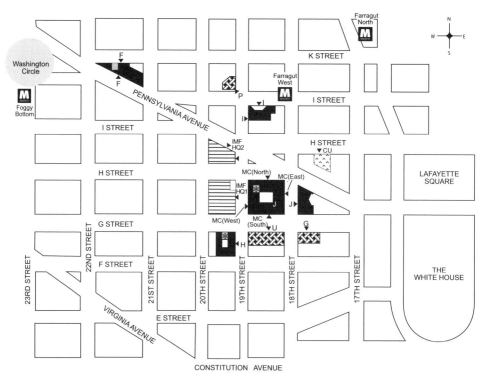

The buildings of World Bank Group headquarters.

CONTACTING THE WORLD BANK GROUP

Headquarters and General Inquiries

The offices and Web sites listed here are good sources of general information about the five World Bank Group institutions: the International Bank for Reconstruction and Development (IBRD), the International Development Association (IDA), the International Finance Corporation (IFC), the Multilateral Investment Guarantee Agency (MIGA), and the International Centre for Settlement of Investment Disputes (ICSID).

General Contact Information

World Bank Group
1818 H Street NW
Washington DC 20433 USA
Tel: 1-202-473-1000
Fax: 1-202-477-6391
Web: http://www.worldbankgroup.org or
    http://www.worldbank.org

Staff Directory Orders

World Bank Publications
Tel: 1-800-645-7247 or 1-703-661-1580
Fax: 1-703-661-1501
Web: http://www.worldbank.org/publications

IBRD and IDA Contact Information

Same as for the World Bank Group
Contact page: http://www.worldbank.org/
    contacts

IFC Contact Information

International Finance Corporation
2121 Pennsylvania Avenue NW
Washington DC 20433 USA
Tel: 1-202-473-1000
Web: http://www.ifc.org

General Inquiries, IFC Corporate Relations:
Tel: 1-202-473-3800
Fax: 1-202-974-4384
Contact page: http://www.ifc.org/contacts

MIGA Contact Information

Mail: Same as for the World Bank Group

Location:
Multilateral Investment Guarantee Agency
1800 G Street NW, Suite 1200
Washington DC 20433 USA
Tel: 1-202-473-1000
Web: http://www.miga.org

Business Inquiries:
Tel: 1-202-473-1000
Fax: 1-202-522-0316
E-mail: migainquiry@worldbank.org
Contact page: see "Contacts" at
    http://www.miga.org

ICSID Contact Information

Same address as for the World Bank Group
Tel: 1-202-458-1534
Fax: 1-202-522-2615
Web: http://www.worldbank.org/icsid
Contact page: http://www.worldbank.org/icsid/
    contact.htm

Media Relations, News, and Public Affairs

The External Affairs Department of the World Bank and the Corporate Relations units of IFC and MIGA are the key resources for media relations, news, press contacts, public affairs, and access to World Bank Group experts and the Speakers' Bureau. Generally, the Bank Group organizations also feature news stories and major events on their home pages.

IBRD and IDA

The following are links to various World Bank media resources:

- The DevNews Media Center provides press releases, feature stories, reviews of press coverage, speeches and transcripts, issue briefs, and an events calendar. It also provides access to the Speakers' Bureau, to World Bank experts, and to media contacts.

  Web: http://www.worldbank.org/mediacontacts.

- Electronic newsletters offer a wide range of material by free e-mail subscription, including the daily press review; the World Bank weekly update; and many newsletters from specific sectors, regions, and partnerships of the Bank.

  Web: http://www.worldbank.org/subscriptions.

- The Online Media Briefing Center is a password-protected site available only to accredited journalists.

  Web: http://media.worldbank.org.

IFC

The IFC Pressroom provides press releases and links to media contacts, country fact sheets, general information about IFC, publications, speeches, briefs, and project documents. See "News" at http://www.ifc.org.

MIGA

MIGA News and Events provides newsletters, press releases, feature stories, an events calendar, and correspondence with nongovernmental organizations. See "Media" at http://www.miga.org.

ICSID

News from ICSID is a biennial newsletter, with the current issue and archives available online. See http://www.worldbank.org/icsid/news/news.htm.

Public Information

Various offices within the World Bank provide public information.

Public Information Centers

InfoShop/Public Information Center
1818 H Street NW, Room J1-060
Washington DC 20433 USA
Tel: 1-202-458-5454
Fax: 1-202-522-1500
E-mail: pic@worldbank.org
(For public information centers in other countries, go to http://www.worldbank.org/reference/ and select "Public Information Centers" in the "Finding Publications" box.)

World Bank Publications

To order publications:
Tel: 1-800-645-7247 or 1-703-661-1580
Fax: 1-703-661-1501
Web: http://www.worldbank.org/publications

World Bank Group Feedback Service

This service helps Web users locate online information resources, project information, and publications. Although the site does not provide in-depth research, it can guide users to those Web sites most likely to have the replies to their questions. The feedback service also welcomes suggestions on how to make the Web site more useful. To provide feedback:
Web: http://www.worldbank.org/feedback
E-mail: feedback@worldbank.org

Projects, Policies, Strategies, and Research

These database portals provide access to information on World Bank Group projects, policies, and strategies. They are searchable by sector, region, country, or development theme.

- Documents and reports: http://www-wds.worldbank.org
- Projects, policies, and strategies: http://www.worldbank.org/projects

▪ IFC projects: http://www.ifc.org/projects
▪ World Bank *Operational Manual:* http://www.worldbank.org/OpManual
▪ World Bank research: http://econ.worldbank.org
▪ World Bank Group articles of agreement and other basic documents: http://www.worldbank.org/articles

Annual Reports

Annual reports of World Bank Group organizations and programs are available online as PDF files or in HTML format. The reports are published in multiple languages and the Web sites include past editions.

▪ World Bank annual report: http://www.worldbank.org/annualreport
▪ IFC annual report: http://www.ifc.org/ar2006
▪ MIGA annual report: click on "Media" and see "News and Publications" at http://www.miga.org
▪ ICSID annual report: see "ICSID Documents and Publications" at http://www.worldbank.org/icsid

Libraries

The Library Network consists of nine libraries and resource centers that serve the World Bank Group and the International Monetary Fund. The libraries offer the following services, which span the full spectrum of Bank Group and International Monetary Fund business: research, consultation, procurement of information products, content organization, and document delivery. All the libraries are located in Washington, DC, with the exception of the World Bank country office libraries and the public information centers. Some libraries admit visitors by appointment only.

Distinct from the Library Network, the PovertyNet Library is an online library of reports and documents devoted to poverty in the developing world. The library contains a variety of poverty-related documents, including technical reports and papers, abstracts, speeches, interviews, and press releases.

Following are links to Bank Group library resources:

▪ World Bank Group and International Monetary Fund Joint Bank–Fund Library: http://external.worldbankimflib.org. For outside visitor access, see http://library.worldbankimflib.org/Services/ServicesFor/visitors.htm.
▪ PovertyNet Library: see "Poverty Net Library" at http://www.worldbank.org/povertynet.

TIMELINE OF WORLD BANK GROUP HISTORY

1944	The United Nations (UN) Monetary and Financial Conference draws up the World Bank (International Bank for Reconstruction and Development [IBRD]) Articles of Agreement at Bretton Woods, New Hampshire, with 44 countries represented.
1945	Twenty-eight governments sign the Articles of Agreement in Washington, DC.
1946	The World Bank formally begins operations on June 25.
	The first loan applications are received (from Chile, Czechoslovakia, Denmark, France, Luxembourg, and Poland).
1947	The Bank makes its first bond offering—$250 million—in New York City.
	The Bank makes its first loan—$250 million—to France.
1948	The Bank makes its first development loan—$13.5 million—to Chile.
1950	The Bank makes its first loan to a national development bank—$2 million—to Ethiopia.
1951	Finland and Yugoslavia are the first countries to repay their Bank loans in full.
1952	Japan and the Federal Republic of Germany become members.
1953	The first three loans to Japan, totaling $40.2 million, are approved.
1955	The Economic Development Institute (now the World Bank Institute) is established to serve as the Bank's staff college.
1956	The International Finance Corporation (IFC) is established as a private sector affiliate of the Bank, with 31 members and authorized capital of $100 million.
1957	IFC makes its first investment—$2 million—in Siemens in Brazil to expand manufacturing.
1958	In the wake of deterioration in India's balance of payments, the first meeting of the India Aid Consortium takes place in Washington, DC.
1960	India, Pakistan, and the World Bank sign the Indus Water Treaty.
	The International Development Association (IDA) is established as part of the World Bank with initial subscriptions of $912.7 million.

1961   The Bank loans $80 million to Japan to finance the bullet train.

IDA extends its first development credit—$9 million—to Honduras for highway development.

1962   IFC establishes an advisory panel of investment bankers.

The Bank makes its first education loan, a $5 million IDA credit to Tunisia for school construction.

IFC makes its first equity investment in Fabrica Española Magentos S.A. of Spain.

1963   The Bank launches the Junior Professional Recruitment and Training Program (now the Young Professionals Program).

Eighteen newly independent African countries join the Bank.

1966   The International Centre for Settlement of Investment Disputes (ICSID) is established.

1967   Developing countries form the Group of 77 as a convention and a negotiation arm.

France, the Federal Republic of Germany, Japan, the United Kingdom, and the United States form the Group of Five to convene meetings of finance ministers and governors of central banks. (The group became the Group of Seven in 1976 with the addition of Canada and Italy. This group, with the addition of the Russian Federation, is now known as the Group of Eight.)

1970   The Bank makes its first loan for population planning—$2 million—to Jamaica.

The Bank's new commitments exceed $2 billion for the first time.

1971   Japan becomes one of the Bank's five largest shareholders.

The Bank makes its first loan for pollution control—$15 million—to Brazil.

1972   The Bank redeploys project and program staff members into regional departments to enable the institution to function more effectively.

The World Bank Group Staff Association comes into existence.

1974   The Interim Committee of the International Monetary Fund (IMF) and the Development Committee are established to advise the Boards of Governors.

The position of director general of operations evaluation is established to ensure independent evaluation of projects and programs.

President Robert S. McNamara delivers a speech at the Annual Meetings at which, for the first time, poverty is placed at the top of the Bank's agenda.

1975   IBRD and IDA commit nearly $1 billion in one fiscal year for rural development projects.

Shirley Boskey is appointed as the Bank's first female manager at the director level (International Relations Department). (The diversity strategy is extended in 1998 to include gender, nationality, race, sexual orientation, culture, and disability.)

The Project Preparation Facility, which provides borrowing governments an advance for financial and technical help with project preparation, is created.

IFC's first major commercial loans are syndicated for projects in Brazil and the Republic of Korea.

1978 The executive directors endorse a Bank policy to assess the environmental impact of Bank-assisted projects.

The first *World Development Report* team, led by Ernest Stern, publishes a report on the theme of accelerating growth and alleviating poverty.

1979 The Bank's new commitments exceed $10 billion for the first time.

The Bank begins lending for health projects.

The Bank Group suspends operations in Afghanistan after the invasion by the former Soviet Union. (Normal operations resume in 2002.)

1980 IBRD's authorized capital stock increases by $44 billion to $85 billion.

The first structural adjustment loan is approved—$200 million—for Turkey.

The People's Republic of China assumes representation for China and quickly becomes one of the largest borrowers.

1981 The position of World Bank ombudsman is established.

IFC coins the term "emerging markets." The Emerging Markets Database is developed.

1982 Anne Krueger is appointed as the first female vice president (Economics and Research).

A Bank loan for the Polonoroeste Program in Brazil finances a 90-mile highway across the Amazon rain forest, unintentionally attracting a large influx of settlers and spurring deforestation and international outcry.

1983 The Bank establishes a small grants program to fund activities to promote cooperation among nongovernmental organizations (NGOs), governments, academics, and the media.

1984 IFC establishes a $20 billion special fund to stimulate private sector development.

IFC undertakes its first direct borrowings in international capital markets.

1986 The Foreign Investment Advisory Service (FIAS)—a multidonor service of the International Finance Corporation that advises governments of developing and transition countries on how to improve their investment climate for domestic and foreign investors—is formed.

1987 In a major reorganization, all staff members are reselected into positions. New country departments combine functions formerly divided between programs and projects staff. Regional and central environment departments are created.

The Emerging Markets Database is launched commercially.

1988   The Multilateral Investment Guarantee Agency is established.

1989   The Bank's Board of Executive Directors endorses a directive on disclosure of information.

1990   The Global Environment Facility is launched.

1991   China replaces India as the largest IDA borrower.

1992   An independent review of the Sardar Sarovar Project in India (Narmada Dam) is conducted. (Bank participation in the project is canceled in 1995.)

    A task force proposes steps to improve the Bank's portfolio management.

    Excellence through Equality recommends an increase in the proportion of women at higher grade levels.

    Russia and 12 other republics of the former Soviet Union become members of IBRD and IDA.

1993   The Institutional Development Fund is established to support innovative capacity-building initiatives.

    The independent Inspection Panel is established to investigate external complaints from individual groups negatively affected by Bank-funded projects.

    IFC initiates the first environmental training for financial intermediaries.

1994   The first Public Information Center is opened.

    The Bank unveils a three-year, $1.2 billion program to assist Palestinians in the West Bank and Gaza in transition to autonomous rule.

    "Dollar budgeting" is introduced.

    The World Bank celebrates its 50th anniversary while being widely criticized by NGOs and member governments.

1995   The Bank Group emphasizes the importance of girls' education.

1996   A trust fund for Bosnia and Herzegovina is created.

    The Quality Assurance Group is established to provide real-time information on the quality of the Bank's work.

    Knowledge management is launched to connect those who need to know with those who do know, to collect know-how, and to make knowledge accessible.

    The IMF, the World Bank, and donors launch the Heavily Indebted Poor Countries Initiative to alleviate debt. (The framework is significantly enhanced in 1999.)

1997   The Governance Action Plan is introduced. After just two years, more than 600 specific governance and clean government initiatives are started in almost 100 borrower countries.

    Adaptable lending instruments are introduced.

    Bank operations are reorganized into a matrix structure (country departments and networks of related sector families) and begin to decentralize.

The Bank approves a loan of $3 billion to the Republic of Korea and approves other loans to economies affected by the Korean financial crisis to restore investor confidence and minimize the social costs of the crisis.

The Board of Executive Directors approves the Strategic Compact, a fundamental organizational renewal program.

The Extending IFC's Reach Initiative is launched, thereby targeting countries where difficult environments hamper investments.

1998 The Knowledge Bank Initiative is launched.

The Bank approves the Kosovo Special Fund.

The Bank holds the first Development Marketplace to reward innovation in development.

IFC strengthens its environmental and social policies.

1999 The Bank's vision for the new millennium is articulated: "Our dream is a world free of poverty."

The Bank Group adopts the Comprehensive Development Framework, and at their Annual Meetings, the Bank Group and the IMF agree to implement country-owned poverty reduction strategies.

IFC and MIGA appoint a compliance adviser/ombudsman to improve accountability to locally affected communities.

2000 The Bank and IMF Spring Meetings in Washington, DC, and the Annual Meetings in Prague draw large protests.

The Bank commits an additional $500 million to fight HIV/AIDS.

The Inspection Panel reviews the China Western Poverty Project. Chinese authorities decide to use their own resources to implement the controversial component.

The Bank and its partners create the Global Development Gateway, a portal on development where users can find and contribute information, resources, and tools.

The Heavily Indebted Poor Countries Initiative delivers on its promise made in 2000: 22 countries receive more than $34 billion in debt service relief.

Completed Bank projects with satisfactory outcome ratings reach 75 percent for the first time in nearly 20 years (up from 60 percent in 1996).

IFC reaches a record for new investment approvals in Sub-Saharan Africa—$1.2 billion.

The United Nations Millennium Summit establishes the Millennium Development Goals for achievement by 2015.

2001 The IMF and the Bank Group cancel their Annual Meetings following the attacks of September 11.

The Bank and its partners establish the Global Development Learning Network, a distance-learning initiative in developing countries.

Partners in the Global Partnership to Eliminate River Blindness pledge $39 million to eliminate the disease in Africa by 2010.

The Bank Group participates in calls for decreasing agricultural subsidies in developed countries.

The Bank revises its disclosure policy to promote better transparency and accountability in its development work.

2002 The Bank Group participates in the first UN International Conference on Financing for Development, held in Monterrey, Mexico.

With its partners, the World Bank establishes the Education for All Fast-Track Initiative to help ensure that developing countries provide every child with a complete primary school education by 2015.

2003 The Bank lends $505 million to support Brazil's accelerated program of human development reforms.

The Bank Group participates in the World Water Forum in Kyoto, Japan, asserting that water is a key driver of growth and poverty reduction.

IFC and its partners launch a program to help local businesses in Azerbaijan benefit from investments in the oil industry.

Ten leading commercial banks adopt the Equator Principles, choosing to follow World Bank and IFC environmental and social guidelines for all their investment work in developing countries.

The Bank Group participates in UN efforts to rebuild Iraq.

A major conference with youth organizations is held in Paris to discuss the role of young people in peace and development.

The Council of the Global Environment Facility approves $224 million in grants for 19 new projects in developing countries and countries with economies in transition.

The first annual *Doing Business* report is published.

2004 The Bank establishes the Low-Income Countries Under Stress Trust Fund.

The Bank's Board of Executive Directors authorizes the Bank to act as an administrator for the Iraq Trust Fund to finance a program of emergency projects and technical assistance.

The Bank and the IMF adopt a more comprehensive and integrated approach to fighting money laundering and terrorist financing in member countries.

The Bank and the IMF launch the Quarterly External Debt Database, an online database that offers access to external debt statistics for 41 countries.

The first issue of the *Global Monitoring Report* is published, warning that, based on current trends, most developing countries would fail to meet most of the Millennium Development Goals.

The World Bank issues a wide-ranging reform proposal for the World Bank Group's activities in the extractive industries—oil, gas, and mining.

2005 The Bank publishes *Focus on Sustainability 2004,* its first report on sustainability.

Donor countries agree to the IDA-14 replenishment of $34 billion, which represents a 25 percent increase over the previous replenishment and the largest expansion of IDA resources in two decades.

The Bank publishes its first annual report investigating fraud and corruption both internally and in Bank-financed projects.

The Bank approves a $20 million grant to step up the fight against HIV/AIDS in the six countries of the Great Lakes region—Burundi, the Democratic Republic of Congo, Kenya, Rwanda, Tanzania, and Uganda.

The Bank launches a new global approach to help developing countries make faster progress in their fight against malaria.

The Bank issues a revised policy on indigenous peoples that reflects a strategic shift toward a broader and direct engagement with indigenous peoples' communities.

The World Bank makes its first loan to Iraq in three decades.

2006 An avian flu pledging conference—cosponsored by the European Commission, the government of China, and the Bank—is held in Beijing, with pledges amounting to almost $1.9 billion.

Wolfowitz outlines a comprehensive strategy for tackling corruption, a serious impediment to development and effective governance.

The Bank announces the creation of the independent, high-level Commission on Growth and Development comprising leading practitioners from government, business, and the policy-making arena.

To mobilize more resources for the very poorest countries, IBRD and IFC make a record transfer of $950 million to IDA, substantially more than the $500 million to be transferred under the IDA-14 replenishment agreement.

The Board of Executive Directors approves the Multilateral Debt Relief Initiative, an extension of debt relief available under the enhanced Highly Indebted Poor Countries Initiative.

The Bank announces the Bank Gender Action Plan, a four-year, $24.5 million plan to enhance women's economic power in key economic sectors in the developing world.

2007 IFC donates $150 million to IDA, the first such contribution by the private sector arm of the World Bank Group.

The Board of Executive Directors approves a new health, nutrition, and population strategy.

PRESIDENTS OF THE WORLD BANK GROUP

Eugene Meyer (1875–1959). Term: June 1946 to December 1946. Head of a banking house, Eugene Meyer & Company, and owner of the *Washington Post.*

John J. McCloy (1896–1989). Term: March 1947 to April 1949. A lawyer whose firm was counsel to Chase National Bank. Held positions in the U.S. government, including assistant secretary of war. Resigned from the World Bank to become the U.S. high commissioner to Germany.

Eugene Black (1898–1992). Term: July 1949 to December 1962. Investment banker and senior vice president of Chase Manhattan Bank. Had previously been the U.S. executive director to the World Bank and assistant secretary at the U.S. Treasury. Served the longest of any World Bank president.

George Woods (1901–1982). Term: January 1963 to March 1968. Investment banker and chair of the First Boston Corporation.

Robert S. McNamara (b. 1916). Term: April 1968 to June 1981. Was previously director and president of the Ford Motor Company and served as secretary of defense in the Kennedy and Johnson administrations.

A. W. Clausen (b. 1923). Term: July 1981 to June 1986. Held positions at the Bank of America and Bank America Corporation before and after his World Bank tenure. These positions included president, chief executive officer, and chair.

Barber B. Conable (1922–2003). Term: July 1986 to August 1991. Member of the U.S. House of Representatives from 1965 to 1985, where his committee memberships included the House Ways and Means Committee, the Joint Economic Committee, and the House Budget and Ethics committees.

Lewis T. Preston (1926–1995). Term: September 1991 to May 1995. Held positions at J. P. Morgan & Company, including president, board chair, chief executive officer, and chair of the Executive Committee.

James D. Wolfensohn (b. 1933). Term: June 1995 to May 2005. Established his career as an international investment banker with a parallel involvement in development issues and the global environment. Currently holds the position of senior adviser to Citigroup.

Paul D. Wolfowitz (b. 1943). Term: June 2005 to June 2007. Served as a public servant, ambassador, and educator, including 24 years in government service.

Robert B. Zoellick (b. 1953). Term: July 2007 to present. For biography, see box 2.1.

COUNTRY MEMBERSHIP IN WORLD BANK GROUP INSTITUTIONS

Once a country has joined the IMF, it may apply for membership in IBRD. Upon admission, each country makes a capital contribution to IBRD. Only countries belonging to IBRD may apply for membership in the other Bank Group institutions. More information on regions and countries is available in chapter 3, including specific ways that IFC regions differ from those used by IBRD and IDA.

Table D.1 Country Memberships and Voting Shares in Each Institution as of April 2007

| Country | IBRD/IDA region | IBRD (founded 1945) | | | IDA (founded 1960) | | | IFC (founded 1956) | | | MIGA (founded 1988) | | | ICSID (founded 1966) |
		Year joined	Votes	Share of total	Year joined	Votes	Share of total	Year joined	Votes	Share of total	Year joined	Votes	Share of total	Year joined
Afghanistan	SA	1955	550	0.03	1961	16,857	0.10	1957	361	0.02	2003	376	0.17	1968
Albania	ECA	1991	1,080	0.07	1991	36,599	0.22	1991	1,552	0.06	1991	360	0.16	1991
Algeria	MENA	1963	9,502	0.59	1963	27,720	0.17	1990	5,871	0.24	1996	1,402	0.64	1996
Angola	AFR	1989	2,926	0.18	1989	57,909	0.35	1989	1,731	0.07	1989	445	0.20	nm
Antigua and Barbuda	LAC	1983	770	0.05	nm	nm	nm	1987	263	0.01	2005	308	0.14	nm
Argentina	LAC	1956	18,161	1.12	1962	134,439	0.81	1959	38,379	1.59	1992	2,468	1.13	1994
Armenia	ECA	1992	1,389	0.09	1993	15,132	0.09	1995	1,242	0.05	1995	338	0.15	1992
Australia	n.a.	1947	24,714	1.53	1960	211,357	1.27	1956	47,579	1.97	1999	3,277	1.50	1991
Austria	n.a.	1948	11,313	0.70	1961	120,425	0.72	1956	19,991	0.83	1997	1,624	0.74	1971
Azerbaijan	ECA	1992	1,896	0.12	1995	7,860	0.05	1995	2,617	0.11	1992	373	0.17	1992
Bahamas, The	LAC	1973	1,321	0.08	nm	nm	nm	1986	585	0.02	1994	434	0.20	1995
Bahrain	n.a.	1972	1,353	0.08	nm	nm	nm	1995	1,996	0.08	1988	394	0.18	1996
Bangladesh	SA	1972	5,104	0.32	1972	100,314	0.60	1976	9,287	0.39	1988	857	0.39	1980
Barbados	LAC	1974	1,198	0.07	1999	39,219	0.24	1980	611	0.03	1988	378	0.17	1983
Belarus	ECA	1992	3,573	0.22	nm	nm	nm	1992	5,412	0.22	1992	491	0.22	1992
Belgium	n.a.	1945	29,233	1.81	1964	191,827	1.15	1956	50,860	2.11	1992	3,835	1.76	1970
Belize	LAC	1982	836	0.05	1982	13,784	0.08	1982	351	0.01	1992	346	0.16	nm
Benin	AFR	1963	1,118	0.07	1963	23,105	0.14	1987	369	0.02	1994	366	0.17	1966
Bhutan	SA	1981	729	0.05	1981	34,663	0.21	2003	970	0.04	nm	nm	nm	nm
Bolivia	LAC	1945	2,035	0.13	1961	51,788	0.31	1956	2,152	0.09	1991	478	0.22	1995

Bosnia and Herzegovina	ECA	1993	799	0.05	1993	38,077	0.23	1993	870	0.04	1993	338	0.15	1997
Botswana	AFR	1968	865	0.05	1968	32,495	0.19	1979	363	0.02	1990	346	0.16	1970
Brazil	LAC	1946	33,537	2.07	1963	282,228	1.69	1956	39,729	1.65	1993	2,864	1.31	nm
Brunei Darussalam	n.a.	1995	2,623	0.16	nm	nm	nm	nm	nm	nm	nm	nm	nm	2002
Bulgaria	ECA	1990	5,465	0.34	nm	nm	nm	1991	5,117	0.21	1992	901	0.41	2001
Burkina Faso	AFR	1963	1,118	0.07	1963	41,732	0.25	1975	1,086	0.05	1988	319	0.15	1966
Burundi	AFR	1963	966	0.06	1963	36,060	0.22	1979	350	0.01	1998	332	0.15	1969
Cambodia	EAP	1970	464	0.03	1970	22,642	0.14	1997	589	0.02	1999	422	0.19	2005
Cameroon	AFR	1963	1,777	0.11	1964	34,991	0.21	1974	1,135	0.05	1988	365	0.17	1967
Canada	n.a.	1945	45,045	2.78	1960	462,791	2.78	1956	81,592	3.39	1988	5,483	2.51	nm
Cape Verde	AFR	1978	758	0.05	1978	8,320	0.05	1990	265	0.01	1993	308	0.14	nm
Central African Republic	AFR	1963	1,112	0.07	1963	23,029	0.14	1991	369	0.02	2000	318	0.15	1966
Chad	AFR	1963	1,112	0.07	1963	16,890	0.10	1998	1,614	0.07	2002	318	0.15	1966
Chile	LAC	1945	7,181	0.44	1960	31,782	0.19	1957	11,960	0.50	1988	1,113	0.51	1991
China	EAP	1945	45,049	2.78	1960	332,400	1.99	1969	24,750	1.03	1988	5,788	2.65	1993
Colombia	LAC	1946	6,602	0.41	1961	77,701	0.47	1956	12,856	0.53	1995	1,028	0.47	1997
Comoros	AFR	1976	532	0.03	1977	13,141	0.08	1992	264	0.01	nm	nm	nm	1978
Congo, Dem. Rep. of	AFR	1963	2,893	0.18	1963	56,767	0.34	1970	2,409	0.10	1989	854	0.39	1970
Congo, Rep. of	AFR	1963	1,177	0.07	1963	38,923	0.23	1980	381	0.02	1991	373	0.17	1966
Costa Rica	LAC	1946	483	0.03	1961	12,480	0.07	1956	1,202	0.05	1994	464	0.21	1993
Côte d'Ivoire	AFR	1963	2,766	0.17	1963	46,863	0.28	1963	3,794	0.16	1988	568	0.26	1966

(continued)

Table D.1 *continued*

Country	IBRD/IDA region	IBRD (founded 1945) Year joined	Votes	Share of total	IDA (founded 1960) Year joined	Votes	Share of total	IFC (founded 1956) Year joined	Votes	Share of total	MIGA (founded 1988) Year joined	Votes	Share of total	ICSID (founded 1966) Year joined
Croatia	ECA	1993	2,543	0.16	1993	59,878	0.36	1993	3,132	0.13	1993	588	0.27	1998
Cyprus	n.a.	1961	1,711	0.11	1962	48,466	0.29	1962	2,389	0.10	1988	441	0.20	1966
Czech Republic	ECA	1993	6,558	0.40	1993	79,859	0.48	1993	9,163	0.38	1993	1,042	0.48	1993
Denmark	n.a.	1946	13,701	0.85	1960	169,299	1.02	1956	18,804	0.78	1988	1,523	0.70	1968
Djibouti	MENA	1980	809	0.05	1980	6,441	0.04	1980	271	0.01	2007	308	0.14	nm
Dominica	LAC	1980	754	0.05	1980	26,014	0.16	1980	292	0.01	1991	308	0.14	nm
Dominican Republic	LAC	1961	2,342	0.14	1962	27,780	0.17	1961	1,437	0.06	1997	405	0.19	nm
Ecuador	LAC	1945	3,021	0.19	1961	47,252	0.28	1956	2,411	0.10	1988	579	0.27	1986
Egypt, Arab Rep. of	MENA	1945	7,358	0.45	1960	79,574	0.48	1956	12,610	0.52	1988	1,067	0.49	1972
El Salvador	LAC	1946	391	0.02	1962	6,244	0.04	1956	279	0.01	1991	380	0.17	1984
Equatorial Guinea	AFR	1970	965	0.06	1972	6,167	0.04	1992	293	0.01	1994	308	0.14	nm
Eritrea	AFR	1994	843	0.05	1994	31,162	0.19	1995	1,185	0.05	1996	308	0.14	nm
Estonia	ECA	1992	1,173	0.07	nm	nm	nm	1993	1,684	0.07	1992	373	0.17	1992
Ethiopia	AFR	1945	1,228	0.08	1961	39,529	0.24	1956	377	0.02	1991	381	0.17	nm
Fiji	EAP	1971	1,237	0.08	1972	19,462	0.12	1979	537	0.02	1990	329	0.15	1977
Finland	n.a.	1948	8,810	0.54	1960	102,458	0.61	1956	15,947	0.66	1988	1,315	0.60	1969
France	n.a.	1945	69,647	4.30	1960	687,398	4.12	1956	121,265	5.03	1989	8,823	4.04	1967
Gabon	AFR	1963	1,237	0.08	1963	2,093	0.01	1970	1,518	0.06	2003	427	0.20	1966
Gambia, The	AFR	1967	793	0.05	1967	19,444	0.12	1983	344	0.01	1992	308	0.14	1975

Country	Region													
Georgia	ECA	1992	1,834	0.11	1993	41,519	0.25	1995	1,211	0.05	1992	369	0.17	1992
Germany	n.a.	1952	72,649	4.49	1960	1,076,549	6.46	1956	129,158	5.36	1988	9,194	4.21	1969
Ghana	AFR	1957	1,775	0.11	1960	66,391	0.40	1958	5,321	0.22	1988	690	0.32	1966
Greece	n.a.	1945	1,934	0.12	1962	45,962	0.28	1957	7,148	0.30	1993	751	0.34	1969
Grenada	LAC	1975	781	0.05	1975	20,627	0.12	1975	324	0.01	1988	308	0.14	1991
Guatemala	LAC	1945	2,251	0.14	1961	37,397	0.22	1956	1,334	0.06	1996	398	0.18	2003
Guinea	AFR	1963	1,542	0.10	1969	33,987	0.20	1982	589	0.02	1995	349	0.16	1968
Guinea-Bissau	AFR	1977	790	0.05	1977	6,790	0.04	1977	268	0.01	2006	308	0.14	nm
Guyana	LAC	1966	1,308	0.08	1967	23,460	0.14	1967	1,642	0.07	1989	342	0.16	1969
Haiti	LAC	1953	1,317	0.08	1961	24,871	0.15	1956	1,072	0.04	1996	333	0.15	nm
Honduras	LAC	1945	891	0.06	1960	43,282	0.26	1956	745	0.03	1992	436	0.20	1989
Hungary	ECA	1982	8,300	0.51	1985	124,659	0.75	1985	11,182	0.46	1988	1,252	0.57	1987
Iceland	n.a.	1945	1,508	0.09	1961	42,791	0.26	1956	292	0.01	1998	348	0.16	1966
India	SA	1945	45,045	2.78	1960	488,525	2.93	1956	81,592	3.39	1994	5,629	2.58	nm
Indonesia	EAP	1967	15,231	0.94	1968	130,075	0.78	1968	28,789	1.19	1988	2,107	0.96	1968
Iran, Islamic Rep. of	MENA	1945	23,936	1.48	1960	15,455	0.09	1956	1,694	0.07	2003	1,917	0.88	nm
Iraq	MENA	1945	3,058	0.19	1960	15,669	0.09	1956	397	0.02	nm	nm	nm	nm
Ireland	n.a.	1957	5,521	0.34	1960	60,966	0.37	1958	1,540	0.06	1989	908	0.42	1981
Israel	n.a.	1954	5,000	0.31	1960	60,421	0.36	1956	2,385	0.10	1992	1,093	0.50	1983
Italy	n.a.	1947	45,045	2.78	1960	432,716	2.60	1956	81,592	3.39	1988	5,228	2.39	1971
Jamaica	LAC	1963	2,828	0.17	nm	nm	nm	1964	4,532	0.19	1988	577	0.26	1966
Japan	n.a.	1952	127,250	7.86	1960	1,676,530	10.06	1956	141,424	5.87	1988	9,237	4.23	1967
Jordan	MENA	1952	1,638	0.10	1960	24,865	0.15	1956	1,191	0.05	1988	429	0.20	1972
Kazakhstan	ECA	1992	3,235	0.20	1992	4,106	0.02	1993	4,887	0.20	1993	626	0.29	2000
Kenya	AFR	1964	2,711	0.17	1964	58,781	0.35	1964	4,291	0.18	1988	561	0.26	1967
Kiribati	EAP	1986	715	0.04	1986	11,777	0.07	1986	262	0.01	nm	nm	nm	1967

(continued)

Table D.1 continued

Country	IBRD/IDA region	IBRD (founded 1945) Year joined	Votes	Share of total	IDA (founded 1960) Year joined	Votes	Share of total	IFC (founded 1956) Year joined	Votes	Share of total	MIGA (founded 1988) Year joined	Votes	Share of total	ICSID (founded 1966) Year joined
Korea, Rep. of	EAP	1955	16,067	0.99	1961	107,096	0.64	1964	16,196	0.67	1988	1,049	0.48	1967
Kuwait	MENA	1962	13,530	0.84	1962	90,524	0.54	1962	10,197	0.42	1988	1,897	0.87	1979
Kyrgyz Republic	ECA	1992	1,357	0.08	1992	8,751	0.05	1993	1,970	0.08	1993	335	0.15	nm
Lao PDR	EAP	1961	428	0.03	1963	22,867	0.14	1992	528	0.02	2000	318	0.15	nm
Latvia	ECA	1992	1,634	0.10	1992	40,225	0.24	1993	2,400	0.10	1998	429	0.20	1997
Lebanon	MENA	1947	590	0.04	1962	8,562	0.05	1956	385	0.02	1994	508	0.23	2003
Lesotho	AFR	1968	913	0.06	1968	38,272	0.23	1972	321	0.01	1988	346	0.16	1969
Liberia	AFR	1962	713	0.04	1962	22,467	0.13	1962	333	0.01	2007	342	0.16	1970
Libya	AFR	1958	8,090	0.50	1961	17,478	0.10	1958	305	0.01	1993	807	0.37	nm
Lithuania	ECA	1992	1,757	0.11	nm	nm	nm	1993	2,591	0.11	1993	445	0.20	1992
Luxembourg	n.a.	1945	1,902	0.12	1964	47,099	0.28	1956	2,389	0.10	1991	462	0.21	1970
Macedonia, FYR	ECA	1993	677	0.04	1993	34,011	0.20	1993	786	0.03	1993	346	0.16	1998
Madagascar	AFR	1963	1,672	0.10	1963	44,794	0.27	1963	682	0.03	1988	434	0.20	1966
Malawi	AFR	1965	1,344	0.08	1965	44,374	0.27	1965	2,072	0.09	1988	335	0.15	1966
Malaysia	EAP	1958	8,494	0.52	1960	68,189	0.41	1958	15,472	0.64	1991	1,278	0.59	1966
Maldives	SA	1978	719	0.04	1978	40,284	0.24	1983	266	0.01	2005	308	0.14	nm
Mali	AFR	1963	1,412	0.09	1963	35,336	0.21	1978	701	0.03	1992	401	0.18	1978
Malta	MENA	1983	1,324	0.08	nm	nm	nm	2005	1,865	0.08	1990	390	0.18	2003
Marshall Islands	EAP	1992	719	0.04	1993	4,902	0.03	1992	913	0.04	nm	nm	nm	nm

Country	Region													
Mauritania	AFR	1963	1,150	0.07	1963	35,623	0.21	1967	464	0.02	1992	369	0.17	1966
Mauritius	AFR	1968	1,492	0.09	1968	49,657	0.30	1968	1,915	0.08	1990	411	0.19	1969
Mexico	LAC	1945	19,054	1.18	1961	102,666	0.62	1956	27,839	1.16	nm	nm	nm	nm
Micronesia, Federated States of	EAP	1993	729	0.05	1993	18,424	0.11	1993	994	0.04	1993	308	0.14	1993
Moldova	ECA	1992	1,618	0.10	1994	612	0.00	1995	1,110	0.05	1993	354	0.16	nm
Mongolia	ECA	1991	716	0.04	1991	24,389	0.15	1991	394	0.02	1999	316	0.14	1991
Montenegro	ECA	2007	938	0.06	2007	44,271	0.27	2007	1,285	0.05	2007	319	0.15	nm
Morocco	MENA	1958	5,223	0.32	1960	79,602	0.48	1962	9,287	0.39	1992	871	0.40	1967
Mozambique	AFR	1984	1,180	0.07	1984	19,523	0.12	1984	572	0.02	1994	429	0.20	1995
Myanmar	EAP	1952	2,734	0.17	1962	55,655	0.33	1956	916	0.04	nm	nm	nm	nm
Namibia	AFR	1990	1,773	0.11	nm	nm	nm	1990	654	0.03	1990	365	0.17	nm
Nepal	SA	1961	1,218	0.08	1963	41,409	0.25	1966	1,072	0.04	1994	380	0.17	1969
Netherlands	n.a.	1945	35,753	2.21	1961	346,481	2.08	1956	56,381	2.34	1988	4,080	1.87	1966
New Zealand	n.a.	1961	7,486	0.46	1974	51,753	0.31	1961	3,833	0.16	nm	nm	nm	1980
Nicaragua	LAC	1946	858	0.05	1960	43,282	0.26	1956	965	0.04	1992	438	0.20	1995
Niger	AFR	1963	1,102	0.07	1963	19,302	0.12	1980	397	0.02	nm	nm	nm	1966
Nigeria	AFR	1961	12,905	0.80	1961	74,183	0.45	1961	21,893	0.91	1988	1,745	0.80	1966
Norway	n.a.	1945	10,232	0.63	1960	172,928	1.04	1956	17,849	0.74	1989	1,490	0.68	1967
Oman	MENA	1971	1,811	0.11	1973	37,068	0.22	1973	1,437	0.06	1989	424	0.19	1995
Pakistan	SA	1950	9,589	0.59	1960	156,805	0.94	1956	19,630	0.81	1988	1,421	0.65	1966
Palau	EAP	1997	266	0.02	1997	3,804	0.02	1997	275	0.01	1997	308	0.14	nm
Panama	LAC	1946	635	0.04	1961	10,185	0.06	1956	1,257	0.05	1997	489	0.22	1996
Papua New Guinea	EAP	1975	1,544	0.10	1975	45,445	0.27	1975	1,397	0.06	1991	354	0.16	1978
Paraguay	LAC	1945	1,479	0.09	1961	20,258	0.12	1956	686	0.03	1992	399	0.18	1983
Peru	LAC	1945	5,581	0.34	1961	29,494	0.18	1956	7,148	0.30	1991	915	0.42	1983

(continued)

211

Table D.1 *continued*

Country	IBRD (founded 1945)				IDA (founded 1960)			IFC (founded 1956)			MIGA (founded 1988)			ICSID (founded 1966)
	IBRD/IDA region	Year joined	Votes	Share of total	Year joined	Votes	Share of total	Year joined	Votes	Share of total	Year joined	Votes	Share of total	Year joined
Philippines	EAP	1945	7,094	0.44	1960	16,583	0.10	1957	12,856	0.53	1994	742	0.34	1989
Poland	ECA	1986	11,158	0.69	1988	361,284	2.17	1987	7,486	0.31	1990	1,022	0.47	nm
Portugal	n.a.	1961	5,710	0.35	1992	48,714	0.29	1966	8,574	0.36	1988	931	0.43	1984
Qatar	MENA	1972	1,346	0.08	nm	nm	nm	nm	nm	nm	1996	499	0.23	nm
Romania	ECA	1972	4,261	0.26	nm	nm	nm	1990	2,911	0.12	1992	1,236	0.57	1975
Russian Federation	ECA	1992	45,045	2.78	1992	51,361	0.31	1993	81,592	3.39	1992	5,786	2.65	nm
Rwanda	AFR	1963	1,296	0.08	1963	23,612	0.14	1975	556	0.02	2002	390	0.18	1979
Samoa	EAP	1974	781	0.05	1974	21,741	0.13	1974	285	0.01	1988	308	0.14	1978
San Marino	n.a.	2000	845	0.05	nm	nm	nm	nm	nm	nm	nm	nm	nm	nm
São Tomé and Príncipe	AFR	1977	745	0.05	1977	9,714	0.06	nm	nm	nm	nm	nm	nm	nm
Saudi Arabia	MENA	1957	45,045	2.78	1960	556,643	3.34	1962	30,312	1.26	1988	5,786	2.65	1980
Senegal	AFR	1962	2,322	0.14	1962	50,925	0.31	1962	2,549	0.11	1988	514	0.24	1967
Serbia	ECA	1993	3,096	0.19	1993	52,017	0.31	1993	2,053	0.09	1993	665	0.30	nm
Seychelles	AFR	1980	513	0.03	nm	nm	nm	1981	277	0.01	1992	308	0.14	1978
Sierra Leone	AFR	1962	968	0.06	1962	38,112	0.23	1962	473	0.02	1996	390	0.18	1966
Singapore	n.a.	1966	570	0.04	2002	11,000	0.07	1968	427	0.02	1998	530	0.24	1968
Slovak Republic	ECA	1993	3,466	0.21	1993	53,523	0.32	1993	4,707	0.20	1993	649	0.30	1994
Slovenia	ECA	1993	1,511	0.09	1993	40,878	0.25	1993	1,835	0.08	1993	438	0.20	1994
Solomon Islands	EAP	1978	763	0.05	1980	518	0.00	1980	287	0.01	2005	308	0.14	1981

Somalia	AFR	1962	802	0.05	1962	10,506	0.06	1962	333	0.01	nm	nm	nm	1968
South Africa	AFR	1945	13,712	0.85	1960	50,798	0.30	1957	16,198	0.67	1994	1,920	0.88	nm
Spain	n.a.	1958	28,247	1.74	1960	122,219	0.73	1960	37,276	1.55	1988	2,523	1.16	1994
Sri Lanka	SA	1950	4,067	0.25	1961	72,188	0.43	1956	7,385	0.31	1988	736	0.34	1967
St. Kitts and Nevis	LAC	1984	525	0.03	1987	13,778	0.08	1996	888	0.04	1999	308	0.14	1995
St. Lucia	LAC	1980	802	0.05	1982	30,531	0.18	1982	324	0.01	1988	346	0.16	1984
St. Vincent and the Grenadines	LAC	1982	528	0.03	1982	34,787	0.21	nm	nm	nm	1990	346	0.16	2003
Sudan	AFR	1957	1,100	0.07	1960	25,784	0.15	1960	361	0.02	1991	464	0.21	1973
Suriname	LAC	1978	662	0.04	nm	nm	nm	nm	nm	nm	2003	340	0.16	nm
Swaziland	AFR	1969	690	0.04	1969	19,022	0.11	1969	934	0.04	1990	316	0.14	1971
Sweden	n.a.	1951	15,224	0.94	1960	328,687	1.97	1956	27,126	1.13	1988	2,107	0.96	1967
Switzerland	n.a.	1992	26,856	1.66	1992	182,197	1.09	1992	41,830	1.74	1988	2,901	1.33	1968
Syrian Arab Rep.	MENA	1947	2,452	0.15	1962	10,351	0.06	1962	444	0.02	2002	554	0.25	2006
Tajikistan	ECA	1993	1,310	0.08	1993	20,568	0.12	1994	1,462	0.06	2002	388	0.18	nm
Tanzania	AFR	1962	1,545	0.10	1962	53,758	0.32	1962	1,253	0.05	1992	506	0.23	1992
Thailand	EAP	1949	6,599	0.41	1960	75,798	0.45	1956	11,191	0.46	2000	1,000	0.46	nm
Timor-Leste	EAP	2002	767	0.05	2002	558	0.00	2004	1,027	0.04	2002	308	0.14	2002
Togo	AFR	1962	1,355	0.08	1962	23,243	0.14	1962	1,058	0.04	1988	335	0.15	1967
Tonga	EAP	1985	744	0.05	1985	26,061	0.16	1985	284	0.01	nm	nm	nm	1990
Trinidad and Tobago	LAC	1963	2,914	0.18	1972	14,309	0.09	1971	4,362	0.18	1992	616	0.28	1967
Tunisia	MENA	1958	969	0.06	1960	2,793	0.02	1962	3,816	0.16	1988	533	0.24	1966
Turkey	ECA	1947	8,578	0.53	1960	107,538	0.65	1956	14,795	0.61	1988	1,072	0.49	1989
Turkmenistan	ECA	1992	776	0.05	nm	nm	nm	1997	1,060	0.04	1993	324	0.15	1992

(continued)

213

Table D.1 *continued*

Country	IBRD/IDA region	IBRD (founded 1945)			IDA (founded 1960)			IFC (founded 1956)			MIGA (founded 1988)			ICSID (founded 1966)
		Year joined	Votes	Share of total	Year joined	Votes	Share of total	Year joined	Votes	Share of total	Year joined	Votes	Share of total	Year joined
Uganda	AFR	1963	867	0.05	1963	48,099	0.29	1963	985	0.04	1992	491	0.22	1966
Ukraine	ECA	1992	11,158	0.69	2004	1,762	0.01	1993	9,755	0.40	1994	1,604	0.73	2000
United Arab Emirates	MENA	1972	2,635	0.16	1981	1,367	0.01	1977	4,283	0.18	1993	914	0.42	1982
United Kingdom	n.a.	1945	69,647	4.30	1960	858,061	5.15	1956	121,265	5.03	1988	8,823	4.04	1967
United States	n.a.	1945	265,219	16.38	1960	2,158,302	12.95	1956	569,629	23.64	1988	32,822	15.03	1966
Uruguay	LAC	1946	3,062	0.19	nm	nm	nm	1968	3,819	0.16	1993	460	0.21	2000
Uzbekistan	ECA	1992	2,743	0.17	1992	746	0.00	1993	4,123	0.17	1993	433	0.20	1995
Vanuatu	EAP	1981	836	0.05	1981	13,821	0.08	1981	305	0.01	1988	308	0.14	nm
Venezuela, R.B. de	LAC	1946	20,611	1.27	nm	nm	nm	1956	27,838	1.16	1994	1,685	0.77	1995
Vietnam	EAP	1956	1,218	0.08	1960	19,203	0.12	1967	696	0.03	1994	646	0.30	nm
Yemen, Republic of	MENA	1969	2,462	0.15	1970	49,574	0.30	1970	965	0.04	1996	413	0.19	2004
Zambia	AFR	1965	3,060	0.19	1965	60,030	0.36	1965	1,536	0.06	1988	576	0.26	1970
Zimbabwe	AFR	1980	3,575	0.22	1980	20,957	0.13	1980	2,370	0.10	1992	494	0.23	1994
TOTALS		185	1,619,599	100	166	16,671,072	100	179	2,409,852	100	171	218,384	100	143

Source: World Bank Group Corporate Secretariat.

Note: Totals may not add to 100 because of rounding. Also, 0.00 signifies less than 0.005 percent. AFR = Africa, EAP = East Asia and Pacific, ECA = Europe and Central Asia, LAC = Latin America and the Caribbean, MENA = Middle East and North Africa, SA = South Asia, n.a. = high-income country that does not currently borrow or receive financing from the World Bank or IFC (these countries are not necessarily classified as Part I relative to IDA), nm = nonmember.

CONSTITUENCIES OF THE EXECUTIVE DIRECTORS

IBRD's general operations are delegated to the Board of Executive Directors. Under IBRD's Articles of Agreement, the five member countries holding the largest number of shares each appoint one executive director, and the remaining member countries elect the other executive directors. At present, IBRD's Board consists of 24 executive directors. Of these, five were appointed by the largest shareholders—the United States, Japan, Germany, France, and the United Kingdom (figure E.1) and 19 were elected by other country constituencies. (See chapter 1 for more information.)

Under the Articles of Agreement for IDA and IFC, respectively, the executive directors of IBRD serve ex officio on IDA's Board of Executive Directors and on IFC's Board of Directors. Members of MIGA's Board of Directors are elected separately, but it is customary for the directors of MIGA to be the same individuals as the executive directors of IBRD. (See chapter 1 for more information.)

Regular elections of executive directors are held every two years, normally at the time of the Annual Meetings. Elections are coordinated by the Bank Group's Corporate Secretariat, which anticipates changes in constituency groupings resulting from new memberships or political events, as well as increases in members' capital subscriptions and the corresponding changes in voting power. The Corporate Secretariat also verifies the credentials of governors who are entitled to vote.

In the event that an executive director elected during the regular election terminates his or her service before the next regular election, the constituency affected by the vacancy holds an interim election for a successor. The interim election is conducted either by mail vote or during an Annual Meetings session that does not fall on a regular election year.

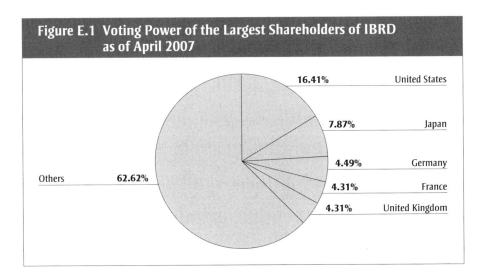

Figure E.1 Voting Power of the Largest Shareholders of IBRD as of April 2007

- 16.41% United States
- 7.87% Japan
- 4.49% Germany
- 4.31% France
- 4.31% United Kingdom
- Others 62.62%

Table E.1 Voting Shares of Executive Directors of IBRD as of April 2007

	Nationality of executive director	Constituency	Number of votes	Percentage of total votes
Appointed directors				
1	United States	United States	265,219	16.41
2	Japan	Japan	127,250	7.87
3	Germany	Germany	72,649	4.49
4	France	France	69,647	4.31
5	United Kingdom	United Kingdom	69,647	4.31
Elected directors				
6	Belgium, casting the votes of	Austria, Belarus, Belgium, Czech Republic, Hungary, Kazakhstan, Luxembourg, Slovak Republic, Slovenia, and Turkey	77,669	4.81
7	Mexico, casting the votes of	Costa Rica, El Salvador, Guatemala, Honduras, Mexico, Nicaragua, Spain, and República Bolivariana de Venezuela	72,786	4.50
8	Netherlands, casting the votes of	Armenia, Bosnia and Herzegovina, Bulgaria, Croatia, Cyprus, Georgia, Israel, former Yugoslav Republic of Macedonia, Moldova, Netherlands, Romania, and Ukraine	72,208	4.47

	Nationality of executive director	Constituency	Number of votes	Percentage of total votes
Elected directors *continued*				
9	Canada, casting the votes of	Antigua and Barbuda, The Bahamas, Barbados, Belize, Canada, Dominica, Grenada, Guyana, Ireland, Jamaica, St. Kitts and Nevis, St. Lucia, and St. Vincent and the Grenadines	62,217	3.85
10	Brazil, casting the votes of	Brazil, Colombia, Dominican Republic, Ecuador, Haiti, Panama, Philippines, and Trinidad and Tobago	57,462	3.56
11	Italy, casting the votes of	Albania, Greece, Italy, Malta, Portugal, San Marino, and Timor-Leste	56,705	3.51
12	Republic of Korea, casting the votes of	Australia, Cambodia, Kiribati, Republic of Korea, Marshall Islands, Federated States of Micronesia, Mongolia, New Zealand, Palau, Papua New Guinea, Samoa, Solomon Islands, and Vanuatu	55,800	3.45
13	India, casting the votes of	Bangladesh, Bhutan, India, and Sri Lanka	54,945	3.40
14	Ethiopia, casting the votes of	Angola, Botswana, Burundi, Ethiopia, The Gambia, Kenya, Lesotho, Liberia, Malawi, Mozambique, Namibia, Nigeria, Seychelles, Sierra Leone, South Africa, Sudan, Swaziland, Tanzania, Uganda, Zambia, and Zimbabwe	54,347	3.36
15	Norway, casting the votes of	Denmark, Estonia, Finland, Iceland, Latvia, Lithuania, Norway, and Sweden	54,039	3.34
16	Pakistan, casting the votes of	Afghanistan, Algeria, Ghana, Islamic Republic of Iran, Morocco, Pakistan, and Tunisia	51,544	3.19
17	Switzerland, casting the votes of	Azerbaijan, Kyrgyz Republic, Poland, Serbia, Switzerland, Tajikistan, Turkmenistan, and Uzbekistan	49,192	3.04
18	Kuwait, casting the votes of	Bahrain, Arab Republic of Egypt, Iraq, Jordan, Kuwait, Lebanon, Libya, Maldives, Oman, Qatar, Syrian Arab Republic, United Arab Emirates, and Republic of Yemen	47,042	2.91

(continued)

Table E.1 *continued*

	Nationality of executive director	Constituency	Number of votes	Percentage of total votes
Elected directors *continued*				
19	China, casting the votes of	China	45,049	2.79
20	Saudi Arabia, casting the votes of	Saudi Arabia	45,045	2.79
21	Russian Federation, casting the votes of	Russian Federation	45,045	2.79
22	Malaysia, casting the votes of	Brunei Darussalam, Fiji, Indonesia, Lao People's Democratic Republic, Malaysia, Myanmar, Nepal, Singapore, Thailand, Tonga, and Vietnam	41,096	2.54
23	Argentina, casting the votes of	Argentina, Bolivia, Chile, Paraguay, Peru, and Uruguay	37,499	2.32
24	Mauritius, casting the votes of	Benin, Burkina Faso, Cameroon, Cape Verde, Central African Republic, Chad, Comoros, Democratic Republic of Congo, Republic of Congo, Côte d'Ivoire, Djibouti, Equatorial Guinea, Gabon, Guinea, Guinea-Bissau, Madagascar, Mali, Mauritania, Mauritius, Niger, Rwanda, São Tomé and Principe, Senegal, and Togo	32,252	2.00
			1,616,354	100.00

Source: World Bank Group Corporate Secretariat.
Note: Individual percentages may not total 100 because of rounding. Eritrea, Montenegro, Somalia, and Suriname did not participate in the 2006 regular election of executive directors.

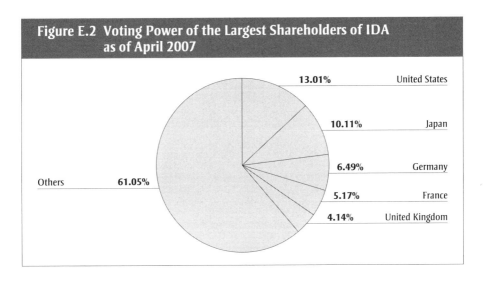

Figure E.2 Voting Power of the Largest Shareholders of IDA as of April 2007

13.01% — United States
10.11% — Japan
6.49% — Germany
5.17% — France
4.14% — United Kingdom
Others — 61.05%

Table E.2 Voting Shares of Executive Directors of IDA as of April 2007

	Nationality of executive director	Constituency	Number of votes	Percentage of total votes
Appointed directors				
1	United States	United States	2,158,302	13.01
2	Japan	Japan	1,676,530	10.11
3	Germany	Germany	1,076,549	6.49
4	United Kingdom	United Kingdom	858,061	5.17
5	France	France	687,398	4.14
Elected directors				
6	Norway, casting the votes of	Denmark, Finland, Iceland, Latvia, Norway, and Sweden	856,388	5.16
7	Belgium, casting the votes of	Austria, Belgium, Czech Republic, Hungary, Kazakhstan, Luxembourg, Slovak Republic, Slovenia, and Turkey	769,914	4.64
8	Ethiopia, casting the votes of	Angola, Botswana, Burundi, Ethiopia, The Gambia, Kenya, Lesotho, Liberia, Malawi, Mozambique, Nigeria, Sierra Leone, South Africa, Sudan, Swaziland, Tanzania, Uganda, Zambia, and Zimbabwe	759,597	4.58

(continued)

Table E.2 *continued*

	Nationality of executive director	Constituency	Number of votes	Percentage of total votes
Elected directors *continued*				
9	Canada, casting the votes of	Barbados, Belize, Canada, Dominica, Grenada, Guyana, Ireland, St. Kitts and Nevis, St. Lucia, and St. Vincent and the Grenadines	725,957	4.38
10	India, casting the votes of	Bangladesh, Bhutan, India, and Sri Lanka	695,690	4.19
11	Mauritius, casting the votes of	Benin, Burkina Faso, Cameroon, Cape Verde, Central African Republic, Chad, Comoros, Democratic Republic of Congo, Republic of Congo, Côte d'Ivoire, Djibouti, Equatorial Guinea, Gabon, Guinea, Guinea-Bissau, Madagascar, Mali, Mauritania, Mauritius, Niger, Rwanda, São Tomé and Principe, Senegal, and Togo	651,445	3.93
12	Netherlands, casting the votes of	Armenia, Bosnia and Herzegovina, Croatia, Cyprus, Georgia, Israel, former Yugoslav Republic of Macedonia, Moldova, Netherlands, and Ukraine	11,646,359	3.90
13	Switzerland, casting the votes of	Azerbaijan, Kyrgyz Republic, Poland, Serbia, Switzerland, Tajikistan, and Uzbekistan	633,423	3.82
14	Italy, casting the votes of	Albania, Greece, Italy, Portugal, and Timor-Leste	564,549	3.40
15	Saudi Arabia, casting the votes of	Saudi Arabia	556,643	3.36
16	Republic of Korea, casting the votes of	Australia, Cambodia, Kiribati, Republic of Korea, Marshall Islands, Federated States of Micronesia, Mongolia, New Zealand, Palau, Papua New Guinea, Samoa, Solomon Islands, and Vanuatu	537,669	3.24
17	Brazil, casting the votes of	Brazil, Colombia, Dominican Republic, Ecuador, Haiti, Panama, Philippines, and Trinidad and Tobago	500,909	3.02

	Nationality of executive director	Constituency	Number of votes	Percentage of total votes
Elected directors *continued*				
18	Malaysia, casting the votes of	Fiji, Indonesia, Lao People's Democratic Republic, Malaysia, Myanmar, Nepal, Singapore, Thailand, Tonga, and Vietnam	469,719	2.83
19	Kuwait, casting the votes of	Arab Republic of Egypt, Iraq, Jordan, Kuwait, Lebanon, Libya, Maldives, Oman, Syrian Arab Republic, United Arab Emirates, and Republic of Yemen	375,316	2.26
20	Mexico, casting the votes of	Costa Rica, El Salvador, Guatemala, Honduras, Mexico, Nicaragua, and Spain	367,570	2.22
21	Pakistan, casting the votes of	Afghanistan, Algeria, Ghana, Islamic Republic of Iran, Morocco, Pakistan, and Tunisia	365,623	2.20
22	China, casting the votes of	China	332,400	2.00
23	Argentina, casting the votes of	Argentina, Bolivia, Chile, Paraguay, and Peru	267,761	1.61
24	Russian Federation, casting the votes of	Russian Federation	51,361	0.31
			16,585,133	100.00

Source: World Bank Group Corporate Secretariat.
Note: Individual percentages may not total 100 because of rounding. Eritrea, Montenegro, and Somalia did not participate in the 2006 regular election of executive directors.

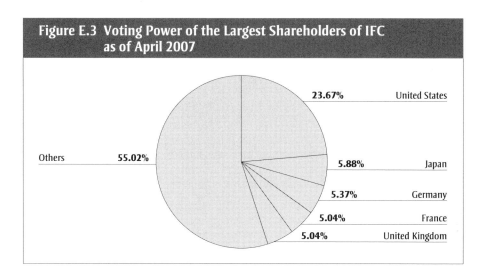

Figure E.3 Voting Power of the Largest Shareholders of IFC as of April 2007

- United States 23.67%
- Japan 5.88%
- Germany 5.37%
- France 5.04%
- United Kingdom 5.04%
- Others 55.02%

Table E.3 Voting Shares of Directors of IFC as of April 2007

	Nationality of executive director	Constituency	Number of votes	Percentage of total votes
Appointed directors				
1	United States	United States	569,629	23.67
2	Japan	Japan	141,424	5.88
3	Germany	Germany	129,158	5.37
4	France	France	121,265	5.04
5	United Kingdom	United Kingdom	121,265	5.04
Elected directors				
6	Belgium, casting the votes of	Austria, Belarus, Belgium, Czech Republic, Hungary, Kazakhstan, Luxembourg, Slovak Republic, Slovenia, and Turkey	125,221	5.20
7	Italy, casting the votes of	Albania, Greece, Italy, Malta, Portugal, and Timor-Leste	101,758	4.23
8	India, casting the votes of	Bangladesh, Bhutan, India, and Sri Lanka	99,234	4.12
9	Mexico, casting the votes of	Costa Rica, El Salvador, Guatemala, Honduras, Mexico, Nicaragua, Spain, and República Bolivariana de Venezuela	97,478	4.05

	Nationality of executive director	Constituency	Number of votes	Percentage of total votes
Elected directors *continued*				
10	Canada, casting the votes of	Antigua and Barbuda, The Bahamas, Barbados, Belize, Canada, Dominica, Grenada, Guyana, Ireland, Jamaica, St. Kitts and Nevis, and St. Lucia	92,944	3.86
11	Netherlands, casting the votes of	Armenia, Bosnia and Herzegovina, Bulgaria, Croatia, Cyprus, Georgia, Israel, former Yugoslav Republic of Macedonia, Moldova, Netherlands, Romania, and Ukraine	87,289	3.63
12	Norway, casting the votes of	Denmark, Estonia, Finland, Iceland, Latvia, Lithuania, Norway, and Sweden	86,693	3.60
13	Russian Federation, casting the votes of	Russian Federation	81,592	3.39
14	Brazil, casting the votes of	Brazil, Colombia, Dominican Republic, Ecuador, Haiti, Panama, Philippines, and Trinidad and Tobago	75,980	3.16
15	Republic of Korea, casting the votes of	Australia, Cambodia, Kiribati, Republic of Korea, Marshall Islands, Federated States of Micronesia, Mongolia, New Zealand, Palau, Papua New Guinea, Samoa, Solomon Islands, and Vanuatu	73,309	3.05
16	Argentina, casting the votes of	Argentina, Bolivia, Chile, Paraguay, Peru, and Uruguay	64,144	2.66
17	Switzerland, casting the votes of	Azerbaijan, Kyrgyz Republic, Poland, Serbia, Switzerland, Tajikistan, Turkmenistan, and Uzbekistan	62,601	2.60
18	Malaysia, casting the votes of	Fiji, Indonesia, Lao People's Democratic Republic, Malaysia, Myanmar, Nepal, Singapore, Thailand, Tonga, and Vietnam	59,912	2.49

(continued)

Table E.3 *continued*

	Nationality of executive director	Constituency	Number of votes	Percentage of total votes
Elected directors *continued*				
19	Ethiopia, casting the votes of	Angola, Botswana, Burundi, Ethiopia, The Gambia, Kenya, Lesotho, Liberia, Malawi, Mozambique, Namibia, Nigeria, Seychelles, Sierra Leone, South Africa, Sudan, Swaziland, Tanzania, Uganda, Zambia, and Zimbabwe	57,688	2.40
20	Pakistan, casting the votes of	Afghanistan, Algeria, Ghana, Islamic Republic of Iran, Morocco, Pakistan, and Tunisia	45,980	1.91
21	Kuwait, casting the votes of	Bahrain, Arab Republic of Egypt, Iraq, Jordan, Kuwait, Lebanon, Libya, Maldives, Oman, Syrian Arab Republic, United Arab Emirates, and Republic of Yemen	34,476	1.43
22	Saudi Arabia, casting the votes of	Saudi Arabia	30,312	1.26
23	China, casting the votes of	China	24,750	1.03
24	Mauritius, casting the votes of	Benin, Burkina Faso, Cameroon, Cape Verde, Central African Republic, Chad, Comoros, Democratic Republic of Congo, Republic of Congo, Côte d'Ivoire, Djibouti, Equatorial Guinea, Gabon, Guinea, Guinea-Bissau, Madagascar, Mali, Mauritania, Mauritius, Niger, Rwanda, Senegal, and Togo	22,947	0.95
			2,407,049	100.00

Source: World Bank Group Corporate Secretariat.
Note: Individual percentages may not total 100 because of rounding. Eritrea, Montenegro, and Somalia did not participate in the 2006 regular election of executive directors.

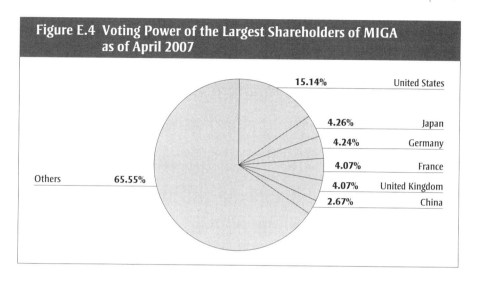

Figure E.4 Voting Power of the Largest Shareholders of MIGA as of April 2007

	15.14%	United States
	4.26%	Japan
	4.24%	Germany
	4.07%	France
Others 65.55%	4.07%	United Kingdom
	2.67%	China

Table E.4 Voting Shares of Directors of MIGA as of April 2007

	Nationality of executive director	Constituency	Number of votes	Percentage of total votes
Directors elected by 6 largest shareholders				
1	United States	United States	32,822	15.14
2	Japan	Japan	9,237	4.26
3	Germany	Germany	9,194	4.24
4	France	France	8,823	4.07
5	United Kingdom	United Kingdom	8,823	4.07
6	China	China	5,788	2.67
Directors elected by other shareholders				
7	Netherlands, casting the votes of	Armenia, Bosnia and Herzegovina, Bulgaria, Croatia, Cyprus, Georgia, Israel, former Yugoslav Republic of Macedonia, Moldova, Netherlands, Romania, and Ukraine	11,688	5.39
8	Belgium, casting the votes of	Austria, Belarus, Belgium, Czech Republic, Hungary, Kazakhstan, Luxembourg, Slovak Republic, Slovenia, and Turkey	11,491	5.30

(continued)

Table E.4 *continued*

	Nationality of executive director	Constituency	Number of votes	Percentage of total votes
Directors elected by other shareholders *continued*				
9	Ethiopia, casting the votes of	Angola, Botswana, Burundi, Ethiopia, The Gambia, Kenya, Lesotho, Malawi, Mozambique, Namibia, Nigeria, Seychelles, Sierra Leone, South Africa, Sudan, Swaziland, Tanzania, Uganda, Zambia, and Zimbabwe	11,058	5.10
10	Canada, casting the votes of	Antigua and Barbuda, The Bahamas, Barbados, Belize, Canada, Dominica, Grenada, Guyana, Ireland, Jamaica, St. Kitts and Nevis, St. Lucia, and St. Vincent and the Grenadines	10,392	4.79
11	Kuwait, casting the votes of	Bahrain, Arab Republic of Egypt, Jordan, Kuwait, Lebanon, Libya, Maldives, Oman, Qatar, Syrian Arab Republic, United Arab Emirates, and Republic of Yemen	8,214	3.79
12	Mauritius, casting the votes of	Benin, Burkina Faso, Cameroon, Cape Verde, Central African Republic, Chad, Democratic Republic of Congo, Republic of Congo, Côte d'Ivoire, Equatorial Guinea, Gabon, Guinea, Guinea-Bissau, Madagascar, Mali, Mauritania, Mauritius, Rwanda, Senegal, and Togo	8,035	3.71
13	Norway, casting the votes of	Denmark, Estonia, Finland, Iceland, Latvia, Lithuania, Norway, and Sweden	8,030	3.70
14	Italy, casting the votes of	Albania, Greece, Italy, Malta, Portugal, and Timor-Leste	7,968	3.68
15	India, casting the votes of	Bangladesh, India, and Sri Lanka	7,222	3.33
16	Pakistan, casting the votes of	Afghanistan, Algeria, Ghana, Islamic Republic of Iran, Morocco, Pakistan, and Tunisia	7,210	3.33

	Nationality of executive director	Constituency	Number of votes	Percentage of total votes
Directors elected by other shareholders *continued*				
17	Brazil, casting the votes of	Brazil, Colombia, Dominican Republic, Ecuador, Haiti, Panama, Philippines, and Trinidad and Tobago	7,056	3.26
18	Republic of Korea, casting the votes of	Australia, Cambodia, Republic of Korea, Federated States of Micronesia, Mongolia, Palau, Papua New Guinea, Samoa, Solomon Islands, and Vanuatu	6,958	3.21
19	Malaysia, casting the votes of	Fiji, Indonesia, Lao People's Democratic Republic, Malaysia, Nepal, Singapore, Thailand, and Vietnam	6,588	3.04
20	Switzerland, casting the votes of	Azerbaijan, Kyrgyz Republic, Poland, Serbia, Switzerland, Tajikistan, Turkmenistan, and Uzbekistan	6,441	2.97
21	Mexico, casting the votes of	Costa Rica, El Salvador, Guatemala, Honduras, Nicaragua, Spain, and República Bolivariana de Venezuela	6,324	2.92
22	Argentina, casting the votes of	Argentina, Bolivia, Chile, Paraguay, Peru, and Uruguay	5,833	2.69
23	Saudi Arabia, casting the votes of	Saudi Arabia	5,786	2.67
24	Russian Federation, casting the votes of	Russian Federation	5,786	2.67
			216,767	100.00

Source: World Bank Group Corporate Secretariat.
Note: Individual percentages may not total 100 because of rounding. Djibouti, Eritrea, Liberia, Montenegro, and Suriname did not participate in the 2006 regular election of directors.

ADDITIONAL COUNTRY RESOURCES

World Bank and IFC regional Web sites serve as portals to country-specific Web sites or pages (box F.1). Those country-specific Web pages typically provide a brief summary of activities and issues in the country, with links to specific projects, economic data and statistics, publications, Web sites of the country's government, and related news.

Additionally, the following resources are available:

- *Bank Group Offices.* For links to country office Web sites, go to http://www.worldbank.org/ and select the "Countries" tab.
- *Public Information Centers (PICs).* These centers disseminate information on the Bank Group's work. They are hosted in either the World Bank offices or in external organizations who work closely with the Bank. Most PICs have project documents and publications specific to the country in which the office is located and will generally have access to World Bank online databases. PIC Europe in Paris and PIC Tokyo offer the complete range of Bank operational documents for all member countries and maintain libraries of recent World Bank publications. For more information go to http://www.worldbank.org/reference/ and select "Public Information Centers" in the "Finding Publications" box.
- *World Bank Depository and Regional Libraries.* Each depository library is entitled to a free copy of each formal publication of the Bank Group. A depository library must make its collection of Bank Group publications available to the public. Each regional library has a similar arrangement but receives only major publications and formal publications that are related to its World Bank region. Go to http://www.worldbank.org/reference/ and select "Worldwide Depository Libraries" in the "Finding Publications" box.
- *Distributors of World Bank Group Publications.* The Bank Group encourages customers outside the United States to order through local distributors. For a list of distributors go to http://www.worldbank.org/reference/ and select "Book Distibutors" in the "Finding Publications" box. The Bank Group also sells direct to all member countries.

■ *Publication Discount.* Bank Group publications are sold at discounts of 35 percent or 75 percent off the list price to customers in many developing countries, depending on the country's income level. These discounts are assessed biennially on the basis of new economic data. See http://publications.worldbank.org/discounts.

Box F.1 Regional Web Sites

Sub-Saharan Africa
World Bank vice presidency: http://www.worldbank.org/afr
IFC regional department: http://www.ifc.org/africa

East Asia and the Pacific
World Bank vice presidency: http://www.worldbank.org/eap
IFC regional department: http://www.ifc.org/eastasia

South Asia
World Bank vice presidency: http://www.worldbank.org/sar
IFC regional department: http://www.ifc.org/southasia

Europe and Central Asia
World Bank vice presidency: http://www.worldbank.org/eca
IFC regional department: http://www.ifc.org/europe

Latin America and the Caribbean
World Bank vice presidency: http://www.worldbank.org/lac
IFC regional department: http://www.ifc.org/lac

Middle East and North Africa
World Bank vice presidency: http://www.worldbank.org/mena
IFC regional department: http://www.ifc.org/mena

Western Europe
World Bank EuropeExternal Affairs: http://www.worldbank.org/europe

REFERENCES

IFC (International Finance Corporation). 2006. *IFC Annual Report 2006.* Washington, DC: IFC.

MIGA (Multilateral Investment Guarantee Agency). 2006. *2006 Annual Report.* Washington, DC. MIGA.

United Nations. 2000. *Millennium Declaration,* A/RES/55/2, New York: United Nations.

―――. 2001. *Road Map towards the Implementation of the United Nations Millennium Declaration,* Report of the Secretary General, New York: United Nations.

World Bank. 2006. *World Bank Annual Report 2006.* Washington, DC: World Bank.

INDEX

Boxes, figures, and tables are indicated by "b," "f," and "t."